ROOTS

AND

BRANCHES

The History of the Christian and Missionary Alliance in Brazil

David P. Jones
Editor

PWO PUBLICATIONS
2018

Editor:
David. P. Jones

Layout:
PJ Bogoniewski

Cover Illustration:
Kenneth Shepherd

Cover Layout:
Sophia Lirio

First Edition

ISBN: 978-1986737197

1＞3 9898355

WHAT OTHERS ARE SAYING ABOUT ROOTS AND BRANCHES

"*Roots and Branches* traces the development of C&MA in Brasil from the earliest stages of the ministry of Dr. A. B. Simpson to this day. After much research, with frankness and clarity, David Jones reveals the challenge, victories, frustrations and successes on the way to the C&MA's maturing. It is remarkable that veteran missionary, Sam Barnes, had a vision of the way to proceed, but could not carry it out. Fortunately, God did not give up and He fulfilled it. It recalls Proverb 16:9 that says, " In his heart a man plans his course, but the Lord determines his steps." This book clearly demonstrates how God raised up the Brazil Alliance to take its place alongside partners from other countries in the work of evangelization. This is a very worthwhile book to read."

—Rev. Paul Bryers,
Alliance missionary sent to
Brazil in 1961

"It is a good thing to give thanks unto the Lord, and to sing praises unto thy name, O Most High. (Psalm 92:1) Rare is the book on history that would be considered in the category of "giving thanks," but this is a special case. While it is quite a bit longer than the customary Psalm reading, it is worth the necessary time to read *Roots and Branches*, since it recounts the long and varied journey of those used by the Lord to lay the foundation for The Christian and Missionary Alliance in Brazil – both for the national church of Brazil as well as its missionary endeavor. The writer, pastor, teacher and researcher, David Jones, is to be congratulated for this fine work.

—Rev. Timothy Bubna,
Brazil Field Director
from 1993 to 2014

"*Roots and Branches* is the fascinating story of young men and women from the US, Canada, Japan, Chile, Argentina, Uruguay, Colombia and Hong Kong who, against all odds, were used by God to establish a vibrant faith community in Brazil, rooted in the movement started by A.B. Simpson. You can relate to the twists and turns these passionate missionaries experienced as they proclaimed Christ to a Catholic nation with strong Afro-Indian religious influences. David Jones is himself part of this wonderful story of commitment and sacrifice, and his storytelling abilities are fully displayed in this book. The seeds were sown, the roots were spread, and today the branches are producing much fruit. Read this book so that you can follow the next chapters of this story unfolding before your eyes."

—Rev. Jurandir Yanagihara, President of The Alliance World Fellowship and former President of the Brazil Christian and Missionary Alliance

DEDICATION

This book is dedicated to three people whose lives and ministry had a lasting impact on the establishment of The Brazilian Christian and Missionary Alliance.

Rev. Mutsuko Ninomiya (Sensei) whose vision for the lost of Brazil, her fearless obedience to do God's will and her tenacious commitment to fulfill the call inspire all who follow.

Rev. João Alves da Costa, first Alliance national pastor, a godly, sincere pastor of Christ's flock who gladly served His Lord with no expectation of applause other than The Lord's *"Well done my good and faithful servant."*

Rev. Thomas Buskey Kyle, whose powerful preaching brought the message of salvation to tens of thousands in Brazil and worldwide, and whose leadership enabled the C&MA Mission to pioneer and plant His Church.

CONTENTS

ACKNOWLEDGEMENTS

A book like this, written over a period of almost two years, with contributions from so many, leaves ample opportunity for someone to be overlooked and left out. That is the danger inherent in such literary enterprises. However, one must run the risk of forgetting or offending someone by not giving credit where credit is due. That is a risk that must be taken, because the number of contributors and helpers that collaborated in order to make this book possible are considerable. The order of these names is chronological since I began working three years ago with the first named and then worked down the list over time.

The earliest collaborator who proved to be an extremely valuable and hard-working assistant is a former "MK" from Brazil, Mrs. Ruth Jenks Coddington of Toccoa, Georgia. She spent countless hours researching old family prayer letters, *Brazil Bulletins*, *Aliança em Revistas*, and other field periodicals, then scanning and sending them to me for use in the book. It has been a real joy to work with one of the "missionary kids" who grew up to be a woman of God with a heart for Brazil. Many thanks, "Ruthie."

A second major word of thanks is directed to long-time friend and field colleague, Mrs. Ruth Myers Davis. She researched and wrote Chapter 9 which tells the São Paulo story, a very big job well done. I asked Ruth to write this chapter since I knew that she enjoyed writing, had a feel for history, and was willing to take on this major task. She and husband, Mike, were among the first of a new wave of missionaries sent out by the U.S. Alliance Mission in the mid 1980s to open São Paulo and turn the page to a whole new period of field history.

Two former field colleagues, Dick LaFountain and Steve Renicks, combined to help write a complete and comprehensive chapter on the history of the work in Porto Alegre. The drama and trauma associated with Alliance ministry in the great state of Rio Grande do Sul is well written from their experience and example. Many thanks, Dick and Steve.

Mrs. Loraine Todd graciously provided a comprehensive account of the Alliance ministry in Campinas, recounting the work led by her husband, John, as well as the beginning of the Chinese ministry there under Pastor Koon and his family. I am very grateful for this important contribution.

Longtime field director, Pastor Tim Bubna, provided valuable assistance in recalling the field history of the later decades, and his memory for dates, names and events is legendary.

Three of the earliest missionaries sent out by the North American Alliance provided very helpful information regarding the early 1960s. Rev. Paul Bryers, now retired, was the first North American C&MA missionary to enter Brazil in early 1962. His recollections and records of those earliest years in Goiânia and Brasília filled in many blanks. Mrs. Marilyn Sundeen, along with husband David, arrived in 1963 and helped pioneer in Goiânia and later in Gama, Federal Distirct. Mrs. Ann Hemminger was the daughter of Rev. Samuel Barnes of Argentina, who with wife, Vera, were the pioneer field leaders of the C&MA Mission to Brazil. They arrived in 1962 – not long after the Bryers Family. Ann's memories, family prayer letters and long-time ministry in Brazil contributed greatly toward the unfolding of the story told in this book.

Among the many Brazilians friends and Alliance colleagues who gave information for the book, the name of Pastor Eduardo Toshiaki "Toshi" Yassui must be given special mention. Pastor Toshi's amazing memory helped recreate the story of the Alliance in Rudge Ramos, São Bernardo do Campos, as well as the history of "Dona Mutsuko" Ninomiya Sensei, the first Alliance missionary from Japan to go to Brazil in 1959, pioneer of the pioneers. As a former president of ACEMBRAS and also involved in early missionary efforts of the national church, Pastor Yassui has made a very important contribution to this history.

Mrs. Elsa Costa, widow of ACEMBRAS' first president, Rev. João Alves da Costa, and her son, João Alves da Costa, Junior provided details and dates regarding the early history of Alliance in Brasília.

Pastor Sergio Moraes Pinto, former ACEMBRAS president and longtime pastor of the Vista Verde Alliance Church in São José dos Campos, was interviewed by the editor. He provided color and context to this historical narrative, having had a long and varied ministry in Porto Alegre, Curitiba, Manaus and São José dos Campos.

Pastor José Freitas, of the Airport Alliance Church, provided a treasure trove of recollections regarding the early years of the pioneer church plant in São Paulo on its pilgrimage around the South Zone of the city before finding the "promised land" and purchasing property near the Congonhas Airport.

Pastor Akira Fukuura, as well as pastoring the Paraíso Alliance Church, is also the former chairman of the Department of Missions for ACEMBRAS. He emailed me many files, photos and other important material for Chapter 10, which covers the mission heart and outreach of the Brazil Alliance.

I am very grateful to God for the highly professional and personal work done by my new "best friend," Rev. Jim "PJ" Bogoniewski, who did the layout and copy editing for this English edition of *Roots and Branches*. PJ's huge contribution toward the publishing of this book came as an answer to prayer. God bless you, my friend.

The translators that the Lord provided were truly a Godsend. As the chapters were completed in English, revised and edited, they were then sent to the translators who put the English into good Portuguese prose in a timely manner. Chapter 1 – Pastor Leialdo Pulz; Chapters 2, 7 and 8 – Mr. Flávio Campos; Chapter 3 – Mr. Cesar Umekita; Chapter 4 – Mr. Marcos Alves; Chapter 5 – Mrs. Denise Clark; Chapter 9 – Miss Beatrice Koopman; Chapter 6, 10 and 11 were done by the editor.

Special mention must be made of two men who provided vital and precious material for Chapter Two – *Bananal*. Through the miracle of Google search, I came across the name of Dr. Lloyd Cooke, a professor at the Regent College of the Caribbean (formerly the Jamaica Bible College), and author of a book recounting the amazing story of Jamaica's role as a missionary-sending island nation. Rev. Cooke provided valuable material for the second chapter of this book. More importantly, he informed me that Rev. David Clark, son of Rev. Ray Clark, the leader of the Bananal venture in 1923 was still alive and well in Fort Wayne, Indiana. David Clark provided rare documents, original diary entries that his father wrote more than ninety years ago.

While not mentioning all of the names of former Brazil C&MA missionary colleagues who answered the queries sent by email and Facebook, I am very grateful for their input. I trust that you will accept my heartfelt thanks while remaining anonymous. I express equal appreciation to my many Brazilian friends, some former students at IBA/SEMIBA while others were members of churches that we planted or pastored during our many years in Brazil. Many thanks for your stories, testimonies, recollections and words of encouragement.

It should be pointed out that the cover art, the *Buriti* palm tree, was chosen for symbolic reasons. This species of palm (*Mauritia Flexuosa*) is found all over the "cerrado" highlands of Brazil, where much of the early history of the C&MA occurred. The *buriti* is noted for its many roots, and its numerous branches which produce abundant fruit. The Brazil Alliance is the result of many "roots" coming from many Alliance churches from various parts around the world. The seed planted from different lands took root and became a body of Brazilian believers today, who are part of the Alliance World Fellowship. The many branches on the Brazil Alliance *buriti* are producing more seeds and good fruit on various continents around the world.

Last, but certainly not least, I must thank my dear wife and companion of years of life together in the Lord, Judy Jones, for her long-suffering patience in doing the first proof reading of all of this work. She is my best critic, memory corrector and encourager. Many thanks, Judy, for listening to me when my enthusiasm for history far exceeds yours. Blessings on you, Jude.

In most of the Apostle Paul's epistles, the closing chapter contains words of salutation to friends near and far, to companions with him in prison, to young pastors that he placed in ministry and to apostolic colleagues at work all over the Roman Empire. This writer is "no Paul," but to all who read this, "May the Lord bless you with His grace and peace, and may this narrative of the story of God's work in Brazil through the C&MA

be an encouragement as you continue to bless others with the gospel.

David P. Jones, Editor

PREFACE

The Splendid Cradle

Brazil's *Hino Nacional Brasileiro* (Brazilian National Hymn) was written in 1843 as requested by Dom Pedro I, Brazil's first emperor, the rebel son of the King João VI of Portugal. In 1822, he was ordered by his father and the *Cortes* of Portugal to return to the mother country. Dom Pedro I's famous proclamation, "Independence or Death," shouted out on the banks of the Ipiranga River near São Paulo became the country's rallying cry for freedom from Portuguese rule. Thus in 1822, Brazil freed itself from the country whose great explorer and navigator, Pedro Alvarez Cabral, had "discovered" Brazil hundreds of years before in 1500. For more than three centuries, Portugal treated Brazil as its private treasure trove. Brazil's wood, gold, silver, precious stones, sugar, coffee, rubber and the natural wealth of its biggest colony enriched the mother country and beggared the daughter land.

When Brazil became a republic in 1889 with the peaceful removal of the first emperor's son, Dom Pedro II and his family, new words were written to the old hymn tune. The second verse begins with words that prophetically evoke the hard-to-kill optimism and enduring hope that characterize the people of Brazil:

Eternally lying in a splendid cradle,
To the sound of the sea and under deep sky light,
Thou flarest, O Brazil,
ornament of America,
Illuminated by the sun of the New World!

At various times in her history, Brazil's long-suffering citizens have thought: "Our time has come. Brazil is getting up from the splendid cradle to take its place among the nations." It seemed to happen when slavery was abolished in 1888 by Princess Isabel, daughter of Dom Pedro II. Influenced by French ideals of *liberté, egalité* and *fraternité* and challenged by the dynamism of the United States of America, another former colony finally broke the shackles of slavery. With the Declaration of the Republic on November 15, 1889, the newly-minted Republic of Brazil seemed to be ready to take its rightful place among the great nations.

These momentous developments occurring in the "giant to the south" were keenly noticed by a young Presbyterian minister who recently had moved to New York City to pastor the prestigious Thirteenth Street Presbyterian Church. A dynamic preacher and impassioned evangelist, Rev. Albert B. Simpson, Canadian born and late of the Chestnut Street Presbyterian Church in Louisville, Kentucky, had moved to the metropolis because there the heart of the world mission movement beat strongest. God had expanded the vision of this once-proper Presbyterian pastor. Like Peter in the home of Simon the Tanner, Simpson's spiritual "band-width" had broadened, and his heart was for the whole world. Thus, he launched the first illustrated missions magazine of North America, *The Gospel in All Lands* [GAL]. This personal journalistic enterprise purposed to inform and inflame the evangelical churches of America about the needs of the nations of the world without the Gospel.

The first issue of *The Gospel in All Lands,* with the subtitle: *An Evangelical Monthly Magazine of Universal Missions,* was published by Simpson in February 1880, two short months after he arrived in New York. The periodical, co-edited with Eugene R. Smith, was financed by Simpson through offerings and subscriptions. This was the first of his many

A.B. Simpson

publishing ventures. Simpson produced the magazine through the November 1881 issue, at which point he turned it over to Smith due to failing health. Smith continued publication of the magazine for some years.

In the inaugural issue of *GAL,* Brazil is mentioned as one of the many fields where the *Missionary Society of the Methodist Episcopal Church* carried on its evangelistic outreach ministry. In the July issue, notice was given of the *American Bible Society's* cooperation with "the revision of the *Almeida* Portuguese version of the New Testament which has been completed." Month after month, snippets of information were given: missionaries shipping out for Brazil, missionary offerings being received with candidates coming forward for service. Mention of many of the notable names of Protestant mission pioneers in Brazil were given: Ashbel Simonton and G. W. Chamberlain of the Northern Presbyterians, William Taylor and Daniel Kidder of the Methodist Church South, and W. B. Bagby of the Southern Baptists are mentioned as the country continued to open under the relatively enlightened leadership of Dom Pedro II.

In the March 1881 issue, Mrs. Dabney, of the *American Presbyterian (South) Mission* writes "from Campinas of 'a very interesting case of a clever, clear-headed young man, 18 years of age, whose parents are people of the best social position and Romanists. In direct opposition to the will of his father, he is making the Bible a book of diligent study, and has, we have every reason to believe, had that study blessed to him by the Holy Spirit, and has learned the truth. He has not yet made a public profession of his faith but there is no doubt about his intention to do so. He expresses a strong desire to preach and to go as a missionary among the Indians. His knowledge of the Bible is wonderful.'" This unnamed youth showed the promise of a new day dawning among the well-educated upper-class youth of Brazil who were abandoning the Catholic Church while not abandoning their belief in God and the Bible. Perhaps another stirring in the splendid cradle.

The April 1881 issue of Simpson's *The Gospel to All Lands* followed, which featured a photogravure of Dom Pedro II dominating the cover page! The whole issue reported on Protestant missions in South America in general and Brazil in particular. The major part of that first issue covered the five protestant missions in Brazil: *The Presbyterian Board (North)*, *The Southern Presbyterians*, *The South American Missionary Society* [British], *The Southern Methodists* and *The Southern Baptists.*

Both the Southern Baptists and the Southern Methodists were working in the interior of the province of São Paulo, directing their ministry toward Brazilians as well as the recent North American immigrants who left the U.S. when slavery was banned under Lincoln's Union Government after the Confederates States were defeated. *Piracicaba, Santa Bárbara do Oeste* and the town of *Americana* were among the centers where the defeated "rebels" put down roots. Slavery was legal, cotton grew well in the red soil of São Paulo, and Brazil needed a textile industry that soon was introduced by the former citizens of the American South.

A. B. Simpson's eye had fallen on Brazil in a big way. Fascinating information filled the pages of the April 1881 issue. As is apparent from the names of the five missions working at that time, a "great divide" between the North and the South of the United

Dom Pedro II

States was obvious. The Presbyterian, Baptist and Methodist Churches were still split over the issue of states' rights and slavery, but they were brought together in a country where slavery was still legal, only to be ended by the signature of Princess Isabel, Dom Pedro's daughter to the *Golden Law*, in 1888, while her father, Dom Pedro II was absent from the country. Simpson, of Canadian birth, saw beyond the racial divide and antipathy between the American North and South. His burden was to reach the millions who lived in spiritual darkness, led by a corrupt clergy who fought against the entrance of the hated Protestants.

From these earliest *GAL* notes, it is clear that Simpson's attention was being drawn to Brazil even as he was increasingly targeting the Congo as the initial site for the fledgling missionary society of the newly-founded Gospel Tabernacle. The South American "sleeping giant," Brazil, never was far from his mind. Following his resignation from the Thirteenth Street Presbyterian Church in November of 1881, Simpson founded the Gospel Tabernacle and began a new missions periodical, *The Word, The Work and The World* [*WWW*]. A February 1882 article, "Romanism in South America" decried the small number of mission societies working in Brazil. In a later edition, November: "The Empire of Brazil is really larger than the whole United States, and its natural resources in agriculture and minerals are exhaustless. *The people are overshadowed by ignorance, superstition and imbecility. Much of this is due to the Roman Catholic Church* (editor's italics)."

In an article in the July-August *WWW* issue of 1885, Dr. J. T. Gracey, president of the *International Missionary Union*, describes the "Open Door in South America," writing several paragraphs describing Brazil's size, and the potential of its "splendid cradle." Yet it goes on to describe the deplorably low rate of literacy, lack of schools, legality of slavery at that late date and many other social ills. "Romanism has held sway for more than three hundred years, and yet this is the educational status." This fact is brought out since the Roman Catholic Church still had the monopoly on public education and continued to be the "official religion" of the Brazilian Empire.

In 1887, following a meeting of Gospel Tabernacle members and followers of Simpson's vision, *The Christian Alliance* and *The International Missionary Alliance* were founded and organized, to carry on their vision of "the whole gospel for the whole man and for the whole world." Subsequent issues of *The Christian Alliance* magazine, the house organ for the newly-created Alliances, cry out: "Priest-ridden Brazil with its fourteen millions is calling for the gospel." "Our missions [Presbyterian] have been the uncompromising foes of Roman Catholicism, the curse of Brazil during the Empire." In *The Christian Alliance*, January 1892, an article by Simpson's colleague, F.W. Farr, asks the question: "Are Romanists

Salvable?"

Thus for more than ten years after Simpson arrived in New York and began to immerse himself in the global movement for world evangelization, his missionary periodicals were focusing the evangelical church's attention on the desperate spiritual and social needs of Brazil. The intense antipathy between Protestants and Catholics shocks today's reader. However at that time, the Reformation battles of the fifteen hundreds were still being fought more than three hundred years later. The Catholic clergy in Brazil stated that to be a "Brazilian protestant" was to be a traitor to the emperor and the country. Memories of the bloody Inquisition sponsored by the church and states of Spain and Portugal were still fresh in their citizen's minds, and that mindset carried over to their colonies.

Brazil was beginning to assume its rightful role among the other countries in South America. Rio de Janeiro was a beautiful capital city and cultural center. São Paulo was called the "Athens of Brazil" with its universities, law schools and Catholic seminaries. Immigrants from Italy, Spain, Germany and Portugal were bringing new technology and industry to the backward, agricultural economy. The Republic had been declared in 1889; religious liberty for all faiths and creeds came into effect and the Catholic Church had lost its rights and privileges and was no longer the official religion of Brazil. Freedom of faith and practice was guaranteed by the new constitution. The young nation had awakened, sat up and was climbing out of its splendid cradle. It is in this historical context that A. B. Simpson's interest and initiative to begin a missionary endeavor in Brazil is found shortly after the founding of his fledgling missionary society.

CHAPTER ONE
AN OPEN DOOR
1893-1903

The *Christian and Missionary Alliance*, the name eventually adopted when the two *"Alliances"* became one organization in 1897, was born of A. B. Simpson's vision and burden for the lost worldwide. He was a true "spiritual son" of Dr. Hudson Taylor, the English physician/missionary who founded the *China Inland Mission.* Taylor's emphasis on reaching the interior of the non-Christian lands around the world was not lost on Simpson. Up to that time, most Protestant and Catholic missions had followed the colonial powers and established their mission stations on or near the coast. Taylor knew that the vast majority of those unreached by the gospel were not found on the easy-to-reach coastal areas, but within the distant "inlands." This perception became a major missiological principle that many other "faith missions" followed. Thus Simpson limned in prose and poem this burden for "the regions beyond," where the gospel "story had never had been told." This became the watchword for the emerging C&MA mission.

The Alliance's entrance into Latin America was somewhat delayed, despite Simpson's early awareness of the needs and opportunities there. At that time, some "mission authorities" opined that Central and South America should not be considered as legitimate objectives for Protestant missions from Europe and the United States. Since the South American continent had been colonized by the Spanish and Portuguese, both Roman Catholic countries, the continent was to be considered "evangelized." This opinion was not accepted by the majority of Protestant mission societies of that era, both denominational and interdenominational. They rejected such an idea because of the clear evidence of the failure of the Catholic Church to preach the gospel message of salvation by grace through faith, the moral decadence of the clergy, the spiritual poverty of the populations, the high level of illiteracy that resulted from the Church's hold on education and the political instability that resulted from unjust governments supported by the Roman Church. Thus, by the mid to late 1800s, missionaries were sent out by the Presbyterians, Methodists, Baptists, Anglicans and Congregationalists. Non-denominational and interdenominational missions were soon to follow.

Not many years after the "Alliances" were first organized in 1887, the eyes of the Alliance mission began to look more closely at this needy region of the world where millions of men, women and children lived in spiritual darkness and physical destitution while the Roman Catholic Church maintained an almost 100% spiritual monopoly over the soul of the continent. Among the indigenous populations, various forms of animism were practiced, and Spiritism manifested itself, especially in Brazil with variants of African and Amerindian occult animism and French Kardecism. Many who practiced the different varieties of Spiritism in Brazil also considered themselves members in good standing with the Catholic Church. Christian catechism in Brazil was cursory at best.

The Annual Report of the C&MA of 1892 gives the first glimmer of a more serious commitment by the Alliance to South America. In the report, financial considerations as to the costs for sending missionaries to South America were discussed among the potential "new fields" to be opened. This was the first official mention of such a possibility.

The following year's *Annual Report for 1893*, presented "Perspective Work – South America:"

The Board has had under consideration for many months the opening of mission stations in South America. This continent is our nearest neighbor and is almost destitute of the gospel. Among fifty or sixty millions of people there are not five thousands adherents of the various Protestant missions, and very many of these are English and American people connected with the various chaplaincies. There are from three to five millions of aboriginal Indians without any missionary among them. There are also several states without any missionaries: Peru, Bolivia, Ecuador and Venezuela are almost, if not altogether without laborers.

Rev. Mr. Bright, of Mexico, an experienced missionary who understands the Spanish language and publishes a religious paper in that language, has been invited to undertake a journey of missionary exploration with a view to the opening up of stations in this land, and already several volunteers have offered themselves, and some have been accepted. We hope, before the close of the year, and certainly before the next annual meeting, to have a number of missions established in this land.

In this connection, we are glad to call attention to the *Central American Missionary Society* under the direction of Rev. Dr. Scofield [editor of the *Scofield Study Bible*], of Dallas, Texas, a member of our Board, and a brother in full sympathy and fellowship with us. We desire to recognize this work, as in fraternal affiliation with us, and we rejoice to be able to report that under this Society there are already two or three laborers in Nicaragua and that perhaps a dozen more will go to Central America and possibly to Cuba before the close of the present year.

An interesting note here is that the aforementioned "Rev. Mr. Bright" of the Mexico project disappeared from view without another trace. It would appear that the early Alliance, with A. B. Simpson as its leader, was a bit like "David's band" of the restless, rebellious, and rootless adventurers who were looking for a leader but not necessarily interested in being led. Such missionary volunteers cropped up time after time on various new mission fields that were opened. Since the Alliance had no experienced field personnel, Simpson often readily received those whose later service explained why they were "free lancers" rather than part of an established mission. While Dr. C. I. Scofield certainly should not be cast in the same kind of mold, his association with the Alliance soon vanished as his mission became stronger and better known because of his name recognition.

Despite Brazil's not being on this first list of potential missionary destinations, a rising interest by the Alliance in the Americas grew evident. Even before there were any C&MA missionaries in South America, there already was a sub-committee responsible for opening the work in South America, with C. I. Scofield as one of the five members along with Rev. Stephen Merritt, Mr. G. S. Fisher, Mr. F. W. Perry and Rev. F. W. Farr.

The First Attempt in 1894 with J. B. Howell

The *1894 Annual Report* showed how the new Alliance Mission was agile in adjusting to new opportunities and possibilities. The following excerpt explains the rapid entrance of the Alliance in Brazil:

> A most hopeful and encouraging beginning has been made in Brazil. Rev. J. B. Howells [Howell], a former missionary of the Presbyterian Board [North] has returned to that country with a party of laborers, under the auspices of the Alliance, to establish a Missionary Training School in San Paolo (sic), with a view of preparing and sending out native evangelist to labor among their own people.

> The new party consists of Rev. J. B. Howells and his wife, who remains at present in America, Mr. Smart, and Mr. and Mrs. Emory. Two other missionaries, viz.: Miss Felton and Miss White, are under appointment to South American and will soon, we trust, leave for the field.

Rev. J.B. Howell

The first question to answer is who was Rev. J. B. Howell? According to information provided by Rev. Alderi Souza de Matos, Presbyterian historian for the *Igreja Presbiteriana Brasileira* (*Brazilian Presbyterian Church*) and other available information: John Beatty Howell was born in March of 1847 in Allentown, New Jersey. He received a B.A. degree from New Jersey College and became a school teacher. He later felt led to study at Princeton Seminary where he graduated and became part of the Lackawanna PA Presbytery. Blue-eyed and almost six feet tall, John B. Howell had a strong face, square chin and fair complexion, as expected from one of English extraction.

His United States passport application was made in New York shortly before he was sent as a missionary to Brazil by the New York Presbyterian Mission Board, arriving in Rio de Janeiro on August 19, 1873. He worked first in Petrópolis with Rev. A. L. Blackford, was received into the Rio Presbytery in January of 1874 and then transferred to São Paulo where he worked with the noted Presbyterian pioneer, Rev. George Chamberlain. For the next ten years he remained in São Paulo, often traveling to the interior for preaching ministries. He was director of the American School [later renamed *Mackenzie Presbyterian University*] and also editor of the *Imprensa Evangélica* (*Evangelical Press*). (http://www.ebenezer.org.br/wp-content/uploads/2015/09/Parte-1-Mission%C3%A1rios-PCUSA.pdf)

In 1877, Howell returned to the United States on furlough where he married Elizabeth Hibler Day in Wilkes-Barre PA on June 14 and soon returned to Brazil. Picking up from his previous term, he worked in São Paulo with Rev. Chamberlain teaching theology at the American School. In fact, while he was director of the American School, Dom Pedro II, Emperor of Brazil, visited the school and was received by Howell, a high honor for a Protestant missionary. While at the *Training School* he taught some of the leading lights of the young Presbyterian movement who sat under his teaching.

Though teaching and pastoring the first Presbyterian Church in the great city of São Paulo, he continued his evangelistic sorties into the interior of the great-coffee-producing state. It was at this time that Howell began to write regularly for *The Foreign Missionary*, a Presbyterian periodical, regarding his views on pastoral training. He envisioned training promising young men from the interior regions, to serve as teachers and evangelists or, as he called them "Bible readers." These youth would teach in local church schools for eight months and then spend the other four studying with Howell in *Brotas*, an interior town, during the vacation period. Their training would prioritize biblical interpretation and exposition. He first visited *Jaú*, not far from Brotas, in 1878 where he preached; only the previous year before his visit, the Brazilian evangelist, *Sr. da Gama*, had been attacked, had his beard pulled and was forbidden to preach. Research reveals that the actual assault occurred on April 26, 1877, when the evangelist, João Fernandes da Gama, originally from Madeira, a likely convert of Dr. Robert Kalley, and a colporteur, was threatened and forbidden to proselytize in Brotas.

In 1885 Howell was transferred to the Brotas field where he ministered at the many preaching points in the region. In

1887, at the nearby town of *Jaú*, Howell purchased a farm property a few miles outside of town in a place called *Ortigal* or *Capim Fino*, and opened his proposed school for the training of national workers. At Jaú, Howell actually invested his own money in order to test his theory for ministerial preparation. He had two young men teaching at the school, while he did itinerant preaching all over the interior of São Paulo and nearby *Minas Gerais* state. While serving with the Presbyterians, he trained many local leaders and organized the Presbyterian Church of Jaú on April 14, 1889. The next year, Howell returned to the United States and took up a Presbyterian pastorate in New Jersey. For the next four years, Howell and family lived in Burlington, NJ where he pastored the local Presbyterian church. It was near the end of that period that he began to have contact with the C&MA and Dr. Simpson. From all accounts, Howell was a valuable and valorous Christian man, energetic, visionary, experienced, still able and willing to serve his beloved country of adoption.

A. B. Simpson met up with the still-young Howell during the summer at the Asbury Park NJ Alliance Convention. In the July 28, 1893 issue of *The Christian Alliance*, Howell is introduced to the Alliance family, under the title: "The Lord's Work in Brazil." Howell addressed an Alliance audience as a member of the "Presbyterian Board." In the article, he recounted several fascinating stories relating to his seventeen years in Brazil and the openness of the Brazilian people to the gospel. He related:

> "In the city of São Paulo, where I was then living, a man had his attention arrested by some words on the stray leaf of a Bible wrapped about some little article that he had brought from the

grocery. So interested was he that he returned and secured the remnants of the Bible from which the leaf was taken by the study of which he was led to purchase a complete copy, through which he found Christ as His Lord and Savior. He became at once a most zealous evangelist . . . and devoted his life to the work of telling men of Jesus both in Brazil and in his native land too, Portugal. . . ."

Another account tells of "A Brazilian lady, a member of the church in the same town, which I was then serving, had a brother who was a traveling Lottery Ticket Seller." The lady slipped a Bible into the man's bag with a prayer that God would use it. While on his trip through the interior, the man was storm-bound in a farmhouse. Looking in his bag, he found the Bible, showed it to his hosts and began to read it aloud. "The lady of the house, as soon as he had read a few verses said, 'Why this is just the kind of a book that I have been wanting to see for years!'" She asked the ticket seller to send his sister to her farm and that she would pay for the sister's travel. "The sister came; and you may imagine her surprise when she found fifty or sixty people gathered in the large dining room to hear her tell of Jesus." Many came to Christ and a church was founded right there on the farm. Sounds like a Cornelius-type of story right out of the Book of Acts!

Howell ended his address by saying "It seems to me that this is a missionary field which the Christian Alliance may properly take up, as it is one in which God Himself is already manifestly working." Later in December of the same year, 1893, Howells wrote to *The Christian Alliance and Missionary Weekly* (*CAMW*) that "the great majority of the Brazilian people, while nominally Catholics, are practically heathen." He went on to describe the corruption of the local priests with their common-law wives and children, and their ignorance of biblical truth. Howells optimistically opined that "Romanism in Brazil is not a stronghold that must be battered down; it has crumbled of itself, and is but a mass of ruins." He went on in the periodical to state: "I have not the slightest doubt that within six months from the time we should open a school for training evangelists in such studies as could be pursued in their own language, I could gather over a dozen young men of proved ability and character, anxious to take up the course, and willing to make some sacrifices in order to obtain it."

The March 2, 1894 issue of the *CAMW*, the "Editor," Dr. Simpson, wrote an article titled: "Brazil as a Mission Field" and announced that "We have just appointed Rev. Mr. Howells, formerly a member of the Presbyterian Church in Brazil, to take charge of the new mission about to be opened in this republic." Thus it would appear that John B. Howell, a seventeen-year veteran missionary, middle-aged, experienced and energetic, brimming with confidence and possessing a strategic plan for Brazil, had come forward as the man whom the Alliance was seeking to open the door to the "sleeping giant" to the south. With his years of experience, contacts, ability with the language, and even a property to begin a mission station, it appeared that this was God's provision for the opening of a new field. A few months later it was announced that Howell and three missionaries from the U.S. and one from England would be sailing on June 10 for Brazil.

On June 10, 1894, *The Christian Alliance and Foreign Missionary Weekly* (*CAFMW*) announced the farewell service held at the Gospel Tabernacle on the night of June 7. Dr. Simpson and Rev. Stephen Merritt both gave short addresses.

Rev. Howell was introduced and "gave a short and excellent address. He said that the motto of the Mission was, 'The Holy Ghost, Manager in Chief, and the One to whom shall be referred all details and arrangements.' 'He said that the object of the Mission was to train native evangelists and send them out to carry the Gospel to their own people.' He said another object of the Mission was to teach the Brazilians industrial work and train them in living simple country style. One of the features of the Mission would be a farm, under the care of Mr. and Mrs. Emory."

Howell then went on to describe a problem that has faced missions and churches for years: "How do you keep them down on the farm once they've been to São Paulo?" "One of the difficulties," Howell explained, "of the present training system in South America is that nearly all the preachers are trained in cities, where they learn expensive habits of living, and are unable to go back among their people and live in the simple style in which they were born. When evangelists are used to the people's way of living, they can be maintained at much less expense."

Howell was followed by Mr. Smart, "a child of the Alliance work" from Syracuse, New York who had sensed God's calling on his life while attending an Alliance Convention in 1889, had trained at the Missionary Training Institute (MTI) in New York City and was ready to leave all and go. Mr. Emory, who was to run the farm with his wife, also gave a brief word, as did his wife, who related a dream in which 'she had seen the Lord coming in the clouds, and how in her sleep she cried out that God would send her to help hasten His coming, and would help to prepare her for the work.'" The farewell service concluded with the missionaries kneeling and being commissioned to God for "His blessing and keeping as they went forth to obey His last command." Thus the first missionary team to Brazil under the C&MA shipped out three days later to enter Brazil's open door.

Consequently in mid-1894, Howell returned to the province of São Paulo to the interior that he loved, and made his home again at the farm and property that he had purchased some years before. His wife, Lizzie, did not accompany him, perhaps due to the total lack of adequate educational opportunities for their children whose ages ranged from fifteen to seven years of age. Before proceeding further, another question might be posed. Why would an established, experienced Presbyterian missionary, entering middle age with several children leave the Presbyterian Board of Missions in 1890? There is no indication from the information available that he was "fired" and told not to return to the field. Yet it appears that Howell did have serious misgivings regarding the serious issue of Masonry that split the Presbyterian Mission and national church less than ten years later? This became a major problem for missionaries and the church. Howell likely left the Presbyterian Mission over this issue and returned to the pastorate in New Jersey.

Howell had taught for ten years in São Paulo at what eventually became one of Brazil's most prestigious universities, *Mackenzie University*. In fact, Rev. Eduardo Carlos Pereira, who some years later became the founding president of the *Igreja Presbiteriana Independente do Brasil* (*The Independent Presbyterian Church of Brazil*), numbered as one of Howell's students in São Paulo that he trained and influenced. The Independent Presbyterians broke off from their Presbyterian Church of Brazil colleagues over that very issue of membership in the Masons as well as the heavy hand of the American missionaries in the life of the Brazilian church.

Howell had given up the big city and gone to the primitive interior to preach, teach and train national workers to stay put and reach their people locally. The matter of how and where to educate Brazilian pastors had become another divisive topic among national Presbyterian pastors and missionaries on both sides of the controversy. Perhaps all of these difficult questions caused him to resign from the New York Board in 1890. Future events would show that he did not break his ties with Presbyterian pastors and missionaries since he maintained fraternal relations with them while serving with the C&MA Mission in Brazil and years beyond.

As a result of meeting Simpson, and the warm reception that he received from the Alliance family, not many months passed before Howell was named the Field Superintendent of the soon-to-be opened Brazil Field of the C&MA. Consequently, less than a year after Simpson and Howell first met at the Asbury Park, John Beatty Howell was leaving the United States to return to Brazil. With him went three first term missionaries: Mr. William Smart and Mr. and Mrs. John Emory. Soon to follow was Miss Sallie Felton of England.

Howell's Strategy in Jaú, São Paulo

The December 14, 1894 issues of *The CAFMW* outlined Howell's strategy for reaching Brazil's interior with the gospel:

> My plan of operations would be (leaving out of account the River Toncantins at present) to take as a base line the two rivers, São Francisco and Paraná, establish native evangelists or Bible readers at as many points as possible along these rivers to work back from the river in each direction, and then to have at least two

missionaries continually travelling up and down, stopping in turn at each station for a week or more, making, if possible, quarterly visits, with a grand annual rally at each place for an eight or ten days' convention, at which the institute professors, missionaries and adjacent local preachers would come together. . . . This is entirely unoccupied territory. There is no mission or society working along this line, and the great part of it has scarcely ever been visited by a minister.

At the end of this long article, Howell makes a request that reflects his vision for the work's future:

I ask for four men, but twice or three times that number could be profitably employed along the same lines. The present location of the Institute is much preferable for teaching purposes, as it is within easy reach of the material from which the native laborers are to be formed; later, when we have a larger membership of our own along these rivers, it might be advisable to change it. I may say, in passing, that the farm is only four miles from the Tiete, one of the largest branches of the Paraná, which at this point is navigable for large steamers. The young men should come out at once, so as to be learning the language.

Once back in Jaú with Mr. Smart and the Emorys, he began to put into practice what he had envisioned and tried to do for a few years while serving the Presbyterian Board. *The*

1895 Annual Report of the C&MA gave a glowing review of the first year of activity of their new mission in Brazil:

> First of all, we have special cause for thankfulness for the safe arrival and settlement of our pioneer band of missionaries to Brazil, and the commencement of their work at *Jahu*, in the province of San Paulo. It is a matter for thanksgiving that the President of the Republic of Brazil is a friend of Protestantism, and some of his family have been educated in a Protestant college. Still more it is a matter for gratitude to God that our missionaries have been received so heartily in various parts of the republic, and that God has opened the hearts of the people to receive the gospel. The superintendent, Mr. Howells (sic), was able to begin work immediately, through his former residence in the country and his thorough knowledge of the language and he has held many meetings during the year which have been well attended. Mr. Howells has already baptized nineteen persons. He has also taken one or two important journeys into the interior, and has had very remarkable evidences of the work of the Holy Spirit and the preparation of the hearts of persons in different places for the reception of Christ. Some of the incidents are almost like the story of apostolic times. In remote districts, little companies have sent for him to come and preach and baptize those who have accepted Christ, and little churches have been formed where no minister had ever previously come. The special object of

our work in Brazil has at length been attained at least in its initial sage by the opening of a *Missionary Training Institute*, called "*The Bíblico Institute Carolina Greer.*" Two recruits, namely, Miss [Sally] Felton and Mr. [William Azel] Cook, have been sent to Brazil during the year, and have already entered upon their work. Miss Felton, having a thorough knowledge of the Spanish language, was soon ready for service, and Mr. Cook is rapidly acquiring the language. Finally, a door seems to have been opened for a chain of evangelistic stations along the great San Francisco River, and the hearts of the people are said to be quite open to the truth. Thank God for the first chapter in the story of the Alliance mission in Brazil.

The *CAFMW* dated March 20, 1895 gives a description of the Jaú station:

The farm containing the Missionary Home and school buildings is situated in the State of São Paulo about five miles from the city of Jahú, which is the terminus of a rail road, and lies about 400 miles northwest of Rio de Janeiro and 250 miles north of Santos, the nearest seaport. The farm is an unsurveyed tract of an undivided plantation, and practically includes 150 acres of good farming land, with three or four well-marked varieties of soil . . . . The Missionary Home is an old plantation house containing eight bedrooms, parlor, dining room and kitchen, built in Brazilian style, with clay walls plastered and

white-washed board floors, glass windows and
tile roof. The school building is of the same style,
one half being taken up with the school room,
which is also used as a church hall, with seats
accommodating eighty persons; and a regular
pulpit; the other half is divided into six rooms,
and with some additions will serve as the home of
the students.

The rest of the article describes the twice-weekly
religious services held, on Sundays with from seventy to eighty
in attendance, and the Wednesday evening with twenty-five to
thirty coming to pray. Howell generally did the preaching while
William Smart, picking up the language well, was able to lead
in prayers. The region around the farm was thickly settled with
about thirty Protestant families and a few congregations. While
there was still a great deal of religious prejudice, the outright
opposition and persecution of the past was increasingly rare as
the new Republic of the United States of Brazil guaranteed
religious freedom to all faiths.

The 1895 report stated that the Bible Institute had
opened with eleven students, and that one of the newly-opened
"little churches" already had twelve members. The Brazil
Mission had received $2,821.44 according to the Financial
Report and had sufficient funds to function. Thus the beginning
of the mission to Brazil was auspicious and encouraging.

The *1896 Annual Report of the C&MA*, despite its
optimistic tone, began to show the first signs of a crisis of
leadership and strategy:

Our work in Jahu, Brazil, is chiefly preparatory
to the more aggressive plans of the future. The

home on [the] farm has been managed with much economy and success, and affords a place of rest and study at moderate expense for our new missionaries, and the native whom we are training for future work. Two new missionaries, Mr. and Mrs. [John and Elizabeth] Price, have gone to the field, and Mr. Howells has returned to this country. God is opening our way to open a mission among the Indians of South America. A wealthy friend abroad has offered the necessary means to sustain such a mission. We have found a native Brazilian specially fitted for this work, and are only waiting to find the right leader to go forward and give the gospel to some of the millions of aboriginal tribes on the Upper Amazon, who have such good cause to say, "No man cared for my soul."

The 1896 report concluded with another good word concerning the Brazil Mission's finances with $3,394.07 having come into the coffers. There were now seven missionaries on the field: Mr. W. B. Smart, Miss Sallie P. Felton, a school teacher, Mr. and Mrs. John Emory who were in charge of the Jaú farm, the newly arrived Mr. and Mrs. John Price, and Mr. William Cook. Yet Rev. John Howell, the "field superintendent" who had only arrived in mid-1894, had left the field with no explanation in the report and returned to the United States in June, 1896, just two years after leaving with his missionary team for Jaú.

Howell's Rapid Departure

Questions arise, "What could have been the reason for Howell's rapid departure?" Was it because he served alone for more than two years, and that his wife and children were not going to return to Brazil? Was he frustrated with the Alliance because the resources, human and financial, were not forthcoming at the speed he desired? Were his absences for long periods from Jaú when he left seven brand-new missionaries, all in language study, making the adjustment to life in the primitive interior, learning how to live and work in a completely new culture and context . . . were all of these frustrations felt by his colleagues causing a strain on his role as leader?

The 1896 report then stated cryptically: "We are only waiting to find the right leader to go forward and give the gospel to some of the millions of aboriginal tribes on the Upper Amazon . . . ." It had appeared two years before that Howell was the right leader with the right stuff for Brazil; now he was gone with the Jaú team leaderless. And then there was the remark about the mysterious "wealthy friend abroad [who] has offered the necessary means to sustain such a mission [among the Indians of the Upper Amazon]. Who might that be? Was this the famous "miser of Leeds," the British missions champion and major donor, Robert Arthington? It was reported that he paid for the construction of a river steamer built in the United States to be used on the rivers of Brazil. Perhaps Simpson had met him on one of his trips to Europe. What is known is that Simpson had republished in *The Gospel in All Lands* part of a document by Arthington, "An Appeal," which did just that, appealed to the various mission boards and protestant denominations to unite in an effort to evangelize the world. Simpson knew who Arthington was, since he had been a generous and ardent backer of British missions.

What is known about Rev. Howell following his return to North America is that he returned to pastor the *Tennent*

Memorial Presbyterian Church in Philadelphia, from 1897 to 1904. He then became chaplain of the Presbyterian Hospital in the same city, from 1903 to 1912. Still sensing his missionary calling late in life, and taking advantage of his command of Portuguese, Howell went to Portugal where he worked with Rev. João Marques da Mota Sobrinho, the first Brazilian Presbyterian missionary to that needy nation. While there, Howell helped publish an evangelical periodical, *O Endoutrinador* (*The Doctrinator*), wrote a commentary on the *Gospel of Matthew* and worked on another, the *Epistles to the Romans,* which was never published. Howell returned to North America definitively in 1919, residing in Newtown, Connecticut until his death in 1924.

To try and ascertain just what happened that caused this sudden departure by Howell, at best, can only be accomplished by an attempt to deduce from the Alliance literature available. Following the sanguine *Annual Reports* and articles in the Alliance periodicals of 1895, the April 6, 1896 issue of the *CAFW* included on the "Requests for Prayer" section the following note: "SOUTH AMERICA, Pray for special guidance and blessing to be granted to our workers in Brazil in settling some matters of great moment at this time." This same prayer request was repeated for five issues in a row. The phrase, "settling some matters of great moment at this time," apparently indicated a serious level of dissonance and distress among the staff. Two months later, the June 19, 1896 issue of the *CAFMW* gave brief notice to "Mr. Howells (sic), of the Brasil Mission" having returned for furlough. The next months (07/24/96) issue published an article, apparently written by Howell on his return:

As the mission in Brazil was only started two years ago, the work there is still in an initial and experimental stage; nevertheless encouraging beginnings have been made. The Farm-School for the training of native evangelists, which in view of the peculiar needs of the country, was thought to be the most important work with the I. M. A. [International Missionary Alliance], could undertake, has been inaugurated and closed the first year with an attendance of seven young men, ranging in age from nineteen to thirty years. The proposed course of study has been tested, and *various questions relating to the inter-relation of the industrial and literary departments have received a practical solution. . . .* (author's italics).

A flourishing mission day-school under the direction of Miss Felton, in which careful daily religious instruction is given, is in operation with an enrollment of from thirty-five to forty boys and girls, and more anxious to enter as soon as a place can be found for them.

A Sabbath audience varying from eighty to one hundred and thirty, with an almost equal number at the weekly prayer meeting, and a Sabbath school in which the attendance has from sixty to eighty, are regarded as evidence of the Divine favor.

We have been blessed with abundant crops; the farm, under the efficient management of Mr.

Emory, having yielded so bountifully, and the increase of stock having been such as to warrant the hope of a considerable money return from the place in the near future.

A special cause for gratitude has been the preservation in excellent health of the whole missionary party during the year, although an epidemic of yellow fever in a very malignant form has been raging all around us. With God's blessing upon the branches of work already initiated, we hope soon to be able to report tangible results.

In the October 16, 1896 issue of the *CAFMW* a general report of all of the C&MA missions fields gave note of "Our work in Jahu, Brazil, is chiefly preparatory to the more aggressive plans of the future." The piece basically repeated the information given earlier in Howell's July article. It was mentioned that "Mr. Howells (sic) has returned to this country." It is worthy of mention that the *CAFMW* and the *Annual Reports* never managed to spell correctly his name, "Howell," always referring to him as "Mr. Howells." Later in that same general overview of Alliance fields, the mysterious "wealthy friend abroad" and the goal of working on the Upper Amazon received mention again. For all intents and purposes, the October 16 article was a fresh presentation of old news. Thus ends the association of Rev. John Beatty Howell, a veteran missionary with vision and energy to reach the lost in "the regions beyond" of Brazil's interior. One can only wonder what might have been if he had remained to give leadership to the newly-opened Brazil Mission of the C&MA.

Emílio Olsson, Visionary Leader

Just as John Howell passes off the scene, a new face appears; a charismatic figure who took command of the Alliance advance in South America. *The 1897 Retrospect and Annual Report of the C&MA* introduces this new personage:

> Perhaps the most marked aggressive movement of the year has been in connection with the South American mission. A few months ago the Lord sent us one of His most honored missionaries, Mr. Emílio Olsson, who has already labored successfully for about fifteen years in South America, especially with the Bible Society and pioneer evangelism. His earnest spirit and his ideas and methods of mission work at once recommended him to us and the aims and methods of the Board in turn attracted him and in due time, after mature consideration, he was accepted as a missionary of the Board, and appointed to lead a new party of workers to the Neglected Continent and to take oversight of our entire mission work in South America.

"Emil" Emílio Olsson, Swedish born, had been a rough sailor for twenty years who miraculously was saved after hearing the gospel while in port at the Falkland Islands. Sensing God's call on his life to serve in South America, he Latinized his name to "Emílio." Veteran Alliance missionary to Argentina, Jack Shannon, tells Olsson's story in the article, "Simpson and Emílio Olsson: The Birth and Death of a Great Plan" (*His Dominion*, 1989, Vol. 16, No. 1). After his dramatic conversion, Olsson became an impassioned evangelist with a burden for souls. He soon arrived in Buenos Aires where he apparently perfected his rough "seaman's Spanish," and by 1889 had worked with the YMCA, and had become a colporteur with the *British and Foreign Bible Society*. He took his boxes of Bibles and Scripture portions to the whole of the province of Buenos Aires and as far north as Bolivia and westward to Chile.

Olsson's Grand Plan

Eventually, after also spending time working with both the Presbyterians and Baptists in Argentina, Olsson went to New York with his wife and their two small children, and there they met Simpson. Olsson shared his vision and strategy for the evangelization of South America with Simpson. It was an audacious proposal. Olsson shared in the *CAFW* of December 4, 1896 his vision: "I think eighty-five earnest workers could evangelize South America in four years . . . I know from experience that one man, working hard, can reach by preaching

Olsson, and new missionaries for South America
(Olsson, seated front and center)

the gospel and by circulating the Holy Scriptures there, 100,000 persons a year which would be 34,000,000 at the end of the nineteenth century." Olsson calculated that the whole project could be paid for with 100,000 pounds sterling, or half a million dollars.

Simpson was taken by this bold, ambitious project laid before him. As a result within a few weeks it was announced that the Alliance was to embark on this continental campaign and that Olsson would be leader over the whole of South America. In a short time, Simpson authorized Olsson to go to Britain and Europe to raise resources for this project. Simpson sent him off as "commended, therefore, to the confidence of all who are interested in this great field and authorized to communicate with volunteers for missionary work and receive contributions for the work in connection with the...Alliance..." In the May 21, 1897 issue of the *Christian and Missionary Alliance* (the latest iteration of the Alliance periodical's name), Olsson gave a report of his fund- and friend-raising trip to Europe. His trip began on January 20 and he returned to New York by the end of April. On the trip, he visited London, Liverpool, Edinburgh and Glasgow, Scotland, ending up in Sweden, his native land that he had left twenty years before. While in Liverpool, he visited the un-named "friend of the mission" who had promised a sizeable investment in the Alliance's efforts to reach the indigenous peoples of South America. By mid-June, Olsson and his family would be leaving for South America with a sizeable party of missionaries who would be going to Chile, Peru, Paraguay, Uruguay, Bolivia, Equator, Colombia, Venezuela, Brazil and Argentina. It was at this time that the first inkling of the transfer of the Jaú mission team to Buenos Aires was in the offing.

Before proceeding with this staggering strategy for the

evangelization of South America in four years, something of Simpson's missiology needs to be understood at that point. As pointed out in Shannon's article in *His Dominion*, "Before making harsh judgments regarding Simpson's naiveté in buying into a plan for evangelizing an entire continent in four years, the missionary purpose of the C&MA at that time should be taken into consideration." Grandiose goal-setting was prevalent. *The Student Volunteer Movement* begun in 1886 clearly stated: "The evangelization of the world in this generation." The great missionary "scramble for Africa" had that same kind of driving desire to see all the tribes of the heart of Africa reached within just a few years. Thus Simpson was simply reflecting that same desire and goal, and Olsson's strategy seemed a way of reaching South America.

Shannon goes on to comment on this chiliastic drive and expectation that Simpson and Olsson both had:

> Franklin Pyles has shown that a Biblical key to his [Simpson's] attitude with regard to the mission of the Church is Matthew 24:14, 'For this Gospel of the Kingdom shall be preached to the whole world as a witness to all the nations, and then the end shall come.' Simpson believed that during the millennium Christian Jews would be used for the conversion of the world. Before that time, however, the task of the Church was to give every tribe and nation at least one chance to hear the gospel and to see some from every group converted.' Thus missionaries were sent out for the purpose of getting a few people converted 'as a witness' and thus prepare the way for the second coming of Christ and the evangelization of

the world by the Jews in Christ's millennial reign. Simpson, at first, had little interest in planting churches and in indigenous principles. Neither was he concerned about 'encumbering missionary fellowships with ecclesiastical structure.' The Alliance was not a denomination in North America and Simpson did not desire that it become one in the regions beyond. Pyles said that 'it was not expected that a national church would rise up, but only that a few would be converted as a testimony.'

Such a perspective of this rather restricted role of "the Church" and its mission greatly influenced Simpson's decision-making in those "early days." Intrepid pioneer types such as Howell, Olsson, and William Cook, who trekked hundreds and thousands of miles doing the colporteur's work of distributing and selling Scripture portions and Bibles, witnessed to as many as they were able. For those who would listen and believe, the gospel was to be preached with power and a decision for Christ was to be sought. Thus over the miles of their journeys, one here and another there came to faith and followed Christ. However, Jesus, through the gospel writer *Matthew*, also had another word to give to the Church: "Go and make disciples of all the nations, baptizing them in the name of the Father, the Son and the Holy Ghost, teaching them to observe all that I have commanded you. And behold, I will be with you always, till the end of the age." *Matthew 28:18-20* gives a much broader explanation of the missionary task: As you go, empowered and authorized by Jesus Christ Himself, you will make disciples of all the nations and people groups of the world, as the gospel is proclaimed and believed. Those new believers then are to be discipled, nurtured, taught and baptized into the visible local body that is the tangible representation of Christ's universal Church. It is interesting to discover that A. B. Simpson, a man with a lifelong relationship to the visible church would not see the necessity of church planting as an essential part of the basic missionary task. This is an excellent example of eschatology trumping ecclesiology to its detriment.

As a result of this somewhat truncated theology of mission, in just five short months after Olsson met Simpson, the "Grand Plan" was presented to the larger Alliance constituency, and well before the end of the year, Olsson was stationed in Buenos Aires, the newly-established "headquarters" of the South American field. Soon there were new Alliance missionaries in Venezuela, Ecuador, Uruguay, Paraguay, Bolivia, Peru and Chile. On the voyage to Argentina with some of the new recruits, Olsson stopped off for a short visit to Belém, the capitol of the Province of Pará in northern Brazil with its countless unreached tribes and *mestiço* river-dwellers. He met independent Baptist missionary, Rev. Eric Nelson, who had been working for more than five years in the interior with various tribes and had a command of some tribal languages. Nelson, like Olsson, was a Swede by birth but had been a cowboy in Kansas when he sensed God's call on his life to be a missionary to Brazil. Thus, with his wife and family, he sold all and sailed to Belém do Pará. It was there that he was met by the newly-appointed Director of the Alliance work in South America.

By the end of the visit, Olsson had invited Nelson and wife to become Alliance missionaries and appointed them to head up the work to reach the indigenous of the Amazon. He eventually reached the port of Santos and took the train to Jaú and visited the farm. In short order, all of the Jaú staff: the

Emorys, Mr. Smart, Miss Felton and Mr. and Mrs. John Price, had been transferred to Buenos Aires.

Jaú No More

At this point, it is fair to ask what happened to the Jaú station and why was it closed so quickly? What had begun so auspiciously seemed to evaporate like ice cream in the hot Brazilian sun, and was no more. A hint as to what occurred had been published in the May 22 issue of the *CAFMW*, earlier that same year of 1896. In an interesting article, *"Facts Concerning Brazil,"* William Cook further described the Jaú station and farm. He told about the location of the farm a few miles from the railroad tracks, outside of the town of Jaú, in "a very healthy place." This was noteworthy given that the region had a lot of yellow fever and the town of Jaú itself had been decimated by the fever. The elementary school, recently organized by Miss Sallie Felton, had twenty-four pupils with potential for another forty if facilities could be obtained. In the midst of this newsy piece, Cook wrote: "We have nearly all necessary equipment for carrying on a successful work. All things considered, the expense of establishing ourselves here has been remarkably light, and there need be but slight further expenses. If we owned the property that we have established ourselves upon, as I thoroughly believe we should, we could sell at any time, receiving fair return for all moneys invested."

What was strange about that statement is that, in May of 1896, it did not seem that anyone was thinking of selling the property, or was there someone? J. B. Howell had left Brazil and was back in the U. S. by June 19. In a brief article, "Brazil Mission," written by Howell for the July 27 issue of the *CAFMW*, he reiterated what had been said previously, that "As the mission in Brazil was only started two years ago, the work there is still in an initial and experimental stage; nevertheless encouraging beginnings have been made." He goes on to talk about the farm and the training of seven native evangelists. He then adds that "The proposed course of study has been tested, and various questions relating to the inter-relation of the industrial and literary departments have received a practical solution." This rather opaque statement apparently alluded to the previous prayer request that had been mentioned in five consecutive issues of the *CAFMW* in March and April of 1896. "Pray for special guidance and blessing to be granted to our workers in Brazil in settling some matters of great moment at this time." Apparently the "various questions relating to the inter-relation of the industrial and literary departments" referred to the farm operation run by Mr. John Emory and the colporteur ministry led by Mr. William Cook. It would appear that there had been a problem integrating or coordinating these two ministries while Howell was on his preaching tours. It looked as if the resolution to the ongoing problem was part of Howell's reason for leaving Jaú and the C&MA Mission. From Cook's comment about the purchase of the property, Howell must have offered the Jaú farm to the C&MA for purchase. At the same time, the new vision brought forward by Emilio Olsson apparently took precedence over the Howell strategy; thus the Jaú mission station and farm were not purchased. Only William Cook remained in Brazil. The Jaú station was no more.

John and Elizabeth Price
Pioneers in Cuiabá, Mato Grosso

Among the Jaú mission's staff that left for Buenos Aires were Mr. and Mrs. John Price. Shortly after arriving in the beautiful capitol city of Argentina, by far the richest and most advanced city on the South American continent, Price wrote for the *CMA* of February 9, 1896 an article describing the efforts of the former Brazil missionaries to establish themselves in Argentina. He wrote about the advantages and disadvantages of learning Spanish after having

John & Elizabeth Price

studied Portuguese. He mentioned that with the former Brazil Mission staff, "We have with us our native worker [da Silva], who by his sweet disposition and earnestness has done a great deal for our work." On the "Correspondence" page of the *CMA*, dated March 23, 1898, it reads: "Mr. Price feels led to believe God would have him go to Western Brazil, Cuigoba (sic), its capitol [of the province of Mato Grosso], has 16,000 inhabitants. There is no worker there. He is praying for light and guidance and desires to know the feeling of the Board in this matter." A short time later in the September 28, 1898 issue of the *CMA*, they had traveled some twenty-five hundred miles from Buenos Aires to "Cuyaba, Matto Grosso," in far western Brazil, a month of travel, mostly by river boat. Price wrote: "This is a very important center, with some twenty-five large Indian villages nearby. In [his] last letter Mr. Price says, 'If at all possible, send us help, for we want to claim this territory for God. We are the only missionaries here. Send us men and money to advance at once. What an opportunity!'"

The Alliance history written in 1939, *After Fifty Years*, gives a thumbnail historical sketch of the first attempt to maintain a mission in Brazil. After outlining the work at Jaú, it goes on: "In the meantime some rather extensive pioneering was done in the Matto Grosso, and for two years among the jungle Indians." Mr. and Mrs. Price were indeed the first protestant missionary pioneers in the far western frontier town.

At this point, John and Elizabeth Price deserve a fuller treatment since they did not quietly ride off into the sunset of missionary anonymity. Research reveals that John Watkin Price was born in Tamaqua, PA in January, 1870. He studied for three years at *Oberlin Academy* in north-central Ohio in the early 1890s and was a starting player on the Academy's excellent 1893 football team, but did not graduate. Instead, he transferred to the *Christian Training School* (later *Malone College*) in Cleveland where he prepared for the ministry and graduated. He met his wife, Elizabeth Wittman, while at Cleveland. They were married June 18, 1895 and eventually had four children. Through his reading of Henry Guinness's book, *The Neglected Continent*, Price felt a definite call to Brazil where he and Elizabeth eventually spent more than 30 years as missionaries. The Price family formed deep roots in Brazil and one of Price's great grandsons today is a medical doctor and hospital chaplain in Rio Grande do Sul. According to the *Christian Alliance* of May 15, 1896, the Prices farewelled from the Gospel Tabernacle on May 3. The news note goes on:

> "A new missionary party for South America has just sailed [on May 7] The farewell meeting was held in the Gospel Tabernacle on Sabbath evening, May 3, to bid adieu to Mr. and Mrs. Price on their departure to Brazil. Mr. Price comes to us from our beloved Quaker friends, and was for some time the assistant of our dear brother, Mr. Walter Malone, in Cleveland, Ohio. He and his wife have been tried and proved as consecrated and effective workers who know the Holy Spirit,

and have been much used in winning souls for Christ."

Price and family sailed from Brooklyn on the *Coleridge* and docked in Brazil about the end of that same month, and soon joined the rest of the missionary staff in Jaú. Shortly thereafter, Olsson arrived at Jaú, quickly closed the station and took the whole staff to Buenos Aires which he established as the head station for South America.

The Door Opens in Argentina

Thus, 1896 is the "official" starting date for the Christian and Missionary Alliance work in Argentina. After more than more than a year in Buenos Aires province, the Price's move to Cuiabá, Mato Grosso was approved. He traveled alone up the Paraná River to *Corrientes*, then following the Paraguai River to *Assuncion*, Paraguay. From there he traveled to frontier town of *Corumbá*, Mato Grosso and then on to the last leg of the trip on the Caxipós River to *Cuiabá*. The total journey took twenty-three days. He soon returned to get Elizabeth and their young daughter and retraced his steps to Cuiabá in July of the same year. While in Cuiabá, Price, a man of culture and well educated for such a wilderness town, made a good impression on the intellectuals and helped found the *Sociedade Geográfica* for the region. The next step on Price's missionary pilgrimage is a bit confusing, since there are two conflicting tales on what happened next.

In the *Rebirth of the Paraguayan Republic: The First Colorado Era, 1878-1904* by Harris Gaylord Warren, it is stated that in 1899, missionary John Price and a local land-grant farmer, Mr. E. Kirk, had joined two British explorers, Williamson and Foster, who were exploring south of Cuiabá in hostile tribal forest lands, where Price and Kirk were murdered. However, like Mark Twain, it appears that Price's demise was prematurely announced, since several sources unequivocally confirm that he actually lived to a ripe old age and died in 1951 in Denver, Colorado. It is possible that he indeed was part of the Williamson Expedition, since he was an adventurous sort, but whatever happened on the ill-fated expedition, Price definitely survived.

The more prosaic version of his life, confirmed by several sources, states that the Prices left Mato Grosso and became a Methodist missionary in May 1899, moving down to Rio Grande do Sul where he served with the Methodist Mission for more than three decades. Shortly before he left Cuiabá with his sick wife, Price was heard by the João Pedro Dias family, later Presbyterian pioneers in the region, who had just moved to the frontier town. With Price and his family's departure, the Alliance initiative in Cuiabá ceased in 1899. Apparently the cause of his joining the Methodist Mission was related to the difficulty that the C&MA had in being able to regularly send the Price's monthly financial allowance from New York to Cuiabá. Lack of dependable communications and bank-transfer technology apparently was the cause of this failure to keep their support arriving regularly.

While all of these moves and changes were taking place over a period of about two years, 1897-1898, it would appear at first that the dynamic new leader of the C&MA's South American Mission was giving positive leadership to his scattered missionary band all over the continent. However, disturbing reports soon started arriving at the New York Alliance headquarters. A single male missionary in Paraguay, Mr. Irving Hathaway, became deranged and took his life while suffering from a "malignant fever." The missionary team left in

Buenos Aires rebelled against Olsson's dictatorial leadership style and told the mission leaders at the New York headquarters that they would not accept his leadership anymore and provided a long list of grievances. Like J. B. Howell, Olsson had taken long trips to preach and distribute Bibles and Scripture portions leaving his colleagues in Buenos Aires for months at a time in financial and personal distress.

Early in 1899, a report from Olsson found him surfacing after months of silence following a long trek inland. Once again the peripatetic, former sailor had traveled through Paraguay and Bolivia to the headwaters of the Amazon. From there he moved on down the mighty river, preaching, selling Bibles and hunting out new tribes in need of evangelization. Once again his voyage was characterized by "adventure and narrow escapes." (Shannon, p. 18) All was not well on the South America field.

Olsson Dismissed

In a short time, Olsson was back in New York where he had been summoned in early April 1899, by the Alliance Board, to answer questions regarding his leadership and arbitrary decisions. The July 1, 1899 issue of CAMA tersely stated that Mr. Olsson had been "dismissed as a missionary of the Christian and Missionary Alliance." The following issue, July 8, 1899, carried almost three full pages of the charges and countercharges on this imbroglio. In essence, there were three major areas of failure by Olsson. (1) Administrative excess and arbitrary misuses of his authority. He had invited and appointed missionaries, i.e., the Nelsons in Pará, to become full-fledged missionaries of the C&MA without Board approval and solely on his authority. He opened and closed stations without consultation, reassigned and "fired" missionaries who did not agree with his decisions. (2) He was charged with financial malfeasance since he misused mission funds that had been raised in the U. S. and Europe. In fact, he had visited the "mysterious friend of the mission" while in Europe before taking his missionary team to South America.

Indeed it was Robert Arthington, the missionary philanthropist, who had indicated his desire to give major funding to the Alliance for the evangelization of South America. The meeting between Olsson and Arthington apparently did not go well and resulted in such an "unfavorable impression made by Mr. Olsson and his plan of work on Mr. Arthington that the latter gentlemen withdrew his promised gift and has not sent us a single dollar toward the mission." Olsson used the funds raised in Britain and Sweden without consultation with the Alliance. As a result, he was found to have made personal expenditures with mission funds. (3) His long absences from Buenos Aires and rash decisions had caused a revolt by the Argentine mission staff who would no longer accept his leadership, forcing the mission to act in order to save the work and workers in South America. (4) Finally, he was charged with insubordination for refusing to meet with the Board to resolve the issues and give him the opportunity to still serve with the Alliance as a "private missionary." This rebellious attitude was apparently the straw that broke the patient camel's back.

Apparently Olsson had met with the board once where he was defiant, refusing to accept the board's authority, while confirming the substance of the charges made against him by the Buenos Aires staff. Rather than showing humility and a desire to make amends, Olsson went to the secular and religious press and made serious countercharges against A. B. Simpson and his co-workers. As a result, Simpson made a public response in the C&MA periodical as well as in one of the New York newspapers. *The Baptist Examiner*, which had published Olsson's charges without first contacting the Alliance, refused to print the C&MA's rebuttal. All in all, the whole affair left the South American fields in disarray for some time. Some missionaries from Argentina left the field. William Cook, the only Alliance missionary still in Brazil, continued to soldier on alone.

William Cook – Evangelist Explorer

Of all of the Jaú station staff that remained on the farm after Howell left the field, William Azel Cook is doubtless the most noteworthy in terms of energy and accomplishments. Cook, in his amazing book, *Through the Wildernesses of Brazil by Horse, Canoe and Float*, published in 1909 by the American Tract Society, mentions John Beatty Howell: "The first months of my residence in Brazil were passed near the town of Jahú,

William Cook

the terminus of a railway, some three hundred miles west of São Paulo. The missionary who first preached the Gospel here was dragged through the streets by the beard. Afterward, Dr. Chamberlain evangelized here, and the Rev. J. Beatty Howell labored devotedly and successfully for many years in this region, going from place to place on horseback. . . . A lady missionary [Miss Sally Felton] conducted a school for a time for the children of the poor country folk in the district where I stayed [Jaú], the attendance at which was large as there was a strong church here. It was a bitter grief to these children when the school was permanently given up . . . ." Thus Cook described what happened in 1897 when Olsson transferred all of the staff from Jaú to Buenos Aires to open the Alliance Mission there.

Cook remained in Brazil until 1902. Essentially, his ministry, described in his book *Through the Wildernesses . . .* took him all over Central and Western Brazil. He traveled by horse and mule, canoe and on foot through the "provinces" of Goiás and Minas Gerais, as well those known now known as Mato Grosso and Mato Grosso do Sul. He spent many months at a time out of contact with all means of communication. On one trip, he even collected specimens of native art, flora and fauna, and indigenous artifacts from the Bororó Indians for the *Smithsonian Institute* in Washington. He preached and taught those who would listen, sold Bibles and Scripture portions. Being a single man, he traveled light and roughed it, sleeping in his tent, in homes of friendly interior farm folk, abandoned hovels and Indian huts. Malaria and tropical fevers were occasional travel companions and lice and bedbugs were daily fellow travelers. William Cook, infected by the travel bug, clocked thousands of miles evangelizing Brazil's hinterland populations.

Over the years he was associated with the Alliance, Cook sent in many amazing accounts of his travels and travails while working as an itinerant evangelist and colporteur. An example was found both in Cook's book, *Through the Wildernesses . . .* and also the C&MA publication, *Living Truths*, the October edition of 1902. Cook recounts the story of a "Spanish sailor who had lived a very dissolute and reckless life [who] came in contact with what the Apostle Paul declares is the "power" or dynamite of God unto salvation. . . ." This former sailor became a representative of the *British and Foreign Bible Society* and traveled all over Brazil's interior and "penetrated into the heart of Brazil with the Bible. There he met a man from the far-away state of Goyaz who was one of the respected chiefs of a very numerous family extending to the third and fourth generation. To this man the transformed mariner told the story of his life and what had produced the great change, which profoundly impressed [the respected family patriarch], and he also embraced the great salvation. . . ."As a result, this man purchased many Bibles and distributed them to family members and friends, which resulted in a spontaneous people movement among the farmers and ranchers of the region where he lived.

Cook continues his story: "When we visited this region in 1900 we went first to the large cattle ranch owned by the one who was grandfather, great grandfather and elder of the church, and his children, spiritual and natural – celestial and terrestrial – began to gather in. Forty-four grandchildren were present. The women and girls swarmed into the huge kitchen and backyard, while the men filled up the large hall-like front room and occupied the front yard, the corn-crib and other outbuildings." During four days, these simple believers, much like the members of the primitive church, met regularly for worship, the preaching and teaching of the Word, for fellowship and mutual encouragement. The congregation that met at the *Retiro* Ranch, about 25 miles from Santa Luzia, was the "mother church" for another three congregations of Bible believers in that region of Goiás.

The churches had come into being simply through the testimony of the "Spanish Sailor." Is it conceivable that this "sailor" was none other than Emílio Olsson on one of his long itinerant tramps through Brazil's interior before he met

Simpson and joined the Alliance in 1896? It is possible that Olsson related this conversion story to Cook, giving him the name and location of the patriarch's ranch. These churches eventually became part of the Brazilian Presbyterian Church. Thus William Cook described this amazing instance of the power of God unto salvation to all who believe.

C&MA publications carried many other journal accounts of his trips and trials as he shared the Gospel in word and print to those he encountered. While meritorious in terms of sacrifice and service, he finished his work in 1902 when the C&MA decided that the ministry was not bringing visible, lasting results. After furlough in the United States, Cook returned to Brazil with the Presbyterian Board of Foreign Mission and continued his itinerant ministry for more than a decade all over the Center-Western interior of Brazil. According to family genealogical information, "Dr. William A. Cook" became a Presbyterian pastor "in a little town" north of Springfield, Massachusetts, after serving a total of seventeen years in Brazil. After leaving the Alliance, he apparently returned and was involved in various expeditions to Brazil where he collected native artifacts that are found in the National Museum of Natural History in Washington, D.C. He also excelled as a photographer and a collection of his photographs taken on the expeditions are found in the *National Anthropological Archives* in Washington.

The Door Closed in Brazil

As a result, 1904 was the last year for Brazil to appear as an Alliance mission on the field list even though there were no Alliance missionaries present in the country. Its absence was to be prominent for many years since such a great effort had been made to establish the Brazil C&MA Mission to no avail. None the less, A. B. Simpson had a long memory and Brazil was never out of his heart and mind. Thus after almost a decade in Brazil, The C&MA left the country with little to show for the years of initiative and investment made by the Brazil mission staff from 1894 to 1904.

Yet despite this lack of permanent presence in Brazil, Olsson's lasting effect on the Alliance can be seen in the fact there are strong Alliance national churches in Argentina, Chile and Ecuador, all of which were opened by his "Great Plan" for the Americas. On the other hand, Brazil, Paraguay, Uruguay and Bolivia were still-born efforts. It was many years later that these countries were reached again by the Alliance Churches in Argentina, Chile and Peru. Rev, and Mrs. Nelson of Pará, had been "appointed" by Olsson over the Amazon River Basin work among the tribes and were even listed in Alliance publications as Brazil missionaries, but they soon disappeared from view as quickly as they had appeared, although they continued to work in Belém for many years.

Less than a decade later, in 1910 , Dr. A. B. Simpson took an extensive ocean voyage and toured the South American fields aboard the *S. S. Moltke*. While sailing down the coast of Central America, after just passing the equator, he wrote for the March 5, 1910 *C&MA* publication: "The Alliance has no missionaries in Brazil. For some years it maintained a single station near São Paulo [Jaú], but the work was transferred to Argentina many years ago and concentrated there. . . . Our last Brazilian missionary was Mr. Cook

S.S. Moltke

whose volume on South America was recently reviewed in these columns and is for sale by the Alliance Press Co. But Mr. Cook was so much of a traveler and explorer in the interior of Brazil, that our Board finally questioned the utility of maintaining his costly and extended journeys without our being able to follow them up by established mission stations, and in consequence the mission was closed." Thus Simpson explains the reason for Cook's leaving the mission due the lack of permanent results from his evangelistic forays in the hinterlands.

A natural question must be asked at this end of this once -promising C&MA Mission in Brazil. Why, after so many years of interest and intercession on Simpson's part and the seeming providential meeting of John Bailey Howell with A. B. Simpson in 1893, did this venture eventually tail off with no lasting effects despite appearing to have required considerable expenditure of missionaries, money and manpower? More than a century separates us from those involved, but a few tentative reasons may be ventured: (1) the great vision and passion evidenced by Simpson was not accompanied by a commensurate amount of "on-the-ground" experience and knowledge. As was the case with the ill-fated sending of the Congo Band to Cabinda in 1885, the senders and the sent were woefully unaware of the difficulties and dangers to be faced while establishing a new mission. (2) There also was an apparent lack of coherent strategic planning for the mission to be established. As a result, the vision and drive of Howell and Olsson became the strategies that Simpson and his infant mission were to follow. The hyper-ambitious plan of Olsson to evangelize all of South America in four years with eighty five missionaries was not only unrealistic; it was impossible, given the limited resources of the new Alliance mission and the enormity of the task. (3) Another serious problem occurred in the establishment of the Brazil

Alliance Mission because Simpson's mission lacked experienced veterans. Thus he received missionaries whose roots and reasons for being free and available should have been investigated more closely and thoroughly before receiving them into leadership positions with the C&MA. Both Howell and Olsson were accepted and commissioned by the Alliance just a few months after contacting Simpson. As was the case on other newly-opened fields, the C&MA became a flag of convenience for venturesome missionaries that sought freedom from the rules and regulations of more established missions. And finally, (4) there was a distinct lack of capable headquarter Alliance administrative staff to manage the newly opened South American Missions of the C&MA.

Neither Howell nor Olsson demonstrated leadership gifting and ability in relation to the missionaries that they were tasked to direct. Their responsibility was to give direction to workers who would be doing the work. Instead, these two men were "doers," pioneer path-finders, each seeking to make his mark and prove his methodology and philosophy of mission. (5) The final flaw of this initial venture into Brazil directly relates to the eventual failure of the mission. Emílio Olsson and William Cook, and even John Price, were cut from the same cloth as relates to their desire to reach the lost at any cost. Since they also shared Simpson's understanding that the task of the mission was "seed scattering" and not "church planting," their strategy and activities revolved around that missiological mind set. The less than desirable results of such an approach were foreseeable when seen in a broader understanding of the task of world evangelization. The "witness to all the nations" of Matthew 24:14 was not just throwing and sowing the seed, but also the job of working the soil and plowing through prayer. Then comes the careful planting of the evangelistic seed and the vital disciple-making component which eventually leads to the raising up of an indigenous church that can reproduce itself. This more biblically broad-based understanding of the whole task of mission eventually came to be understood and accepted by Simpson and the C&MA. But in its earliest years, the "get-it-done-now" mindset handicapped the work of the Alliance in many newly-opened fields.

One can only imagine what might have happened had that first staff stayed in Jaú and followed John Howell's plan to train and prepare native evangelists to reach their own people with the gospel, planting churches and raising up what would eventually be a strong national church built on a firm foundation. Simple biological growth over more than a century would have numbered the Brazilian Alliance Church among the major evangelical bodies in Brazil. However, it appears that Providence did not smile upon the fleeting efforts of those missionaries involved in "the first try." However, God hadn't forgotten Brazil, nor had the C&MA.

Simpson's Lasting Vision For Brazil

In the March 26, 1910 issue of the *C&MA*, Simpson continues his travel journal logging his voyage down the west coast of South America. His first port of call was at *Belém do Pará*, where the mighty Amazon plunges its watery dagger into the heart of the South Atlantic, staining its bosom with a muddy-bloody blotch for more than 50 miles out to sea. Meditating during his visit to this northern Brazilian state capital, Simpson writes:

> We cannot help thinking what a splendid base Pará would make for such a mission [to the Amazon River valley]. It is one of the healthiest

cities in the world and commands this whole region. A wise and enterprising missionary here with one or two young men and as many native helpers could establish a base in Pará and with a good steam launch and a supply of literature, could go up this river system in various directions and within a reasonable distance reach great numbers not only of the natives but also Indians, of whom there are more than a million on the tributaries of the Amazon.

Simpson then goes on with his prophetic musing:

We at least commend the valley of the Amazons to earnest prayers of some of the young men who read these lines, and some of the people of means who would like to have the honor of giving the Gospel to the Indians of South America. . . We have humbly dared to set the sole of our foot upon the Amazon valley and claim it for God, by whomsoever He may send.

So ends the account of the "first try" by the C&MA Mission to establish a missionary ministry in Brazil with lasting effects. Only God in eternity may reveal the fruit of the Jaú mission station, of Howell and Cook's extensive journeys through Brazil's interior, Olsson's Homeric trips up and trips down the Amazon River and John Price's short-lived pioneer penetration to Cuiabá, Mato Grosso.

CHAPTER TWO

BANANAL

The last few years of Dr. A. B. Simpson's life saw the great leader's health enter into gradual decline. Simpson wearily wore the role of founder and beloved father of the movement. This dwindling of energy came to the fore in 1918. Simpson's granddaughter, Katherine Alberta Brennen described a major reason for his rapid decline in *The Wife or Love Stands*, a biographical sketch of Simpson's wife, Margret Henry Simpson. "When General Allenby entered Jerusalem in 1918 [actual date was December 1917], Grandfather [Simpson] suffered a stroke of paralysis while seated at his desk. The rapture of the event, coupled with fifty years of a supernaturally active life, was such a terrific shock to his whole system that he never recovered." In the early 1900s, those looking for signs of Christ's return understood Allenby's triumphant march into Jerusalem to be hugely significant, just as the 1948 United Nations' decision to recognize the founding of the modern state of Israel deeply impacted another generation of *Maranatha* seekers.

The winter of 1917-1918 was difficult for Simpson because Nyack's winters could be severe and long. According to biographer A. E. Thompson, "He submitted to urgent solicitation and, accompanied by Mrs. Simpson, spent a few weeks with his friends of other days at Clifton Springs, New

York. He did not, as some have suggested, take medical treatment. Dr. Sanders of the sanitarium was an old friend and a former attendant at the Tabernacle, and thoroughly understood Dr. Simpson's position." During the rest of the year he resumed limited activity at the New York headquarters and Missionary Training Institute, but he had already begun to hand over the reins to others to forward the world evangelization movement that he had founded.

Before the next Annual Council of the C&MA, held in May, 1918 at Nyack, Dr. Simpson requested that Mr. Ulysses Lewis, Vice-President, preside over the Council and lead the business sessions, most of which Dr. Simpson attended, but not as an active participant. At that Council, he turned over the rest of his business affairs to the Alliance and watched as trusted younger leaders stepped forward. Paul King's monumental work of research, *"Genuine Gold – The Cautiously Charismatic Story of the Early Christian and Missionary Alliance,"* describes Simpson's last year:

> As Simpson aged, more responsibilities were shifted to other Alliance leaders, and they began to consider who would succeed Simpson; in January 1919, Simpson suffered [another] stroke. Though he continued without pain, he became unable to function   actively as the leader of the C&MA. On May 31, 1919, Paul Rader, pastor of Moody Memorial Church, was elected Vice President of the C&MA.

Simpson missed attending 1919 Annual Council at the Institute in Toccoa Falls, GA. The rest the spring and summer of 1919, Simpson remained in his Nyack home with

Margaret, his loving wife and partner in the yoke of service to their Lord. He was faithfully cared for by one of the MTI graduates, Levin Keller Brubaker of Lancaster PA, who graduated from the last MTI class in New York City. For 16 years he was Business Manager and Treasurer of the Institute.

A. E. Thompson Describes Simpson's Last Day

On Tuesday, October 28, [Simpson] spent the morning on his veranda and received a visit from Judge Clark, of Jamaica, conversing freely, and praying fervently for Rev. and Mrs. George H. A. McClare, our Alliance missionaries in Jamaica, and for the missionaries in other fields, who were always in his mind. After the Judge left him, he suddenly lost consciousness and was carried to his room. His daughter, Margaret, and a little group of friends watched by his bedside with Mrs. Simpson till his great spirit took leave of his worn out body and returned to God who gave it, early on Wednesday morning, October 29, 1919.

A Coincidence?

Amazingly, Simpson's last visitor, Judge William P. Clark, pioneer leader of the C&MA in Jamaica, was the father of the man who was to spearhead the second Alliance effort to enter Brazil where no C&MA missionaries had worked for at least fifteen years. It is likely Simpson and the senior Clark talked about Brazil and his son, Ray, a tent-maker missionary in São Paulo who sensed a heavy burden for the great nation. Perhaps they recalled together Simpson's 1910 visit to the port city of Belém, capital of the State of Pará and his prophetic word: "We . . . commend the valley of the Amazons to earnest prayers of some of the young men who read these lines, and some of the people of means who would like to have the honor of giving the Gospel to the Indians of South America. . . . We have humbly dared to set the sole of our foot upon the Amazon valley and claim it for God, by whomsoever He may send." It would appear that Simpson's commitment to Brazil was not ready to die even though he was about to leave this world.

So who were these Clarks and how did the tiny Jamaican Alliance have such influence on the Alliance Mission's plans for the enormous country of Brazil? Many of the answers to these queries are found in a just-published book, *A Godly Heritage: Jamaican Planter Families Planting the Church at Home and Abroad*, by Lloyd A. Cooke. Dr. Cooke is professor of Bible and Theology at *Regent College of the Caribbean* (formerly known as *Jamaica Bible College*). Dr. Cooke chronicles the amazing world mission contribution made by the island nation of Jamaica. Among the numerous missionaries who ministered the world over are the Clarks, who had originally come to Jamaica from England.

The following narrative from Cooke's book paints a picture of the Judge's first son:

> It was with the C&MA that the first son of Judge William P. Clark would serve as a missionary for most of his life. But when he first went to Brazil in 1911, it was as an independent College teacher of Engineering at McKenzie (sic) College at São Paulo that Ray B. would go. He wanted to be a 'tentmaker' missionary. Ray, like many a Jamaican planter's child, had been sent to

England for his formal education. He studied at Dulwich College, England and later at McGill University in Quebec, where he graduated as a Civil Engineer. Jamaica's *Daily Gleaner* of November 7th 1911 carried the story of Ray's going to Brazil telling us that ". . . He proceeds there [Brazil] in January to take up his duties in February 1912. Mr. Clark has given up brighter financial prospects in Canada to do Missionary work at his own charge."

David Clark, Ray Clark's son, continues his father's story relating how he began to teach at Mackenzie College, as well as working with colporteurs and missionaries of the *Evangelical Union of South America (EUSA)*. He learned Portuguese and gained much practical experience selling and distributing Scriptures during his vacations.

After a few years in São Paulo, Ray met and fell in love with a beautiful young Brazilian, Lucy Shalders. She was the daughter of Dr. Carlos Gomes de Souza Shalders, also a professor of Civil Engineering at Mackenzie. Shalders was son of the British Consul General who had married a Brazilian lady. Thus Lucy was Anglo-Brazilian. Ray and Lucy married in 1914. Sadly they lost twin boys prematurely, with one dying at birth and the other two days later.

Lucy Shalders

Despite this huge blow to their hearts, they continued to trust the Lord. They worked with other Mackenzie faculty members and helped found a "weekly missionary prayer meeting," which eventually evolved into the São Paulo Union Church. By 1917 they were able to purchase a plot of land and constructed a "pretty little house" in the new *Higienóplis* neighborhood. After several years of marriage and ministry in Brazil, they were blessed with a son, David Brooke Clark in 1919. Within a few months that same year, Alliance leaders began conversations about the possibility of entering Brazil, with Ray to spearhead to the initiative. Ray and Lucy sailed to New York with their infant son in late 1919, not long after Simpson's death. Interestingly enough, Ray recorded: "Prior to our leaving Brazil I had been invited by the Evangelical Union of South America to return to Brazil to cooperate in starting a Bible Institute in São Paulo. That was a definite confirmation from the Lord of our decision to return as missionaries." It was apparent that God had been preparing Ray and Lucy for their next step as missionaries.

Their infant son, David, was born during the terrible 1919 plague of *Spanish Influenza*. Ray writes:

During the month of November 1918, toward the end of World War I, I was called to help at Mackenzie College, then converted into an Emergency Hospital. The Spanish Flu was raging around the world and São Paulo was experiencing 75% epidemic. Among other duties that fell to me was loading corpses, wrapped in sheets onto the trucks. That was going on day and night for weeks. It was a terrible experience for me. This was specially so as my little wife was looking forward to the arrival of our baby. . . But day by day we lived by faith, and our faith was rewarded. The testing made the arrival of little David even more welcome.

The Influenza pandemic of 1918-1919 took 20 to 40 million lives worldwide, more than the bloody trench warfare of WWI. The Clark family sailed from Santos to escape the deadly epidemic in São Paulo for the colder, healthier climate of North America. However, after arriving in New York and traveling up the Hudson River to Nyack, the deadly virus caught up with the Clark family and took Lucy's life shortly after their arrival. She died on February 8, 1920, leaving a grieving father and motherless child. "Devastated, the young father could not begin a new missionary career burdened with a less than year-old son. Ray Clark buried Lucy in the Oak Hill cemetery in Nyack, New York, and then took his son David home to his parents in Mandeville, Kendal, Jamaica. He spent the next year and a half helping Rev. McClare pastor the Devon C&MA Church, and in planting a new outreach in the city of Kingston."

Hope Never Dies

Amazingly, "Baby David" Clark, the infant son of Ray and Lucy Clark is 99 years old, still alive and well at the time of this writing (2017), living in Fort Wayne, Indiana. He has provided invaluable information and insight into his father's life and ministry. Ray's diary was transcribed by David and has provided an abundance of personal experiences from Ray's life that give color and context to the *Bananal* story. Following Lucy's death, Ray journaled his thoughts and questions: "Two years followed during which time I was waiting for the guiding light from the Lord. Was it still to be Brazil as I was hoping?"

While waiting in Jamaica and helping the infant Alliance churches, Ray was contacted by the C&MA Board following the February 21, 1921 meeting where the Foreign Department Committee's (FDC) recommendation that the question of [the] possible opening of work in Brazil in connection with the plan of the Clark-Lord party to engage in work there, be held in abeyance until further consultation is had with the members of the party and with the *Committee of Co-operation in Latin American* concerning the Brazil Field."

The Committee of Cooperation for Latin America (CoC) had come into being in 1916. It was part of the response to the 1910 Edinburg Missionary Conference which considered Latin America to be "evangelized" by the Roman Catholic Church. The Protestant missions working on the Southern Continent, including the C&MA, strongly disagreed with this position, and as a result they founded the CoC. Its purpose was to coordinate the many evangelical missions working in Central and South American countries and purposed to encourage cooperation between missions rather than competition. Questions of "comity," defined as "courtesy and considerate behavior toward others," were presented to and resolved by the CoC, which helped missions avoid "stepping on each other's toes" as well as unnecessary duplication of effort resulting in confusion and conflict. Cooperative efforts through the Bible Societies, literature publication, Bible Institutes and Seminaries were also a part of CoC's brief.

In Brazil, Dr. Erasmo Braga, son of one of Brazil's first Presbyterian pastors, headed up the Brazilian office of the CoC called the *Comissão Brasileira de Cooperação (Brazilian Commission of Cooperation).* Braga ably represented the Protestant church of his country. After consultation to ensure that the Alliance's objective of working among unreached people groups in Brazil met with the goals of the CoC and that no other mission had laid claim to the Island of Bananal, the C&MA received the green light to move forward with the intent to re-enter Brazil after almost 20 years of absence. A few months later, Ray wrote: ". . . I was asked by the New York Board of the Christian and Missionary Alliance to consider leading a group to open up work in Brazil for the . . . Alliance. I was then called to New York to talk to the Board and formulate definite plans."

The C&MA Board of Manager's meeting of June 15, 1921 gave approval to the FDC's recommendation: "That the Board approve the entrance of the Alliance into Brazil as a new Mission Field and that the following plan be approved in general, development of details to be worked out. Mr. R. B. Clark to be recognized as the Leader of the party who will first enter Brazil . . . It is expected that Messrs. R. B. Clark and John D. Clark will go to the field for the purpose of opening up the work in the Spring of 1922, . . . It is suggested that the field of labor chosen be south of the Amazon with [Belém do] Pará as a base. . . . " In just a few weeks, Ray was put on allowance following the June 28 meeting of the FDC: "That Mr. R. B. Clark be granted an allowance of $30.00 [monthly] furlough allowance plus $10 rental allowance dating as of June 1st since he is regularly appointed as a Missionary to Brazil and is now in deputational service for the Foreign Department.

The June 18, 1921 issue of *The Alliance Weekly* (*AW*) presented the "Annual Report of the Foreign Department for 1920." As a result of the call sent out by Rev. Paul Rader, the dynamic new president of the C&MA, the report stated that sixty new missionaries, including twenty-five men, were appointed and ready to be deployed overseas. The report went on to say that during the past year a group had offered themselves for Missionary service in Brazil, providing the Alliance is led of God to open work in that great needy field. Clearly the vision shared by Simpson and Judge Clark two years before was considered viable still.

Brazil Bound

By the fall of 1921, Ray was back in the United States preparing to go to Brazil. The *Alliance Weekly* began to mention him regularly as one of the missionary speakers at the missionary conventions in Pennsylvania and New Jersey, listed as a missionary from Brazil. The November 19 issue of the AW featured a major article, "Our New Mission Field, Brazil," by R. B Clark. In this extensive report of the potential of Brazil, the spiritual needs and challenges, Ray presents the strategic aims of this new effort: ". . . the objective of the Alliance in entering Brazil is *two-fold*, namely: the evangelizing of these neglected portions of the Portuguese-speaking Catholics, and also the opening up later on should Jesus tarry – of a work among the pagan Indians of the hinterland."

> The doorway into these neglected regions to which the Lord has definitely pointed us is at the mouth of the mighty Amazon . . . the City of Para, (the real name still very frequently used is Belem, or Bethlehem) a city of a quarter of a million people. This city is an outstanding exception to most of the large sea-coast towns in that there is practically no missionary work being carried on there. [This is] The city we hope to make our headquarters.

The December 10 issue of the AW records the travel journal of Rev. W. M. Turnbull, dean of the MTI, and recently appointed Deputation secretary for the C&MA by Rev. Rader. Sent by the Board, Turnbull surveyed the South American fields and reported back to the Mission leaders about the needs and challenges being faced on the southern continent. In this lengthy article, Turnbull mentions three distinct confirmations that the Alliance Board took into consideration when deciding whether or not to open the Brazil field:

A Portal in Pará

The story of God's leading in connection with this city [Belém do Pará] is one of the refreshing instances of providential guiding. When Mr. R. V. (sic) Clark, who is to lead the new party, was praying over the plans for entering northern Brazil, Para was impressed upon his mind as the Lord's thought for a base of operations. He asked God to confirm his leading by bringing the Board to the same decision without any expression of his own convictions. When the Board prayerfully went over the field with accurate maps on hand, by unanimous choice this city was chosen, and thus the guidance of God confirmed. Not till several months after this clear leading did any member of the Board know of the article from Dr. Simpson's pen concerning Para. When the writer found the paragraphs . . . they seemed like a voice from beyond the grave.

Later in the article, Turnbull described his short stay in Belém do Pará with his wife, finding the city amazingly beautiful and surprisingly comfortable for a tropical city, and seemingly an excellent location in terms of health and modernity. He then commented: "It was impossible in the short time at our disposal, and without proper introductions and addresses, to obtain much desired information about the precise missionary conditions and possibilities of this vast region." He added near the end of the report: "A wise and enterprising missionary here with one or two young men and as many native helpers could establish a base in Para and, with a good steam launch and a supply of literature, could go up this river system in various directions and within a reasonable distance reach great numbers not only the natives but also Indians, of whom there are more than a million on the tributaries of the Amazon."

Several months, later, on May 6, 1922, another Turnbull-authored article appeared in the AW, "*Through the Argentine and the Voyage Home*," where he recounts his return to the United States with his wife. Their ship stopped in Rio for a few days and they were able to do some sightseeing in Brazil's breathtakingly beautiful capital city. They saw the preparations being made for the celebration of Brazil's Centennial later that same year and admired the level of comfort enjoyed by the city dwellers. He judged that the wealth of Brazil had made Rio the beautiful city that it was, to the expense of the rest of the country, and he was correct in his assessment. He wrote: "We learned [while in Rio] that the north of Brazil is almost entirely without missionary effort. It was not possible for us to visit Para without a long delay. We had to sail by the mouth of the Amazon without even a glimpse of the shores at this point. But we carefully gathered all the information which was available and were profoundly moved to discover that the most neglected portion of the continent is that which lies north of the equator and therefore nearest to us.

Thus it appears that Rev. Turnbull's total time spent in Belém was about one day. The shortness of their stay in the "doorway to the Amazon" was later to be regretted because of the brief time he had to gather accurate information as to the number of missions based in Belém. The lack of factual, on-the-ground data would prove to bear serious consequences to the success of the "Clark Party" that was soon to depart from Jamaica for Brazil.

David Clark's transcription of Ray's diary follows all of the developments up to the moment of departure from Jamaica to Brasil:

> Early in May of the following year, 1922, was the time set for going to Brazil. Deep down in my soul I felt happy and grateful to the Lord for calling me back to Brazil, and this time as a full-time missionary. But there was another side of the picture. My little baby was now a beautiful little boy three years of age, and we had become very closely attached to one another. "Are you going to leave me, Daddy?" was a hard question to answer at the age of three. He would be left in capable and devoted hands, I knew, for he already loved "Gramps" and "Grannie." And how they loved him! He would be surrounded by love, but it was *hard* as I looked back to see the little hands waving good-bye. So closed another chapter.

In the next month, the June 10 issue of the *AW* announced: "Mr. R. B. Clark expects to sail for Brazil in June accompanied by Mr. and Mrs. D[avid] S. Clark and Mr. John D.

Clark, to enter upon pioneer work in a portion of that field with Para as a base, and working down the valleys of the Tocantins and Araguaya rivers." Some months later, the December 9 *AW* of 1922 reported on the various advances made into South America "where the Alliance is witnessing to the Savior's love... Brazil – the latter being a recent advance movement, with headquarters in Para, a city of 200,000; and the work will be pushed forward hundreds of miles among the Indians." Thus, the Clark clan had arrived in the great northern capital of Belém do Pará. John and David Clark were Ray's first cousins; John was single and David was already married.

The Amazing Odyssey

R. B. Clark's book, *Bananal or Among the Pagan Indians of Brasil*, which described the amazing odyssey through the heart of Brazil's hinterland, tells what they discovered when the Clark Party arrived in the port city at the mouth of the Amazon:

> On the 17th of June 1922 our party of four sailed for Brazil from New York under the auspices of The Christian and Missionary Alliance. This party consisted of Mr. and Mrs. D. S. Clark and his brother, J. D. Clark and myself. We had as our destination the Port of Pará at the mouth of the Amazon River. Here we intended to make our headquarters while the Portuguese language was being acquired by those who were new to the field while we made a thorough investigation of the whole Amazon Valley in order to find out the field of greatest need and discover just where God was calling us to labour.

At first we thought that it might be Pará itself, but soon found this city to be occupied by missionaries of the Baptist, Presbyterian and Methodist Churches as well as by a Pentecostal Mission. Hence we began to look further afield and made minute investigation into the conditions of the Valley as a whole from the standpoint of the distribution of missionary effort. We found that the Baptists had a considerable work in this region and planned a big forward move. The Presbyterians also, we learned, are located in the Valley. With this information and knowing how small is the population of Amazonia in comparison to its vast area, we began to wonder if our work did not lie rather among the pagan Indians than among the Roman Catholic Brazilians.

At this point, it becomes clear that the initial information Ray Clark had gathered before going to Brazil was faulty. In his two and a half page article written in November of 1921, "Our New Mission Field, Brazil," he stated: "This city is an outstanding exception to most of the large sea-coast towns in that there is practically no missionary work being carried on there. The city we hope to make our headquarters." This inaccurate evaluation, followed by the Turnbull report which seconded the idea that the North of Brazil, principally Pará, as the least reached region of Brazil, was critical. In the May 6, 1922 *Alliance Weekly*, Turnbull reported:

It was not possible for us to visit Para without a long delay. We had to sail by the mouth of the

Amazon without even a glimpse of the shores at this point. But we carefully gather all the information which was available and were profoundly moved to discover that *the most neglected portion of the continent is that which lies north of the equator and therefore nearest to us* (editor's italics).

The brief one-day visit by the Turnbulls to Belém on February 1, 1921 provided little time to gather accurate, on-the-ground information. As reported, their return trip did not even make port in Belém but passed the gaping maw of the Amazon miles out to sea. Thus, the Alliance made a strategic decision to enter Brazil through Belém based on incorrect and incomplete intelligence. The two-fold objective aimed initially (1) to reach the nominally Catholic Brazilian river dwellers in the Amazon Valley, and (2) secondly, to seek out the "pagan" Indian tribes in the Amazon region and to venture onto the Toncantins and Araguaya Rivers to where the "wild" Indian tribes lived. To the Clark's chagrin, they found that Belém had not been missed or ignored by other evangelical missions.

They discovered that there were at least three U. S. missions (Presbyterian, Methodist and Baptist) working in Belém, plus the Swedish-American "Pentecostal Mission," which in fact was the two-man Pentecostal team of Daniel Berg and Gunnar Vingren, founding fathers of the Brazilian Assemblies of God. Clark, in *Bananal*, goes on to say that further study of the "Indian situation" after arriving in Belém do Pará led him to the conclusion their best option was to "make a personal visit to the [least-reached] region. Of the two [regions where indigenous people were found], the country at the headwaters of the Amazon seemed the less favourable. . . . The tribes of the

Central Brazilian Plateau . . . live a much more settled life in their villages, and are therefore much more easily reached."

After receiving approval of his new proposal by the C&MA Board, Ray and J. D. Clark set off on an epic journey down the coast of Brazil to penetrate the Central-West region, specifically, at the headwaters of the Araguaya River in the State of Goiás. Their goal was to survey the Island of Bananal, the largest inland river island in the world, larger than Portugal. As a result, at midnight on September 20, 1922, the Clark cousins set off on the *Lloyde Brasileiro* ship, *Florianópolis*, toward Rio de Janeiro.

Their epic expedition began in Belém, and took them south along the coast of Northern and Northeastern Brazil until reaching Rio. The *Florianópolis* was a flat-bottomed river boat made for rivers rather than ocean travel. As a result, the "Clark boys" got a close-up view of the ocean when their waves of nausea got bigger than the waves of the South Atlantic. The journey took them to the ports of *São Luís do Maranhão*, and *Tutoia*, just north of *Paranaíba,* then capitol of *Piauí.* Their next stop was *Fortaleza, Ceará*, undergoing extensive harbor works by the federal government. Next port on their southward journey was *Natal*, the principal city of *Rio Grande do Norte*. They navigated the dangerous entrance into the harbor between rocks and reefs. After a brief time in port, they moved down the coast to *Cabedelo*, just north of *João Pessoa*, capital of *Paraíba*. Eighteen hours later, they arrived in *Recife* where they spent their hours in port riding out to the lovely suburb of *Olinda*. Three days later after docking briefly in *Maceió*, they entered the massive anchorage of *Salvador, Bahia*, considered the second biggest port in the world after *Rio de Janeiro*. Their next landing took them to *Vitória*, capitol and principal city of *Espírito Santo*, with its beautiful harbor edged by massifs of solid rock. While on this coastal caravan, the Clarks noted the amazing Brazilian fishermen, who ventured far out to sea on their *jangadas*, small rafts of logs lashed together. With their nets, lines and small fire pots for cooking, they remained at sea for days at a time to make a good catch.

Rio de Janeiro

On October 5, 1922, the Clarks awoke "to find ourselves in the most beautiful harbor of the world – Rio de Janeiro." They spent six happy days there with relatives of Ray's deceased wife, Lucy, visiting all of the principal tourist sites such as Sugar Loaf, *Corcovado* (minus the famous statue of Christ dedicated later in 1931). They arrived just in time for the great Centennial commemoration with the International Exhibition on land carved out of a seaside mountain. More importantly, they were able to meet with Dr. Erasmo Braga, the Chairman of the Brazilian Branch of the Committee for Cooperation (BCC) in Latin America. Braga, who had previously communicated with the C&MA's Foreign Department, received the Clarks at his office at downtown Rio de Janeiro. "It was the meeting point for the evangelical leadership of Brazil. The BCC promoted outstanding fellowship and cooperation of the churches around a series of invaluable projects. It represented the Protestant community before the government and served as a link between the churches and the foreign missions working in the country." [1].

Braga introduced Ray and John Clark to the director of the Brazilian Government's *Department for the Protection of the Indians*. The officials they dealt with were "very frank in saying that according to the Constitution they were unable to do

1. (http://www.bu.edu/missiology/missionary-biography/a-c/braga-erasmo-1877-1932/)

any propaganda work for us as a religious body, though they unhesitatingly gave us to understand that the Government looked with greater favor on Protestant effort in this direction than Catholic, as they were of the opinion that the latter had failed badly in doing any lasting good for the Indians, wherever they had attempted to establish a mission. The priests seem to have exploited the Indians rather than sought to help them either materially or spiritually."

Thus they explained their purpose for traveling to the headwaters of the Araguaia River at the river town of Leopoldina. From there, they would then travel downstream to Bananal. They were assured that the local government officials would be able to help them obtain a proper site for the location of an "industrial mission," which would be their base for reaching the unreached tribes of the hinterlands of Brazil. They were told to instruct the indigenous peoples to "wear clothes, to live in houses, to obey the laws of hygiene and cleanliness, to work for his living by cultivating the soil and being industrious with his hands. He must learn to read and write, and be taught something of the great world outside, as well as of the Life beyond, of God and His love for sinful men." Thus having satisfied the important protocol visit with government officials, Ray and John boarded the modern train in Rio heading southwest. After a pleasant day traveling 300 miles through the scenic *Serra do Mar* between the two states, the train pulled into the ornate *Estação Luz* in São Paulo at 7 p.m. that evening. Greeted by Ray's late wife's relatives and missionary friends from his time as a teacher at Mackenzie College, Ray and John were treated royally during their two weeks in the capital of the State of São Paulo.

São Paulo

While in São Paulo, Ray often thought of his eight years spent in what he called, "the Chicago of Brazil." With its great coffee industry, many manufacturing companies, mills, foundries and other industries, large and small, this "locomotive of Brazil" helped pull the rest of the country into the 20th century and greater prosperity. While there, Ray and John purchased the equipment necessary for their upcoming trip. Camping supplies, outdoor clothing, food, articles for trade with the Indians and other important items to pack in boxes and bundles for easy transport were found in the city's many stores.

At last, "Early on the [Tuesday] morning of October 25th, we steamed out of São Paulo City on the very comfortable day train of the Paulista Railroad. For the first time since leaving Para, our faces were turned towards the north." With their baggage aboard, they settled back in their seats to view the countryside tinted deep red by the mineral-rich soil that enriched the powerful "café"

Maria Fumaca

planters. Millions of coffee trees neatly ranked in countless rows extended toward the horizon on both sides of the tracks. They arrived at *Ribeirão Preto*, a prosperous interior "coffee town," at 5 p.m. and spent that night and the next day with more of Ray's Brazilian relatives.

Then boarding the Mogyana Railroad on the 27th, Ray and John rode all day through São Paulo into Minas Gerais, moving out of coffee country and into the cattle –grazing lands of central Brazil where the hardy Zebu, drought and insect-resistant cattle imported from India, survived under the local cattlemen's care. They gradually sensed the train climbing as they watched the soil change from dark red to dusty grey-brown. They arrived that evening at the little town of *Araguary* (now *Araguari*), where they spent the night at the "very modest hotel in the little town" at end of the line for the Mogyana and starting point of the Goyaz Railroad. Ray explains in his book that "the reader is asked to disassociate in his mind anything that would lead him to imagine fine rooms, good meals or efficient service," when using the term "hotel." "One should expect dinner without pudding, coffee without milk, a bed without a sheet and very frequently a night without sleep." On the positive side of the ledger, "the hotel bills for three stops on their trip totaled less than $3.00 for two persons."

At five a.m. the next morning, Friday, October 26, they boarded the "*Maria Fumaça*" (Smoky Mary) train and headed north under a cloud of cinders and black smoke toward the town of *Catalão*, just across the border in Goiás. There the Clark cousins spent the weekend with Mr. Bryce Rankin of the *Evangelical Union of South America* (*EUSA*) which came into being following the 1910 Edinburg Missions Conference, when several British missions in Argentina, Peru, Brazil and other South American republics agreed to merge, thus founding *EUSA*.

Bryce Rankin and his wife had spent years in this hinterland outpost spreading the good news of Christ, battling their bitter enemies, the Catholic priests and nuns, dealing with the scornful Spiritists and superstitious *caboclos* of the interior. The ministry planted by the Rankins greatly affected the region bordering Minas Gerais and Goiás. Ray preached both on Sunday morning and evening at their just-built church building. Against all odds, and with very limited support, the

Rankins were typical of the pioneer missionaries of Brazil's interior that brought light to a spiritual desert that was both dark and dead.

Early Monday morning, the 28th, they were back on the Goyaz Railway train heading for *Roncador* on the banks of the Corumbá River. Arriving at the end of the line by three in the afternoon, they "immediately sought the automobile which we had previously arranged for. The little old Ford Model T looked familiar even in these far away regions, and proved no less heroic than its brothers of the North, for after we and our baggage were on board there was no less a load than eleven hundred pounds!"

Thus began their heroic drive from Roncador to *Goyaz*, then capitol of the State of Goiás. Nothing deserving the name of road was to be found. Driving overland, following wagon ruts, cattle trails and open plains, their valiant Ford "Bigode" (mustache), so-named because of the mustachio-like bar across the radiator), they drove all that day till dark and another two full days to travel the 245 miles. Ray's description in *Bananal* describes the perils of the car driven by a Brazilian "chauffer [who] was extremely reckless and had no consideration for either passengers or car. He drove over holes

Ford "Mustache" used to travel to Goias

and ruts, over stones and fallen trees alike without thinking of shutting off the gas. The result of this fearful combination of bad roads and careless driving will be seen by a description of the car on our arrival in the Capitol. Both front and back springs were broken, both the foot and emergency brakes were useless, the clutch was all but burnt out, necessitating us pushing the car up the hills, the plugs were fouled and the tires in a hopeless condition."

The last day of the trip, they arrived at the isolated state capitol city at 8 p.m. after starting at 4 a.m. under starlight! In the town of *Goyaz* (now *Goiás Velho* and no longer the state capitol), they were greeted by Rev. Archie MacIntyre and his wife, another brave EUSA missionary couple who gave their lives to take Christ's gospel to the far reaches of Brazil's Central Highlands. They had been in the hinterlands of Goiás since 1908, working both among the *Carajá* Indians on the Araguaya River as well as the inhabitants of the capitol of the State of "Goyaz." It was a small town of about 15,000 entirely cut off from the rest of Brazil. Mail came in by pack mules, and telegraph lines had not arrived in the town which also lacked electricity.

Archie was well known and appreciated despite the opposition of the town "padre" and Catholic establishment. It was Archie who introduced and organized the first "football" games in the town, since being English and a passionate player; he helped promote the first games played in the town park. By doing this, Archie was able to enlist the local school boys from the *Lyceu de Goyaz*, thus providing opportunity to share not only his passion for the round leather ball, but also his love for Jesus Christ who came to this world to redeem them.

MacIntyre was able to introduce Ray and J. D. to the "president of the state" who promised to help them obtain a site for their mission and become established on Bananal Island. Since Archie had traveled down the Araguaya many times seeking to reach other Indian tribes, his experience was invaluable helping outfit the two young missionaries for the next leg of their journey. He arranged for a three-man team with two horses and three pack mules to take them to the town of Leopoldina, 120 miles to the west, where they would begin their river ride down the Araguaya to Bananal. *Firmino*, *Raymundo* and *João* proved to be good travel companions over the six day slog westward. The same could not be said for the broken-down nags that the two missionaries rode, and the pack mules displayed the typical disposition of obdurate obstinacy, surly behavior and sudden stampeding which required hours of searching for the errant animals in the dense thickets and brush.

Suffice it to say, their six-day trek required long days in the saddle, short night's of sleep in stinking cattle sheds, humble homes and abandoned hovels. Mrs. MacIntyre fed them royally during their six days in Goyaz, and fattened them up for their odyssey, to be fueled by rice and salt beef, the occasional fish and lots of coffee. The little band of travelers could go no faster than the slowest horse, so they made about six leagues a day, or about 21 miles, from dawn till dusk. Following a sunup cup of black coffee laced with sugary shavings from a block of

Typical caravan using mules

rock-hard brown sugar, they were off on the first leg of their slog, stopping at 11 a.m. or wherever they could find clean water to make their invariable lunch of rice and salt beef. The whole "brunch break" took well over two hours to dismount, unload and pasture the animals, draw water, fix lunch, clean up, get the animals, load and mount up again. This was the routine for nearly a week's travel, punctuated by long night spent trying to sleep while fighting the bedbugs, lice, mosquitos and horse flies.

Their boring ride through the rather bland, flat countryside of the Western Goiás wilderness was relieved by wooded scenery at times, by low *"cerrado"* brush and scrub trees of the highlands. For something to do to break the monotony, Ray and J. D. counted the crude crosses pounded into the ground next to the track they followed. Each cross represented a murder at the site. They counted no less than 125 crosses, representing 125 lives taken violently.

Wildlife consisted mostly of the diverse varieties of parrots and macaws "of which there seemed to be no limit," as Clark observed. Flying in bands of two, three or up to fifty or sixty, the macaws displayed amazing color schemes: "The colouring of the macaws is beyond beautiful, we having observed combinations of dark blue with yellow underside, green with red underside, and blue with red, as well as those only of one colour, red, blue or green." When they finally arrived at the riverside town of *Leopoldina*, now known as *Aruanã*, they bought a supply of *"farinha* (manioc flour), rice, pork-fat and brown brick sugar, which were to be our main articles of diet down the river." They bought an *obá,* a dug-out canoe about 30 feet long and 2 ½ feet wide. Their last night before embarking on the wide river road called the Araguaia, the two Clark cousins thought: "The great outstanding lap of the journey now lay immediately before us. What would it be? —and as we wondered, we crawled into our hammocks and slept until morning."

Interestingly, William Azel Cook, one of the Alliance missionaries sent out by A. B. Simpson in the 1890s, followed the same trail that the Clark cousins were about to embark on. Cook had started in Rio, took the train to São Paulo, and then continued his journey on the *"Maria Fumaça"* through *Ribeirão Preto*, *Araguary*, and *Goiás Velho* and across the wilds of the "cerrado" before finally arriving at the little town of *Leopoldina*. Cook described his impression of the tiny settlement, "a decadent hamlet on the great Araguaya River."

Just as the Clarks were about to do, Cook had canoed down the Araguaya with a party of Brazilians. The same towns that R. B. and cousin John would pass through were visited by the intrepid Cook. A careful reading of his volume, *Through the Wilderness of Brazil by Horse, Canoe and Float*, revealed him to be more of an explorer and adventurer than an itinerant missionary. The C&MA's decision to discontinue their support of his travels was correct since he never seemed to stay long enough anywhere to plant seed and cultivate converts to Christian maturity.

Thus on the next morning, November 15, 1922, "Proclamation of the Republic" day and just 33 years after Brazil deposed the Emperor Dom Pedro II and sent him packing with the royal family into exile in Portugal, R. B. and John Clark set off on their epic journey on the Araguaia River. Their heavily-laden dugout obá, with only two inches of freeboard, was perilously unstable. Loading, boarding and getting out were constant tests in balance and agility. For the next several hundred miles of their trip, R. B., John and their Brazilian crew had to sit still and straight in their unsteady craft.

Down the Araguaia River

R. B. described their first day on the water: "The scenery for most of the way on the Upper-Araguaya is monotonous though very beautiful. The banks are lined with woods and

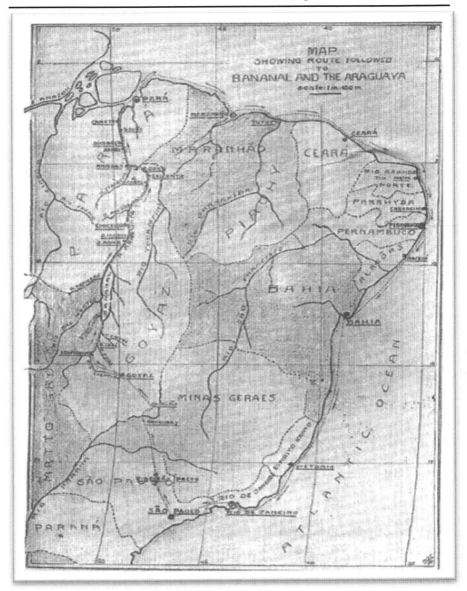

Map of route followed by Clark Party to Bananal Island
on the Araguai River

vegetation of very verdant green which usually come as far as
the water's edge, being reflected in the limpid waters of the
river and so making a picture of rare beauty. This verdure is
broken at frequent intervals by the appearance of long beaches

of white sand which generally occur at the bends of the river. We traveled for over 400 miles from Leopoldina before we saw anything that could be called a hill."

The flora and fauna found in the Araguaia River Valley were varied and interesting. Bird life of all kinds flew over the river and the missionary navigators. Three varieties of ducks, as well as *mutum, jacu,* macaws, parrots, parakeets, gulls and the *mergulhão* fish-diver, accompanied and entertained the Clark team. Small black-tail deer, *onças,* called the "Brazilian tiger," fat *antas* or tapirs, that reminded R. B. of small hippos, as well as wild pigs, live on both banks of the river. The river itself abounded with fish of all sizes, shapes and tastes, from the diminutive but feared *piranha* with its buzz-saw teeth, to the giant *pirarucú,* huge river catfish and the tasty little *pacú.* The *boto,* a fresh-water dolphin, part of local folklore, often followed their canoe, surfacing with a sonorous snort. Turtles, large and small, snakes of all colors and designs, some dangerous but most harmless, were found on the forest shores of the river requiring care when looking for firewood or places to camp for the night.

The *jacaré,* which Clark mislabeled a "crocodile," lay on the beaches sunning themselves as the team floated by. Actually an alligator, the jacaré grows up to eight feet or more. Like their counterparts in Africa and Asia, they prefer the lazy, quiet backwaters and often lay in lairs under the river banks, waiting for their careless prey to float close to their massive maws for lunch. These ever-present predators forced R. B. and team to be careful when they took a swim or spent time washing their clothes on the beautiful, sandy *praias* found at the bends of the river.

Their first day on the river began with gathering wood and starting a wood fire to boil water and make a big mug of café, strong and black like God made it, laced with chunks of hard, dark sugar. Breakfast was always the same: rice, dried salt beef and *farinha*, manioc flour. This unvaried diet quickly became boring, and often they dined on rice and fish caught locally when available. At about 11 o'clock, they would stop for lunch, the same as breakfast, and find shade to escape the brutal midday sun. After a short siesta, there were back on the water. By four in the afternoon of their initial day's canoeing, they had their first glimpse of the objects of their thoughts and prayers for so long, the *Carajás*.

These were members of one of the major tribes found in the hinterlands of West Central Brazil. This first contact with the natives was pleasant, with their chief calling out, "*Olá rapaziada*," the Portuguese equivalent of "Hello boys." Since where these villagers lived was not far from "civilization," many spoke Portuguese more or less well. R. B. describes them:

> This tribe [the Carajá], which we estimate as numbering some eleven hundred, lives on the Araguaya river, scattered over a total distance of no less than 900 miles, though the great majority of them are concentrated on or to the north of Bananal Island over a distance of about 250 miles. They are of a very fine well-built type, tall and muscular and cannot be considered of ugly features. They are kindly in appearance and disposition and always show themselves friendly if well treated.

He goes on to portray them at this first meeting, revealing his initial impressions, some positive and some not so:

> The Carajás are inveterate smokers, both men
> and women, and will smoke almost anything. . . .
> Judging by the type of their small cultivations
> and the shabby appearance of their houses they
> are probably lazy, though we cannot but give
> them credit for a certain degree of ability
> betrayed by the many types of well-made
> ornaments and weapons that the men produce
> and the mats and hammocks made by the
> women. . . . Their huts on the other hand are very
> roughly put together and primitive in the
> extreme.

His depiction of their simple lifestyle is typical of how
most western missionaries and explorers would see them. Their
diet consisted of manioc, a tuber-like root, not very nutritious
but filling, prepared in varied manners. They had plenty of fish,
which they shot with bow and arrow, turtles, roasted in their
shells and an abundance of melons. Bows and arrow, clubs and
sharp lances protected them from their enemies and were part
of every man's kit. The men and boys went without clothes and
the women wore a miniscule *tanga*, a small fiber loin covering.
Wrestling and dancing were a big part of the local culture and
were featured parts of their festive occasions. Clark recorded
their belief system, probably missing the more subtle cues that
are only perceived when observed over time:

> They appear to have very little religion, though
> they believe in a great Invisible Being whom
> they denominate by a name which means, *The*

One Who Cannot Be Seen; they believe in the immortality of the soul, which is seen by the respectful way in which they bury their dead. The corpse is buried in a sitting posture. They are extremely superstitious and frequently suspect each other as responsible for the deaths of their relatives, which accounts for the scattered condition of the tribe.

There is among them the usual medicine man who is supposed to have certain powers to cure the sick and punish the sinful. He is also supposed to have control of the weather, and the like. On one occasion we saw one of these men chew some pieces of root and spit it in the direction of gathering clouds, muttering strange words as he did so in order to stop the approaching rain! Unfortunately for us, the rain came!

Clark summed up his thoughts regarding the Carajá and the missionary task: "Such is the Carajá: a tribe of good physique, many fine qualities and characteristics, yet living uncivilized and pagan; a tribe within reach of the missionary who is willing to lay down his life for their salvation; eager to learn, desirous of better things, yet in danger of complete extinction if left much longer as they are. And

Typical indigenous Careajas

such is the condition of hundreds of other tribes in the forests of Brazil."

Friday, November 17, was much the same as the first two days. Late in the afternoon, the intrepid travelers arrived at *São José*, a "little hamlet situated on the high ground on the right bank of the river, [and] is the last outpost of civilization on the Araguaia as one descends the river and is merely a small group of houses with a small school and church, where the life of the people varies little from that of the Indians themselves; indeed, the Indians who had recently moved from their summer residence on the praia [beach], just above the village were living together with the "*Civilizados.*"

The Clarks decided to spend the weekend in São José and accepted the invitation of a local school-teacher who asked them to preach in his home. This man had been led to Christ by Missionary Archie MacIntyre a year earlier. Before the preaching service, the teacher had asked us to speak using the simplest of terms in order to make the salvation message clear to the town folk whose minds were darkened by ignorance and superstition. "The house in which he lived and where we held the meeting was well filled with perhaps thirty men and women who listened very attentively while we told them the Gospel Story." While the locals listened appreciatively and appeared to grasp the gospel preaching, no visible results were seen. Seed was laid down to be cultivated and cared for by the lone Christian in the town, an unknown school teacher. Eternity will tell the rest of the story.

In São José, the team was able to trade in their narrow *obá* for a more stable dugout about fifteen feet long and three and a half feet wide. It came with a palm-leaf roof that afforded protection to the travelers from the burning tropical sun. Before they could leave town, a little steam launch, one of only two on the whole river, arrived and tied up at the local dock. Thus the missionaries and their crew were able to "hitch a ride" on the steam launch since the owner and pilot agreed to tie them on and give them a tow. For the next day and a half, about 150 miles, they let the launch do the work. On the following Tuesday, November 21, they first sighted the long-contemplated Island of Bananal. Clark describes it:

> This island is formed by the dividing of the waters of the Araguaia, some of which flow in a more easterly direction than those of the main stream which continues almost due north. The eastern and lesser arm of the river is often dry in the summer months along the first part of its course. . . . It is 220 miles long, measured as the crow flies, and some 280 miles from point to point along the course of the main stream. Its width varies considerably, but owing to the fact that the lesser arm has never been explored, no one really knows the true shape of the island. Its width, however, is not likely to be more than fifty or sixty miles at its widest point.

It was at this point, the mouth of the São Luiz River, where they were cut free from the steam launch. Upon arriving at this smaller tributary, only discovered the year before in October of 1921, they paddled down a "*furo*," or hidden branch of the river. They then spent several hours tramping across the flatlands of the island where they saw excellent pasture land. This was the beginning of their search for the best location for establishing their "industrial mission station," which in reality was to be more a farm/ranch proposition. They already knew that the southern part of the island had very few indigenous populations since most tribes tended to keep to the northern half of the islands; thus this first trek was more for survey than a serious site search. The tribes on the northern half were the Carajás who they already had met, as well as the *Javahés*. There was another very savage tribe, the *Canoeiro*s [canoe people] who lived on the mainland on both sides of Bananal. "They were very dark-skinned Indians and of a very bad reputation, being known for habitually killing white cattle-breeders and carrying off their cattle."

On the mainland, west of the southern end of the island, lived the dreaded "*Chavante*," considered the most savage and cruel of the tribes of Brazil. These natives were mortal enemies of the Carajás. Their usual method of killing a Carajá was to break the person's back and leave them to the animals. R. B. and John, with their crew members, witnessed the two wooden crosses that marked the spot on Bananal where two members of the party that had discovered the São Luiz ventured out into the forest to find wild honey. They were surprised by Chavante warriors who quickly killed them with arrows and clubs. This was a sober reminder that those they wished to reach with the gospel of peace were anything but pacific. Years of hatred and resentment against the "Civilizados" for their constant encroachment on native lands and terrible treatment of the original Brazilians had built high barriers that only time, patience, sacrifice and perseverance would overcome.

It was another two days before they came upon another Indian village, located at the mouth of the *Rio das Mortes* (River of Deaths), made famous by Teddy Roosevelt and his party in 1912-13, when the former president and fellow explorers almost perished in the vast wilds of the forest. The river was so named because of fierce *Cinta Larga* Indians who had massacred many miners and treasure seekers trying to find the wealth thought to be found there. In addition, malaria, wild animals and the lack of supplies and communication made the area a natural "black hole" from which few escaped. It was sobering for R. B. and John to

Roosevelt Expedition
The figure with glasses on right is
Theodore Roosevelt

consider where they were venturing in light of the still-fresh memory of Roosevelt's narrow escape from death only a decade before.

The next day, Saturday, November 25, they arrived at the "large Carajá village known to the Brazilians as the village of *Santa Isabel*. "This was the largest village that we had seen, and with the exception of one other, the largest Carajá village on the Araguaya." Clark observed that there were about 100 natives living in this river town, considered a large village. He then adds an interesting detail: "Due to family quarrels and suspicion of one another, the tribe finds it preferable to live scattered and so reduce themselves to small groups that can live more or less at peace among themselves. This incessant internal warfare is having as a result the rapid dwindling of the tribe, from what was once a very large tribe to one that now probably does not number more than eleven hundred souls." Doubtless, these sobering thoughts weighed on the hearts of the young missionaries as these threatened native populations, in rapid decline, were the reason for the survey trip. Time was of the essence.

Through the help of the chief of the Carajá in Santa

Isabel, R. B. and John Clark were eventually able to make contact with the Javahé after an exhausting canoe ride across a big lake on Bananal, only to find the remote village of *Immuty* abandoned. Frustrated, disappointed and very hungry, the small expedition of the two missionaries, the Carajá guides and R. B.'s Brazilian crew bedded down for the night. Much later in the early hours of the morning, they heard the whoops and hollers of the Javahé men who had been fishing all day. At the break of day, their human quarry arrived with obás filled with food. Clark gave a succinct description of the newcomers: "A description of the Javahé Indians is quite unnecessary, it being sufficient to say that they are identical with the Carajás, speaking the same dialect, wearing the same ornaments, living in the same style of hut, though one builds his on the sands of the river and the other on high ground near the lake or river as the case may be."

Though it is likely that his observation was not totally accurate given the fact that the Carajá considered the Javahé to be another tribe, and vice verse, and such a short visit with them would result in superficial similarities, R. B. makes a very apt comment: "From a missionary standpoint, this is most pleasing, for neighboring tribes speaking the same dialect can be considered as the same tribe." Again, this comment oversimplifies the relationship between the two tribes, but the observation from the standpoint of language learning was pertinent. A missionary could easily work with both of these people groups without having to learn two separate languages. He concludes this side-trip to meet the Javahé remarking "of the possibility of future work among these two brother tribes, we started to paddle once more down the Araguaya."

The journey picks up on Sunday, December 3, another beautiful day on the Araguaia. It was on this day, less than three weeks after leaving Leopoldina that the Clark cousins saw hills for the first time in this great inland plain. To their northeast, located in the province of Pará, these were not high mountains, but definitely a long chain of blue hills, a "*serra*," that stood over and above the surrounding flatlands. They paddled to the confluence of another large river, the *Tapirapé*, which flows into the Araguaia from the west, marking the division between Mato Grosso and Pará. At this point, the Araguaia actually divides into four separate streams, called "*quatro bocas*" (four mouths). Just before the mighty river is split four ways, the Araguaia passes through a narrow passage not more than three hundred yards wide between two massive rocky promontories. In this same region another tribe, named the *Tapirapé* after the river, live and were reputed to be friendly to outsiders. Due to the lack of time and funds, the party decided to pass by the three Tapirapé villages, to be visited another time. Looking at their situation from their perspective as missionaries, the Tapirapé merited interest because they stayed in the same place rather than being nomadic as the Carajá and Javahé.

Another four leagues down the river the Clark team came to a tiny village of Brazilians on the left bank of the river. R. B. describes this "most remote outpost of civilization . . . It is hardly to be wondered at that these poor folks live as they do, for most of them are sick and diseased and hundreds of miles away from a doctor and supplies, and living in ignorance and superstition. It must be said, though, they were not so lazy and inert they could make themselves respectable houses to live in and cultivate wholesome food to eat even though unable to obtain good clothes, but all the way down the stretch of river that is inhabited by Brazilians, the most extreme poverty and degradation is met with; disease is universal and ignorance of the deepest dye is widespread."

A Site For The C&MA Mission

It was on December 4, the day after they first spotted the first blue outline of hills on the horizon, that they at last came across a range of hills on the island itself, not as high as those of the *serra*, but definitely higher than the surrounding area on Bananal. Finally after months of travel by ship, train, Model T, horseback and now canoe, their goal seemed to be at hand: a site for the C&MA mission in the Brazilian hinterland. R. B. paints a word picture of what he considered "the site which might, in the providence of God, yet become our home:"

> We found that the range consisted of three quite distinct hills situated near the river and very gradually extending inland, becoming lower as the range receded from the river. The whole extent of high ground, with the exception of one of the hills, which would afford excellent sites for building, was covered with forests. These wooded lands would be ideal for cultivation and also for supplying all the timber that would be necessary for building purposes, and then as far as the eye can reach in all directions there is pasture land of the very best for raising cattle. We climbed the hill that had but little vegetation and found that it started to slope up from the very edge of the water and gradually reached an elevation of perhaps 400 feet above the level of the river. As the river has an elevation of just over 600 feet at this point, the height of this most excellent building site would hardly be less than 1,000 feet

above sea level.

It was at this site, near the poor little village of *Furo de Pedra*, that R. B. and John Clark envisioned the establishment of an "Industrial mission," which essentially was a strategy to reach the indigenous forest dwellers of the Araguaya, establishing a base station where the missionaries would reach out to evangelize the surrounding tribes. In addition, the station would be the missionary's base where they would live, work the land and raise livestock, open a simple school and teach skills and trades. This strategy was in accordance with the directives of the Brazilian government's Indian agency: "the missionaries were to instruct the indigenous peoples to 'wear clothes, to live in houses, to obey the laws of hygiene and cleanliness, to work for his living by cultivating the soil and being industrious with his hands. He must learn to read and write, and be taught something of the great world outside. . . .'" A similar approach had been attempted earlier in the 1890s at the Jaú mission farm in São Paulo under the leadership of former Presbyterian missionary, J. B. Howell. While this first attempt at the founding of the C&MA mission in Brazil was unsuccessful, the "industrial-mission" strategy was one still employed by many faith missions pioneering in primitive areas with pre-industrial cultures.

The elevated location was considered ideal, being situated "about the center of the section inhabited most densely by the Carajá, within two days land journey of the nearest Javahés, and almost at the mouth of the river which is the natural door into Tapirapé territory. These three tribes are, beyond a doubt, the ones to be reached first."

For a few more days, Ray and John, and their Brazilian crew, paddled north down the Araguaia, passing several Carajá villages. Not finding any other site as good as the one at Furo de Pedra, they felt strongly that the elevated site on Bananal was the right place for the C&MA mission station. In another two days, they passed the northernmost point of Bananal Island, where the "lesser arm" of the river to the east finally wound back to the "mother bed" to continue wending its wet way northward. For the next several days, they pushed their canoe downriver toward the town of *Conceição do Araguaya*.

Clark estimated that, at the little town of *Santa Maria*, just a day's journey south of Conceição, they passed their last Carajá village. They were about halfway back to Belém, about four weeks on the river and still had a long way before arriving "home" in the capital of Pará. At Santa Maria, they estimated having already passed at least 1,600 or 1,700 Javahés and almost 1,000 Carajás. R. B. concludes this part of his narrative on a high note: "The most important part of our journey was now at an end, and we were safe and in good health; we recognized that God had been leading us and protecting us in a very marked way, and we felt truly grateful to Him for it all."

At Santa Maria, they left their crew and craft and took passage on a "*bote*," a large boat with a palm-leaf roof, with eight rowers. This was like a power cruiser compared to their smaller two-paddle dugout. Their new boat belonged to the political boss of Conceição, Colonel Norberto de Souza Lima, former "*intendente*" (mayor) of the town. At this point in their journey, they ran into the first of a long series of ever-increasing rapids that went from minor rock ripples to raging torrents. They arrived in Conceição do Araguaya on Tuesday afternoon, December 12, 1922. And they were only about halfway on their way back to Belém do Pará.

They spent five comfortable days in Conceição as guests of Colonel Norberto and family. The Clark cousins were thrilled to eat home cooking to their fill. No salt beef and rice three times a day! They feasted on abundant fresh food, fruits, fish, fresh butchered beef and other local delicacies. While in the Souza Lima home, they shared their Christian faith and the reason for their visit to the region rarely visited by those from the outside world. The de Sousa's were fascinated to hear the Clark's story and reason for being on the river. Since their funds were low, R. B. and John sold most of their camping gear and photographic equipment to the Dominican Friars "with whom they had a pleasant visit," in order to raise funds for the 250-mile next leg of the trip to *Marabá*. From there to Belém do Pará was just a few days more travel.

On Friday, December 18, they set off again on the most adventuresome and dangerous portion of their long river ride. The rocky rapids of the upper Araguaia and Tocantins required experienced crews skilled in the navigation of their frail craft through the rock-strewn river with its violent whirlpools, vicious currents and hidden dangers beneath the roiling river's surface. On Christmas day, December 25, they passed the last Carajá village, and shortly after their noonday meal, the river took the first plunge toward the mighty Amazon lying well to the north. With consummate skill, and years of experience, the pilot and crew raced their boat through the roaring rapids with speeds that the Clarks estimated as being between fifteen and twenty miles per hour! Near the end of that same day, the mighty Araguaia, up to one and a half miles in width at Conceição, had narrowed down to a width of only two hundred feet! At that point, they tied up their valiant little vessel for the night at the little settlement, anticipating another wild ride on the morrow at the *Cachoeira Grande*, or "Great Rapid."

The next day saw them slaloming down the river with a local pilot navigating his own little canoe in front of the boat carrying R. B. and J. D. His skill and knowledge of "every inch of this winding passage among the rocks" amazed the cousins. All breathed a sigh of relief when they arrived that same afternoon, Wednesday, December 27, at next river town, *São Vicente*. "In this settlement, we met two young Brazilian Christians who were faithfully witnessing for Christ in the town and surrounding area," writes R. B. "They had succeeded in starting a Gospel Service in their home every Sunday and Wednesday, and even had a small Sunday School. There are about four or five Christians in this little town, the first we had met on the long stretch of nearly one thousand miles of river that we had covered, with the exception of the school-master at São José, 850 miles away!" Ray and John were invited by the brothers, *Alexandre* and *Raymundo Silva*, to speak to their little "church" in their home, which they did to a good number of listeners despite the heavy rain.

The Clark cousins continued their trip and passed an old town, *São João*, where the Araguaia and the Tocantins Rivers join. Despite the fact that the Tocantins has less volume of water, its name is given to the eventual joining of the two into one mighty waterway. It was in this very region only a week before the Clarks and crew passed through that two Brazil nut-gatherers had been attacked by *Gavião* tribesmen. One of the *castanheiros* had no less than 60 arrows in his body. The other, also wounded, managed to escape with an arrowhead still lodged in his neck when the Clarks met up with him later. Without knowing it, the Clarks camped that night at the same camp site where the two Brazilians had been attacked. Obviously, R. B. and J. D. were glad to get to Marabá on the 28th, the first place on their whole trip that they felt really deserved the name "town."

At Marabá, they had to wait five days before booking

passage on the next river boat that would haul the Brazil nuts harvested from the region's forests. On Monday, January 1, 1923, The Clarks ran into one of their new friends from São Vicente who had attended the gospel service in the two Christian brothers' home the week before. He asked R. B. and J. D. if they would be willing to hold a Gospel meeting in Marabá if he were able to secure the use of the Town Hall. The cousins agreed, and the young man soon had the approval and support of the local mayor, who invited all of the prominent men of the town. Women were not invited. "It was a rare opportunity and great experience to see forty well-dressed and intelligent men, including the Mayor, turn out to hear the Gospel." They were introduced by a local speech-maker who said there were giving a "literary discourse on Religion." R. B. reported that "The attention of those present was excellent and from the discussion that it aroused around town afterward, we judged that many had intelligently grasped what was said. We trust that some may also have got a spiritual grasp of the message."

The next two and a half days, saw the Clarks experience more hair-raising rides through the rapids, including one time when their boat hit a submerged rock and almost sank before the pilot was able to get to shallow water. After beaching their boat, the hole was repaired and soon back on their way. After weeks of slow paddling and calm waters, these last days held thrills-a-minute, threats of crushing crashes and constant soakings from the spray. On their next-to-last day of travel, they arrived at the little port town of *Cametá*. There they cabled their cousins, David and Erma, in Pará that they would be arriving the next day on a river steamboat carrying the *castanha do Pará* (Brazil nuts) to the great port city. The next day, Friday, January 5, 1923, Ray and John Clark arrived in

Belém do Pará after traveling no less than 2,700 miles by steam ship, 960 by railroad, 250 by Model T Ford, 125 on mule-back, 70 miles on foot, 1,000 miles by canoe, another 100 by motor-vessel and 250 by river steam boat, a total of 5,455 miles! Ray concludes the adventure by stating:

> We had passed through much that was untried and unknown, through dangers that we probably never dreamed of; we had passed through the land of the red man in safety, through regions where law is unknown and where life is considered of little value, through sections of river where many refuse to pass, and through zones, on the lower reaches of the river, where malaria holds the population in its grip. Yet by the goodness of God, we came through in perfect health and absolute safety. We had been 'kept by the power of God', and returned home humbly grateful to Him.

In the last chapter of *Bananal*, "A Race Without a Home," R. B. describes the deplorable situation of the indigenous peoples of Brazil. Whether the unreached tribes hounded by rubber tappers or gold seekers in the remote Amazon rain forest or the many tribes that Ray and John had encountered or heard of on their epic journey, all felt the same inexorable encroachment of the so-called "Civilizados." These thoughtless adventurers went there to gouge the ground for gold, strip the land of anything of value, harvest the Brazil nuts or tap the latex-producing trees. None of this benefited the native population. It appeared to the two young missionaries that the only hope for these forest dwellers was the presentation of the Gospel by men and women motivated by the love of Christ, who could introduce a gradual process of integration of the tribes into the larger Brazilian context rather than seeing them simply killed off by the treasure seekers or decimated by the diseases brought in from the outside.

In the eyes of the Clarks and the EUSA missionaries that they had met in *Catalão* and *Goiás Velho*, the Catholic Missions had done little or nothing to better the state of the tribes that they had reached, and the "Romanist Gospel" that they preached was not meeting the soul needs of these unreached people of the forests. The government officials of the Department of Protection of the Indians privately had stated that they preferred evangelical missionaries to reach the primitive peoples of the interior since almost four centuries of Roman Catholic missions had done very little to better the physical, material, educational and spiritual condition of Brazil's indigenous peoples. The last chapter of *Bananal* paints a bleak picture of the hopeless situation in which the original population of Brazil found themselves. Those primitive people groups, who had lived and died there for countless years before Pedro Alvarez Cabral accidental "discovery of Brazil" in 1500, were slowly being decimated and their cultures inexorably destroyed by the *civilizados.* This weighed heavily on Ray's heart.

Ray concludes his slender little book of 130 pages with these words: "In their ignorance and poverty, they continue to wander in the forests, robbed of what is theirs, cheated of their rights, outside the protection of the law, beyond the reach of the preacher's voice, and the hand that would help, waiting – waiting to hear of the Great deliverer and of the Land that lies beyond." But the story doesn't end there. Incredibly, Ray and J. D. never returned to Bananal to plant the gospel standard on

99

the beautiful hill overlooking the Araguaia River.

What Happened to the Bananal Project?

What happened to their detailed survey report, their proposed site for the mission station, their observations and conclusions made on the long journey? Why did The Christian and Missionary Alliance not follow through on its approval of Ray Clark's report and not take up the Bananal banner?

The answer to those questions is not found in Clark's *Bananal.* However, in Ray's personal notes and diary transcribed by his son, David, one finds the answer. Under the title, UNEXPECTED NEWS FROM NEW YORK, a minute from the Foreign Department Committee Meeting, February 15, 1923 is recorded: "In response to the request of Mr. R. B. Clark, Superintendent of the Brazil Work, for us to cable permission for him to return home to consult the Board about the Brazil field, it was recommended that we ask for a full report of their recent trip of exploration before decision is made regarding his coming home in the spring." Apparently between Ray's report being sent and initially approved and the final decision to enter Bananal, something happened that caused the Alliance Mission to reverse its decision.

Comity Or Comedy?

QUESTIONS

Since the Alliance communicated with the Committee on Cooperation in Rio before letting the Clarks enter Brazil . . .

1. Why did Rev. Erasmo Braga, head of the Brazil Commission of Cooperation, not inform the C&MA Mission that there

were three U. S. missions already working in Belém do Pará? The Commission was the clearing house for missions operating in Brazil. That vital information should have been available.

2. Why were R. B. and J. D. not informed by the CoC that the Evangelical Union of South America (EUSA) had already laid claim to Bananal when the Clarks visited with Rev. Braga while in Rio in mid 1922?

3. How did the CoC not know that EUSA had already made a prior claim to Bananal?

4. Why did Revs. Bryce Rankin of Catalão and Archie MacIntyre of Goiás Velho, both EUSA missionaries, not tell R. B. and J. D. that EUSA had already spoken for Bananal since the Clarks stayed with the Rankins and MacIntyres while traveling to the Araguaia River?

5. Was the Alliance's withdrawal from Bananal a result of the Alliance's stated purpose to be a pioneer mission to work where no one else was working, or was the decision a result of agreed-upon mission comity arrangements?

ANSWERS

In the May 16, 1925 issue of The Alliance Weekly, p. 332, a note entitled "Missionary Work" included the following:

> The following kindly furnished by Rev. A. C. Snead, our Foreign Secretary, will be of interest to our readers: In 1922, a party of four under the leadership of Mr. R. B. Clark sailed for Para, Brazil, with a view to undertaking the evangelization of some neglected areas in that great field. A few months later Messrs. R. B. and

J. D Clark made a long trip of exploration through the Indian tribes in the region of the Araguaya and Tocantins Rivers, and it was the intention of the Alliance to enter work among the Indians in some part of this territory. However, after Mr. Dinwiddie's [Co-Secretary of the Foreign Department for Pioneer Fields] visit to England in 1923, letters were received from a British Missionary Society [*World Evangelization Crusade*] stating they had several young men ready to enter the territory in Brazil which the Alliance had expected to occupy, and asking if arrangements could be made for that territory to be allotted to them in case the Alliance was willing to transfer to some other portion. In meeting this request the Board decided to transfer the Alliance missionaries from Para to the needy fields of Ecuador and Peru. Three of the party are now in Ecuador and one, Mr. R. B. Clark, with two others, is enroute to Peru to open a new field of Alliance work among the *Campas* Indians. In the Brazilian field a further readjustment of territory was made between two English Societies, the Worldwide Evangelization Crusade, relinquishing a part of the territory to the Evangelical Union of South America and taking up of another unoccupied territory in a different section of Brazil.

Thus, it is clear that Rev. Braga of the Brazil Commission of Cooperation did not know of EUSA's plans to occupy Bananal because the British-based mission had no plans at the time of R.B. and J.D.'s visit to Rio in 1922. It was only after Rev. Dinwiddie, a C&MA Foreign Department official, visited England in 1923 and apparently announced that the Alliance was about to occupy Bananal that WEC wrote to the Alliance mission headquarters in New York City, asking the C&MA to defer to WEC, since they had "several young men ready to enter the territory in Brazil." Accordingly, following the Alliance policy of respecting comity provisions as well as the aim to pioneer where others were not working, the Clark expedition and resulting Bananal proposal was abandoned.

It is on occasions like this that one has to have a firm grip on Romans 8:28 and a strong belief in God's sovereignty and guidance, even when it would appear otherwise. R. B. Clark eventually ended up in Peru and J. D. and David Stuart Clark and wife, Erma, helped pioneer in Ecuador for the C&MA. Yet what about Bananal, all that effort, the well-laid plans, the hilltop mission site, the industrial mission strategy? What to make of all this? In David Clark's transcription of his father's diary notes, one encounters a "happy ending" and definitely an indication that God was neither frustrated nor handicapped by what might appear to be a "comity comedy."

But this was not to be. [Return to Bananal] Neither JD nor I have ever seen a Carajá again. But our long journey of exploration was not in vain. We reported favorably to the Board of the Christian and Missionary Alliance and recommended that we be permitted to open work among the Carajás and Javahés at the location we had chosen, and our recommendation was favorably considered. But we were never to see those dear people again. Detailed explanation would be out of place here. Sufficient to say that the Christian and Missionary Alliance gave way to the Evangelical Union of South America who promised to start work there as soon as possible. Not very long after, that mission sent a missionary couple down the Araguaya from their base in Goyaz Capital where the McIntyres were still stationed. They decided to establish their first station on the spot we had chosen; and Mr. and Mrs. Wilder were their first missionaries. I do not know how far they had progressed when the Lord took Mr. Wilder to be with Himself; but I concluded that his death from malaria fever brought to an untimely conclusion the work that seemed to have gotten off to a good start. For thirty-five years, more or less, I thought that the Carajás and Javahé were still without knowledge of the Gospel. One can imagine the surprise we had when Mrs. Wilder, still a missionary on Bananal, visited us in our home in Lima, Peru, and showed us slides of the work among the Carajás and what encouraging results their mission was having among them! It surely was good to hear her tell of her experiences and of others who had joined her. It was good to see pictures, not of naked, ignorant savages, but of fine looking men, women and children, dressed and civilized, and also able to read and write, and study God's Word for themselves. We praise God that our trip was bringing forth fruit abundantly. All praise goes to Him!

Now, For Rest Of The "Rest Of The Story

On the night that I finished reading Ray Clark's account of Mrs. Wilder, the missionary widow, who stayed on and worked in Bananal, I wondered where I could learn more about her story. At that moment, I happened to glance at my bookcase and noticed a slender paperback that a friend had given me a few months before. I looked at the title, *Semeando em Lágrimas* (*Sowing in Tears*) and then the name of the author: Rettie Wilding! My reaction was to let out a whoop and a laugh. Talk about coincidence! So I read through the little book that same night.

Sowing in Tears is an amazing story of godly grit and determination. In 1925, Joe Wilding went to Bananal as a single missionary with the Evangelical Union South of America, which had taken responsibility for Bananal when World Evangelization Crusade gave preference to EUSA. Wilding took the long obá ride with Archie Macintyre as the Clarks had a few years before. They built a little cabin on the hill chosen by R. B and J. D. Soon Archie left Joe there alone. Basically he worked as a single missionary with occasional help from outside for his first term. He cared for the Carajá who little by little trusted him. He came down with malaria over and over again, almost dying at one point. The *padre* from the little Brazilian town on the other side of the river opposed him, threatened him and generally tried to make life miserable for him. Eventually Joe became so sick that EUSA sent him back to Britain in 1928 to recuperate.

He returned to Brazil in 1930, and a single lady doctor, Rettie, who heard him while on furlough, followed him later in 1931. She came with another single Brazilian lady who opened a little primary school for the Carajá children. Rettie's story of overwhelming physical needs encountered, surgery by lamplight, cataract operations, draining huge abscesses and removing tumors in the most primitive conditions, is amazing. Eventually they built a little clinic at the hilltop station. And in 1932, Joe and Rettie were married. Tragically, after less than a year of marriage, he fell ill with "*maláría maligna*," likely cerebral malaria with its excruciating headaches and dangerously high fevers. She was pregnant at the time, but cared for him to the end when he died in her arms. She was devastated, but stayed on, praying for a baby boy who would look like his daddy. And God answered that prayer.

That baby, Dr. Joe Wilding Jr., eventually returned to Bananal and opened up a hospital there. New Tribes Mission took over the work on the island some years later after Dr. Rettie had gone to work in Anápolis, Goiás, at the *Hospital Evangélico* founded by the Fanstone family, British evangelicals. She eventually returned to visit the island 27 years after leaving.

The legacy of Joe Wilder and his wife is now found in a thriving church, school, clinic and small hospital on the site first surveyed by R. B. Clark and his cousin, John. Today, the Carajá are among the most developed and integrated Brazilian indigenous peoples in the country and have long since dispensed the need of outside help. They have their own pastors, schools, and have reached out to other Brazilian tribes still untouched by the gospel.

Romans 8:28

Thus the site originally chosen by Ray and J. D. Clark on Bananal was eventually occupied by EUSA's Wildings, later to be turned over to the New Tribes Mission who developed and expanded the ministry. So the original vision to reach the last of the lost in Brazil's hinterland was fulfilled, not by the C&MA

but by another of "God's arms" reaching down to find those unknown to the world but dear to His heart. God paints pictures beautifully, but not always with straight lines and bright colors. The result of His work will always amaze and raise praise.

CHAPTER THREE
THE REDISCOVERY
OF BRAZIL

The 1950s marked a major sea change in Brazil's pilgrimage from a sleeping giant "eternally lying in a splendid cradle" to becoming a modern nation and leader of the Southern Continent. The post WW II years saw Brazil shake off the chains of the fascist-leaning *Estado Novo* (New State) of Getúlio Vargas, a charismatic leader from the rugged southernmost state of *Rio Grande do Sul*. He ruled Brazil from 1930 till 1945 and was deposed by the military, and then was elected president in 1950. Vargas' scandal-ridden government and eventual suicide led to free elections in 1954. So democracy was in the air and a former governor of the great interior state of Minas Gerais, Dr. Juscelino Kubitschek, MD, received the electoral majority and took office in 1956. His campaign theme was "50 years in 5 years," which was a clear reference to the presidential term of five years, with no possibility of reelection.

Under his dynamic leadership, Brazil leaped forward toward the goals that were part of his campaign platform: progress in energy generation, transportation, food production, industrialization, universal education and the main goal, the construction of a new national capital city, Brasília. A spirit of optimism and a renewed sense of national self esteem made itself felt throughout society. In 1958, the "*Seleção*," the Brazilian national soccer team, astounded and enchanted the sports world by winning the World Cup in Sweden. Pelé, their 17-year-old "*futebol*" phenom made his world debut on the grassy stage in Stockholm, scoring two beautiful goals in the final game against Sweden. That was the first of Brazil's five World Cup wins.

On the music scene, the *Bossa Nova* (New Wave or Style) combined the samba beat with cool-jazz influences from America and Europe. The resulting fusion, literally, music to the public's ears, was introduced by João Gilberto, Vinicius de Moraes, Tom Jobim, and many other Brazilian artists. It gained worldwide popularity a few years later through Stan Getz's hit album, *Jazz Samba.* Suddenly the world was swaying to the subtle syncopated beat and whistling tunes beautifully discordant, yet captivating. The soft, sibilant sounds of Brazilian Portuguese soon became familiar to an audience worldwide.

The iconic statute of *Cristo do Corcovado* (Christ of Corcovado) overlooking Rio's massive harbor seemed to smile on the long-suffering populous and nod in agreement with the popular saying, "*Deus é Brasileiro*" (God is Brazilian). This popular expression on the lips of the eternal optimists pointed to the accomplishments of President Kubitschek's five-year plan. The boldly proclaimed goals took form with the installation of the first VW "Bug" factory in São Paulo, followed by automobile factories building Fords, Chevrolets, Peugeot, Renault and the Willys Jeep. New hydro-electric dams were coming on line. Schools were being built around the country.

And most evidently, the new capital city of Brasília

suddenly became a reality in Brazil's great West Central Plateau. Where the desolate, sun bleached *cerrado* (scrub-wood plains) had lain for millennia with nothing more than the wind to stir up the dust, a great modern city reared its head. Daring architectural forms idealized by Oscar Niemeyer combined with a futuristic city plan traced by Lúcio Costa disproved all of the naysayers who did not believe that JK could build and move the capital in just one five-year term.

This was the context of Brazil when it was "rediscovered" in the 1950s by the world-wide movement that The Christian and Missionary Alliance had become. From the frustrating first effort in the 1890s that saw the Alliance leave Brazil with barely a ripple, and the second stirring expedition to Bananal come to naught, there did not appear to be any desire on the part of the C&MA to re-enter Brazil. However, God had other plans; and as is often the case, His plans were as far removed from the mission's plans as heavenly clouds are from earthly clods of dirt.

A Root from Afar

God was raising up missionary vision in the daughter churches of the C&MA that had been planted and carefully nurtured for decades since the last attempt of the early 1920s. Interestingly, God began to turn the eyes and heart of the Alliance to Brazil from far on the other side of the globe, in Japan. In early 1958, God began to touch the heart of a young lady pastor in the Matsuyama Alliance Church where she had been ministering for more than five years. Although her ministry was fruitful, she sensed that God had more for her. She prayed, "Lord, I want to begin a new work in the next year; I will do whatever is needed. So I ask you, open the doors." Suddenly she was surprised by a voice that said one word,

Mutsuko Ninomiya

"Brazil." As a result, she prayed: "God, if this is truly what you want, give me a verse and as I prayed, Mark 16:15 came to my mind." Thus, the doubt disappeared."

Through prayer and godly confirmation from Pastor Ogata, a leading Alliance pastor, along with great encouragement from her spiritual mother and mentor, Missionary Mabel Francis, Miss Mutsuko Ninomiya began to look toward the huge country of Brazil, 38 times larger than Japan. The spiritual plight of tens of thousands of new Japanese immigrants that had gone to Brazil following the close of WW II lay heavy on her heart. War weary and destitute, thousands of families had left the homeland seeking a new life in Brazil's vast interior.

At this point, a word needs to be given concerning the conversion experience of this woman of God. She was born and raised in a Buddhist home and had never heard of Jesus Christ. Her father was a police chief, a man of impeccable character. She was a public school teacher and was working in Hiroshima. Due to the constant raids by the US B29 bombers, the authorities were bulldozing fire lanes in the crowded neighborhoods so that the flimsy wooden houses crowded together would not all catch fire.

On August 5, 1945 at 9:15 a.m., Tokyo time, she was on the outskirts of Hiroshima leading a group of teenage school girls who were clearing rubble. As she leaned over to pick up some debris, at that precise moment, the atomic bomb exploded. With her back turned to the city, the powerful shockwave knocked her down and left her unconscious. When she awoke and turned to see a vast plain of smoldering destruction, the huge mushroom cloud soaring above her head, and the carbonized bodies of the school girls charred by the blast. In panic, young Mutsuko began to run and run and run into the countryside. She survived and eventually was able to make her way back to relative safety at her home town, Matsuyama.

A few years later, the war was over and people were trying to get on with life. Due to the change in curriculum imposed on the Ministry of Education by the US Occupation Government, Mutsuko was frustrated because the changes which affected her status as teacher and her possibilities of becoming a civil servant. At that time, few people had been privileged to graduate from college and begin post graduate work, as she was doing. It was at this time that she involved herself in an extra-curricular activity, taking part in an archery class. She was taught to always maintain an erect posture. For that reason, she was notable for being an "upright" person in her posture—and her person.

Now in her mid-twenties, Mutsuko returned to school in Matsuyama to finish her graduate studies. Daily she walked across a big open square. She soon noted that there was a little old lady who rode across the crowded square on a bicycle almost every day . This was out of the ordinary for several reasons: first, bicycles had been confiscated during the war to provide metal for the war effort. Second, this old lady looked Japanese except for her eyes; yes, definitely she was a westerner. And finally, she was always smiling. In post-war Japan, people didn't smile much. They had lost the war; millions of men and women had died, their economy was in ruins, and their emperor had admitted on radio that he was only a man and not a god.

Why Are You Smiling?

One day, Mutsuko screwed up her courage and stopped

the smiling old lady and asked her, "Why are you always smiling? What's to be happy about?" The little lady on the bicycle, Mabel Francis, who was a single-lady, an Alliance missionary who had stayed in Japan during World War II, said: "I am smiling because my God is alive, and He loves me and He loves you." That simple question and intriguing answer laid the first foundation stone of a bridge of trust and friendship that eventually led Mutsuko Ninomiya to give her heart and life to Christ about a year later. She became a close friend of the legendary "Miss Francis," who served more than 50 years in Japan. Mutsuko soon entered the Alliance Seminary in Hiroshima, graduated, and became a pastor in the Japan Alliance Church, working with Miss Francis in church planting and evangelism. Now after sensing God's call on her life, it was her turn to take a step of faith as Mabel Francis had done years before.

Many obstacles seemed to block her way to Brazil as she began to share her burden and vision with others. Funds for travel to Brazil and regular support were not easy to come by in postwar Japan, still rebuilding after the terrible destruction of more than eight years of war. In addition, the Japan Alliance Church had never sent out a missionary, and now they were going to send a woman as their first! At the Alliance pastor's conference that fall, she went public with her calling. And it was there that

On the ship to Brazil

she received her first public words of encouragement, after which the pastors fervently prayed and laid on hands as they committed her to the Lord's work in Brazil. One pastor wept as he testified that he had prayed for years that the Japan Alliance would send out missionaries. Mutsuko was the first fruit of his prayers.

Shortly thereafter, a special Christmas offering was received for her support. Starting from her home church of Matsuyama, and spreading to the twenty-one other Japan Alliance churches, by early 1959, the $1,100 for her boat ticket and her $50.00 monthly support were raised. Thus, at the age of 36, this intrepid disciple of Jesus set out for Brazil on April 30, 1959 aboard the *Santos Maru*, arriving at the port of Santos on May 23 where she was met by Methodist Missionary Sumiko Miyamoto. "Dona Mutsuko" as she was called in Brazil, went with Sumiko to the interior city of Maringá where she worked with Missionary Miyamoto. After working there for a time to learn how to minister to the expatriate Japanese, Miss Ninomiya went to the *School of Portuguese and Orientation* in Campinas, São Paulo where she studied Portuguese for nine months.

In October 1960, Mutsuko traveled to survey three cities where no work among the Japanese immigrants existed: *Porto Alegre*, the capital of the southernmost state, Rio Grande do Sul; *Belo Horizonte*, capital of the state of Minas Gerais, and *Brasília*, the new nation's capital being built under the dynamic leadership of President Juscelino

Santos Maru

Kubitschek. In her own words: "Brasília was the city that was least attractive to me, since it offered no safety and there was no infrastructure to speak of. Many friends opposed my moving to Brasília. They were right since it was not an appropriate place for a woman to live alone. I was still young and felt insecure listening to their reasons; however, I became convinced [that Brasília was the city] and I went there."

Brasília – Nûcleo Bandeirante

Sensing that this was the field God had chosen for her to work in, Dona Mutsuko moved to the Federal District of Brasília where she was overjoyed to encounter a Japanese Christian family, Mr. Ishikawa and wife, Tokiko. While staying at their home, she sensed "the Macedonian call" to begin to plant the seed in what was then called *Cidade Livre* (Free City). And Cidade Livre (later renamed *Nûcleo Bandeirante* – Pioneer Nucleus) was a wild and wooly place. Dr. Nathan Bailey, then president of the North American C&MA, visited Miss Ninomiya soon after she moved to the new capital city in early 1961. He described her home as a "plywood shack" of a few rooms surrounded by other equally precarious buildings. Cidade Livre was the first workers encampment erected for the laborers who built Brasília, most driven from their homes in the Northeast of Brazil by drought and lack of work. Bars, houses of prostitution and gambling halls were scattered among the rough-wood dormitories set up by the construction companies and the few "private homes," among which was Mutsuko's "plywood palace." As Dr. Bailey recounted

Ninomiya's "Plywood Shack"

what he saw on that visit, he shook his head as he commented on the courage and tenacity of the single-lady Alliance missionary from Japan.

On December 4, 1960, she led the first Alliance church service in what is now called *Núcleo Bandeirante*, the first of Brasilia's many satellite cities, not many months after the new capital's inauguration on April 21, 1960. In order to reach the mostly Buddhist Nikkei population, Mutsuko opened a Japanese school to teach the children of the Japanese who had moved to Brasília. Since they were excellent farmers who could make the barren soil of the Central Plateau yield fruit and vegetables needed for the growing population of the Federal District, President Kubitschek appealed to the Japanese government to send settlers to the new capital and come they did.

Gama, Federal Distirct

In 1961, working all alone with limited Portuguese and minimal funds, Miss Ninomiya obtained a lot in another new satellite city, *Gama*, where she began to evangelize Brazilian working families who had migrated there. This outreach resulted in the *Ebenezer Alliance Church*, now the largest Alliance Church in the Federal District. The testimonies given by senior adults who were children when D. Mutsuko began to evangelize are heartwarming. Despite her sometimes puzzling Portuguese grammar, she conjugated love and concern beautifully. Through meetings held in homes, summer vacation Bible schools, evangelistic campaigns and door-to-door witnessing, the hard-working lady apostle introduced people to Christ who are still following the Lord today.

Eurípedes Dias de Jesus, one of the first converts in Gama remembers "when a lady, rather different, came up [to

Ebenezer Alliance Church

me and my brothers who were playing *futebol* on a Sunday morning], and she asked our names and also if we would like to come to a Sunday school in the Evangelical Church." He was nine years old and faithfully attended each Sunday, even after his brothers stopped. Although he tried, he didn't understand what was being said and taught, but the *"missionária"* persevered in teaching him. A good while passed without making a decision for Christ. In due course, an evangelist from Brazil's northeast, Pastor Gerson Barbosa de Menezes, was holding evangelistic meetings in the various evangelical churches in Gama. Eventually, he came to the big wooden shed that housed the Gama Alliance Church and preached the simple gospel of Jesus. "It was on that day that I gave my life to Jesus. I remember that the *missionária* sat next to me and quietly spoke with me and encouraged me to make my decision." To this day, Euripides, and his wife Francisca Soares, another convert through Dona Mutsuko's ministry, continue to serve the Lord as ACEMBRAS church members in the Federal District.

Consequently, whenever one begins to talk about the "modern history" of the C&MA in Brazil, they have to begin with the ground-breaking work of the Japan Alliance sending Miss Mutsuko Ninomiya to Brazil in 1959. She served the Lord as a missionary till 1996 when she retired from active ministry and returned to Japan, to her beloved Matsuyama, where she served in the local Alliance Church for many years as pastor to the seniors. At the ripe old age of 94, she is still active and lives alone with her memories and her Lord.

Argentine Roots

At about this same time, the Lord continued to "stir the mulberry trees" in another part of the world as another Alliance national church, *La Alianza Cristiana e Misionera* of Argentina, also came under a burden to reach the lost in Brazil. Much of this Brazil vision was cast by C&MA Missionaries Sam and Vera Barnes, who had visited many Brazilian port cities while sailing to and from the field over the course of their long missionary career. For years, Sam and Vera Barnes had been praying about Brazil, this giant neighbor nation of 70 million souls, mostly nominal Roman Catholics, with a slow-growing evangelical church and millions more locked in the grip of Spiritism and a multitude of strange cult groups. Thus a strategy was born in Barnes' heart and passed on to the Argentine Alliance in 1958 to begin a missionary venture of evangelism and church planting in cities that bordered Brazil. In his mind, a strategy for entering Brazil from major Argentine frontier cities began to form in his heart. He shared his vision with his wife, Vera, as well as Myron Voth, a young Alliance missionary to Argentina, and gifted Argentine evangelist, Carmelo Terranova.

In the May 18, 1960 issue of the *Alliance Weekly*, Myron Voth wrote an article, "Missionary Vision Revives a Church," which tells of the enthusiasm and buy-in by the Argentine C&MA Church. A map shows the location of the "Tri-state area – a section of northern Argentina, southeastern Brazil and northwest Uruguay." Stories of God's calling four missionary couples from the pastoral corps, heightened enrollment at the Buenos Aires Bible Institute, sacrificial giving to the missions treasurer of the Argentine Alliance showed how Barnes' vision had spread to the leaders and members of the church.

The Alliance of Argentina sacrificed in order to launch this effort. A poor seamstress had been saving for years to buy a new sewing machine; instead, she gave the money for this challenge. A young couple postponed their wedding and instead gave what they had saved toward missions. Thus, strong evangelistic effort was launched in the town of *Paso de Los Libres* that faced *Uruguaiana* on the other side of the Uruguay River. Another Argentine Alliance couple was sent to *Rivera*, a border city of Uruguay, divided only by a wide avenue and plaza from the Brazilian town of *Santana do Livramento.* Aggressive evangelistic campaigns in these towns resulted in many being saved and churches being planted. While the church planted in Rivera and Paso de los Libres prospered and some Brazilians came across the border and were saved, in neither town on the Brazilian side was a church planted. Unfortunately, the cross border efforts envisioned by Rev. Barnes fell short of the goal of planting an Alliance church on Brazilian soil.

Apparently all of this missionary initiative undertaken by the Alliance churches in Japan and Argentina captured the attention of the North American Alliance. In the January 27, 1960 issue of *The Alliance Witness,* an item under the title, "Mission Leaders on Deputation," stated: Rev. Louis L. King, Foreign Secretary, left New York on January 8 to attend the Latin American Conference. . . Following this Mr. King planned to visit Chile and Argentina. He will then go to the tri-republic area (the border sections of Argentina, Paraguay and Brazil) and Brazilia (sic), Brazil, where the establishing of Alliance missionary work is under consideration." It is interesting to note that the establishment of Alliance missionary work "is now under consideration." That is the first official hint of more to come. Unfortunately, this planned visit to Brasília never materialized. King did visit the Alliance mission works in Chile and Argentina. Included in his itinerary was a visit to Paso de Los Libres bordering the Brazilian town of Uruguaiana followed by a long bus ride to Santana do Livramento, Brazil where he then crossed the plaza and visited the Rivera, Uruguay Alliance Church. After a short visit there, he went to Buenos Aires. Following his visit to Buenos Aires, he flew to the Netherlands.

In the June 15 1960 Portland Council issue of *The Alliance Witness*, Argentina missionary, Myron Voth, gave a stirring address to the council delegates: "When the Church Went Missionary," referring to Argentina's recent outreach to the Tri-Republic border cities with the intent of reaching into Brazil. He threw out the challenge: "Brazil is the greatest missionary opportunity in Latin America." It would seem that Brazil was definitely appearing on the C&MA's radar screen after so many blank decades. Voth was the young protégé that Sam Barnes was preparing for this challenge.

Simpson's Vision Realized

Despite the cancellation of King's visit to Brasília, interest continued to be high in the Foreign Department. Approval was given for a "deputational visit of Dr. Nathan Bailey . . . [to] visit the proposed area for establishing a C&MA work in Brazil." The November 9, 1960 FDSC minute #638 relating to Bailey's visit used the phrase "proposed area for establishing a C&MA work in Brazil." So "consideration" has grown to conviction since there was now a "proposal" on the table. At the subsequent Foreign Department Sub Committee meeting, Minute 706 states: "That approval be granted to open work in Brazil as soon as it is convenient to do so." In a matter of a few short months in 1960, the Foreign Department under Dr. King's leadership progressed from "consideration" to "proposal" to "approval" to establish a new field in Brazil without the personal visit of a representative from the Foreign Department. Thus the question to be answered here is "what proposal," Barnes' or the Foreign Department's? At that same FDSC meeting on November 9, Sam and Vera Barnes were placed on retiral status. The Barneses, 41-year veterans to Argentina with the C&MA, were retired and returned to the United States in August 1959 and were living in Greenville, SC.

Upon his return to the New York C&MA Headquarters, Dr. Bailey wrote up a seven page report which he gave to the Foreign Department. In it, he goes into some detail relating his visit to the Federal District. "You can imagine our joy to be met at the airport in Brasília by the young lady from Japan, Miss Matzuka (sic) Ninomya (sic), a convert of Miss Francis and a member of our Alliance Church in Japan. . . . After our greetings at the airport and exchanging oriental bows, we were invited to accompany her and a lady and gentlemen from her congregation to her home. You can imagine our surprise when we arrived at her "home" to find written across the front of the building in Portuguese: "Iglesius Alianza (sic)." Her home was one room at the back of the church which had been built by the Japanese gentleman on land provided by him. The first [Alliance] church established in Brazil, therefore, is not from North America, but from the Alliance of Japan."

Dr. Bailey was able to talk with some missionaries while in Brasília from whom he received some valuable information concerning the new capital and what it would take for the mission to begin a work there: "There is strict control over the building operations." He then explained that a church or mission, in order to obtain property in the "Pilot Plan," which was the name used for the capital city plan, must already "be working in the country and registered with the government. It must have congregations and churches already functioning." Obviously this would be a problem for a new missionary endeavor as was proposed by the Alliance. If land were obtained, any temporary buildings would have to be replaced by permanent construction within three years. He went on to state: "A number of these denominations are not only building churches, but secular schools as well. All of this is being done with North American funds. *We would have to be prepared to enter on the same basis* (editor's italics). The Nazarene Church will be the first church in the federal district to achieve this goal. Their church is finished. The Mission House and Compound are approximately finished, and they are soon to start building the secular school."

He finished his report on the visit to Brasília with these words: "I do not question the action we have taken in declaring Brazil a field of endeavor for our missionary outreach. It is considered to be the fastest growing and most challenging opportunity in all Latin America. Surely there are vast areas that remain unevangelized and constitute an ever-present challenge to us both in the Tri-State Area to the south and also in the vast jungle areas of the headwaters of the Amazon." This short visit by C&MA president, Nathan Bailey, was the only on-the-ground investigation of the situation in the new capital city by a representative sent by the Foreign Department. In those few days, he did his best to sound out the prospects and present the challenges that would face the new missionaries.

At the April 18 1961 FDSC meeting, Minute 236 reads: "That Mr. and Mrs. D. M. Voth be appointed to Brazil and that they leave for Language school in Campinas, Brazil, in time to attend the next semester of study." This was a strong sign that the Barnes strategy was in view since Sam had shared the "Tri-state" border strategy with Voth. As an experienced two-term veteran missionary to Argentina, Myron Voth was loved and respected by missionary and national alike. Years later, he was called a "living legend" because of his winsome personality, gifts in evangelism, teaching, administration and church planting. He had already served as C&MA board representative and director for the Buenos Aires Bible Institute. He and his wife, Virginia, had gone to Argentina in 1954. Hence, it would appear that the ideal leader for the new field had emerged, a mature, experienced and gifted missionary still young enough to learn Portuguese well who could give many years of service to the new field and break in the new missionary staff.

Amazingly one month later at the May 4, 1961 FDSC meeting, Minute #305 states: "That SC 236/62 be rescinded, appointing Mr. and Mrs. D. M. Voth to Brazil." The very next minute, #306 goes on: "That Mr. D. M. Voth be appointed Board Representative for Argentina and Mr. G. M. Little be named the Director of the Bible Institute." Consequently with one hand, Brazil is given the ideal field leader, and with the other hand he is taken away. It is apparent that the retirement of Sam and Vera Barnes had caused stress on the rest of the Argentine Alliance Mission staff, and Voth was considered too vital to the continued ministry there to be spared for Brazil. Argentina's win was Brazil's loss. At this point, the Foreign Department was moving forward with its plan to open the field of Brazil leaderless. At the Annual General Council of the C&MA, held later that same month in Columbus, Ohio, the June 14 1961 issue of *The AW* dramatically announced: "The moving response of young people . . . the introduction of sixteen missionary appointees . . . the enthusiastic reception of the news that we will enter Brazil . . . ."

Back to Brazil at Last

It was at that Council that Rev. Paul and Claudia Bryers were presented to the Council delegates and members for commissioning as missionaries to Brazil. Paul was from Hamilton, Ontario and a Nyack Missionary College (now Nyack College) grad while Claudia was U.S. born and graduated from St. Paul Bible College (now Crown College). Paul writes: "Toward the end of my last year at Nyack [1960], L. L. King (Foreign Secretary) invited Claudia and me to be missionaries to Brazil. Then he informed us that they would waive the traditional two-year home assignment and send us to Missionary Internship in Detroit to prepare us to quickly get to the field. At the end of the 9 month program in which we served in the Redford Free Methodist Church, our departure had to be delayed as Claudia was then 7 months pregnant."

In the August 29-30 1961 FDSC meeting following the appointment of Paul and Claudia Bryers to the field, the Minute #73 stated: "That SC 21/61 be rescinded [regarding the retiral of the Barneses]. . . and that Mr. and Mrs. S. G. Barnes be appointed to Brazil . . . and that they leave for Brazil not later than January 1, 1962." So it seems that the "great challenge" spoken of the previous year by Myron Voth would have to be carried forward by the visionary veterans, Sam and Vera Barnes. At the October 12, 1961 FDSC meeting, Minute #706 stated that "an amount of up to $3,000 be made available from the Columbus General Council Missionary Sunday special

Paul and Claudia Bryers - Commissioned at 1961 Council

offering to purchase a Camper Volkswagen for Mr. and Mrs. S. G. Barnes and that this be a fully mission-owned vehicle." In November, Sam Barnes was officially appointed "Board Representative for Brazil." Thus the question of who was to lead was answered. Near the end of 1961 as the field budgets were established, the new Brazil Field had a yearly budget for 1962 of $4,000, sufficient for the Barnes and Bryers as the new field was entered.

It becomes clear that sometime following the rescinding of Voth's appointment to Brazil in early May 1961 and the Bryer's commissioning to Brazil just a few weeks later, Dr. King entered into contact with the Barneses. Vera Barnes describes how God was leading in her book, *Miles Beyond in Brazil*: "The conviction [to see the Brazil field opened by the C&MA] grew into a project. The project presented to the Foreign Department and then to the home constituency, was heartily approved and accepted. The burden was shared with others, and God began speaking to His people."

"Then the Reverend L. L. King, foreign secretary, approached us about our going to Brazil for awhile to survey the field and help the young missionaries get a start. God's leadings were unmistakable. We were to go to Brazil. Our hearts burned as intensely, our enthusiasm as keenly as the day we left for the mission field the first time. We even had a map of Brazil hanging in our bedroom at home near enough to see, plan, meditate, talk and pray about where we should go."

From the first glimmer of their missionary call, the burden for Brazil was great. Even after being assigned to Argentina as young C&MA missionaries, the Barnes sensed a deep concern for the port cities that they visited on Brazil's coast going to and from the field. God had laid the plight of this great nation living in spiritual darkness on their souls, and it seemed that at last He was sending them there. Mrs. Barnes's book mentioned another of God's nudges: "More than thirty years ago the foreign secretary of the Christian and Missionary Alliance, Mr. Howard DinWiddie (sic), had written to us a letter about leaving Argentina to go to Brazil to begin a new work there. Although the plan appealed to us tremendously, we were compelled to turn down the offer, at least until the Argentina work be established." God had a plan for Brazil and the Alliance, and Sam and Vera Barnes were part of it. It was just a question of when, not if.

In the November 29, 1961 issue of *The AW*, a lead article, "A New Alliance Mission Field – Brazil," announced that "Four Alliance missionaries are ready to enter the new field of Brazil in January, 1962." The articles went on to explain that the Bryers would study the Portuguese language while the Barnes would "survey an interior section of Brazil southward from the capital of Brasília to the Rio Grande do Sul area. They will be looking for one of the intermediate-size cities in which the Alliance will establish its first work." Thus the Barnes vision and plan birthed in Sam's heart back in 1958 seemed to be coming to fruition.

In the same article, Rev. L. L. King stated: "The Christian and Missionary Alliance will hold to its established tradition of immediately pressing into areas where the gospel witness is seriously lacking and urgently needed . . . . Our 'drive' in Brazil will be to larger towns or cities, as we would call them, rather than in the jungle areas. We will then move into rural and jungle areas, using as our bases the churches that are raised up in these cities."

"The Plan"

The "plan" was repeated in a promotional tract produced

in early 1962, "Sharing the Gospel with BRAZIL," which stated on the back page: "The Alliance missionaries in Brazil, after surveying an area from Brasília southward to Rio Grande do Sul, will establish their first witness of the Gospel in a needy city area, which will serve as a base of operations." Between the publishing of the "plan" and its first steps for execution, disaster struck.

Shortly before Sam and Vera Barnes were to fly to Brazil with Paul and Claudia Bryers in early 1962, the Barneses were involved in a very serious car accident on December 9, 1961. They skidded on an icy road near Richmond, VA, enroute to Baltimore MD to secure their visas for entry into Brazil. Their car slid out of control on an icy patch and crashed. Sam was thrown from the car and suffered serious head trauma and a crushed jaw. Mrs. Barnes was pinned under the steering wheel for three hours and broke 36 bones! Somehow these veterans, now in their late 60's, survived, undergoing many surgeries and a long stay in the hospital. Eventually they were able to return home in order to heal and recover their strength. Just a few months later in May of 1962 at the Miami Annual Council, the Barneses were there and addressed the delegates; they pleaded, "Send us your sons and daughters, your young people and your grandchildren." Vera spoke to the Council while being held up by a man at each side!

Samuel and Vera Barnes

Due to the severity of the accident and the Barnes' long period of recovery, it was decided that Paul and Claudia Bryers would go on to Brazil in early January 1962, with Sam and Vera to come later when they had recuperated from their injuries. When the Bryers arrived on January 17, 1962 at the Viracopos Airport in Campinas, São Paulo, Paul was 24 and Claudia was 25. They were met by a Mennonite missionary couple, Ken and Grace Schwartzentruber, who helped them rent a home and set up housekeeping. They felt very much alone as they began their missionary career in a brand-new Alliance mission field. With help from local missionaries, they were able to rent and furnish a home and begin to study Portuguese at the *Escola de Português e Orientação* (School of Portuguese and Orientation), jointly administered by the Presbyterian, Methodist and Southern Baptist Missions.

Before their departure to Brazil, Paul and Claudia met with the Revs. L. L. King and B. S. King (C&MA Treasurer) and Dr. Nathan Bailey. Paul writes that they were given three instructions at this meeting:

1. "Don't worry about anything, but dedicate yourself to learning the language."

2. "Since we don't know the costs in Brazil, keep track of your expenses for reimbursement. (I wasn't used to writing everything down which made this a very difficult process and pretty much wiped out my savings.) When I needed money, they would see that I get it. Later an arrangement was made with City Bank in New York."

3. "An experienced missionary [couple], Sam and Vera Barnes, would come and essentially mentor

us on beginning the work in Brazil."

Sam, anxious to get on the field as soon as able, flew to Rio de Janeiro on October 11 where he was met by Paul Bryers. They flew on to São Paulo and together bused to Campinas, where the Bryers were in their last few months of Portuguese language study. Soon Sam purchased a Willys Rural Jeep wagon, which he used to travel about the country doing survey work. Ann Barnes Hemminger said that her dad returned to Brazil not totally recovered from the car accident. His neck was still very stiff and he could not turn his head, which must have been disconcerting while driving.

Goiânia, Goiás

In late 1962 at the close of their language study, Paul Bryers and Sam Barnes flew up to Goiânia, the capital of the state of Goiás, where they met Rev. George Constance. While there, they rented housing for each family in the Southern Sector of the city. Shortly thereafter, Vera Barnes arrived on January 14, 1963 to rejoin her husband, Sam. Goiânia was the first city where the North American C&MA established missionary work in Brazil. As capital of the state of Goiás, inaugurated in 1942 and located 120 miles southwest of the brand-new national capital of Brasília, it apparently was chosen because of its proximity to Brasília as well as being on a major north/south highway. In just twenty years, Goiânia already had a population of more than 150,000. Paul and Claudia were told by Sam to "do your own thing, rent a hall and begin a work." Sam met with Paul and mentored him spiritually, but otherwise told him to gain experience, visiting and even preaching to the empty benches if necessary and learn ministry by doing. Thus they rented a store-front hall in their middle-class neighborhood and prepared it for their opening evangelistic campaign. "Claudia and I went door to door to all the homes in the area inviting people to this new work. We were very well received and were very excited. We invited a Presbyterian pastor, a friend of Sam Barnes, to inaugurate the new church with a week of meetings. After sending out invitations, the day came and only four people came, but they were there every night." Thus began the Alliance Mission ministry in Goiânia.

In *Miles Beyond in Brazil*, Vera Barnes relates the story of Maria, a young girl who lived near the Barnes home in Goiânia. She had heard Vera playing hymns on her accordion and came to their door. Fond of music, Maria listened as the veteran missionary played a few more hymns. "The Lord tenderly whispered to me: 'This young girl is hungry for salvation. She will be saved if you witness to her.'" Vera was still trying to learn Portuguese and felt hesitant. Yet each time the girl visited the Barnes home, Vera shared Scripture with her. She attended the opening evangelistic campaign held in the rented hall and declared: "This is the first gospel message I have ever heard." The missionary team gave her a Bible and gospel tracts. The seed fell on the soil but nothing happened apparently. Two months passed and then, one hot, sultry afternoon, Maria came to visit and the Spirit urged Vera that it was time. "I asked Maria if she had time to stay and read the Bible with me. She gladly consented. Together we sat down around God's Word and read John 3:16, Romans 8:8-10 and so on. In a few minutes, Maria spontaneously exclaimed: 'I want Christ now as my personal Savior!'" The good seed planted earlier bore fruit.

The Bryers held a church service each Sunday evening as well as evangelizing children during the week and through Sunday school. Paul also was invited by the

"*Promotor*" (District Attorney) of the nearby town of *Aunicuns*, a contact made by Sam Barnes, to start a preaching point in his house. Weekly, Paul would take the morning bus over to the town about 45 miles northwest of Goiânia. During the afternoon, Paul did visitation and then held a meeting in the DA's home in the evening, attended by 25 to 30 people in this small rural town. This ministry was continued until Paul was instructed by Foreign Department leadership to close the work because the potential for leadership development in the town showed little prospect. One wonders if the DA himself could not have been developed as a leader of the ministry there.

While Paul and Claudia were pioneering at their little hall, Sam and Vera made several survey trips searching for an appropriate city where the eventual Alliance base could be established. The Barneses did not see Goiânia as the ideal city since it was far north from the area to the South that they felt most propitious for establishing a strong mission base, as well as being closer to the Argentine Alliance's efforts on the borders of Brazil. In a January 9, 1963 *Alliance Witness* article, Sam writes: "When we can get the Goiânia burden off our shoulders we will only find ourselves staggering under the burden for the city of Curitiba and the entire state of Paraná. . . . What a city this is! It has a population of 361,000. I noticed, in looking over the city, that the Mormons and other false cults have already arrived. What a challenge to us who have the message of a mighty Christ." In a May 15, 1963 *Alliance Witness* article, Mrs. Barnes writes: "We, too, see a vast multitude of hungry people; and we are so few in number – just the four of us: Paul and Claudia Bryers, and my husband and I. Our hearts are melted before God for speedy reinforcements." That cry was soon to be answered as new missionaries arrived a few months later.

John and Beverly Nicholson and baby daughter, Karen,

arrived on September 7, 1963 on the same flight with David and Marilyn Sundeen, and infant son, Leslie. These were the first of several couples sent to supplement the meager missionary staff. Nicholsons and Sundeens took up residence in Campinas where they began to study at the *Escola de Português e Orientação*. *In Miles Beyond in Brazil*, Mrs. Barnes describes their trip from Goiânia to Campinas: "Early one morning, we started in our Jeep to the city of Campinas, six hundred miles away. We were to meet two new missionary couples [Nicholsons and Sundeens] who had arrived for a year of language study. Although most of the road is paved, some sixty or seventy miles are still dirt road. On the dirt road, we met with clouds of fine red dirt mixed with the dry fog that nearly suffocated us and caused our eyes to smart and burn. Our hair looked as though it had been dyed red. When we arrived, we looked for a room with a shower. We spent a pleasant evening with our missionaries; then after a few hours rest, we continued our journey south toward Curitiba."

In a letter written to his daughter Ann, Sam wrote: "From the very first, well before we went to Brazil, I felt strongly drawn toward the great State of Paraná. Both Londrina and Curitiba were focal points for my interest, my studies and for waiting prayer, before the Presence of my wonderful Father. As soon as possible, after arriving in Brazil, I headed for Curitiba. I was there four times; once, with just Him; again with Myron Voth; and I was there with George Constance; finally, I went with our Vera."

Not One, But Two Strategies

He and Vera had been specifically commissioned to go to Brazil, open the field and chose the area where the Alliance would concentrate its forces. Sam saw Goiânia as only a first step, while his eyes looked south. That this was apparently not the vision of the Foreign Department is revealed in correspondence with his daughter: "I had plans to rent a little home in Curitiba where we could begin our work. Then the Board, like so many mission groups in those days, wanted a window-display as having a work in Brasília. And I went to Goiânia, which was very near the famous, new city. I went to further the thought of the Board about Brasília." From this comment, one can deduce that there were two, not one, strategies in play at this time.

On his first visit to Curitiba, alone, Sam saw the potential of Curitiba, the beautiful capital city of Paraná. However, he spent a day in prayer at the Hotel Iguaçu "alone with my Father in that room . . . . When the storm was passed and submission came, He told me that I would have to go with the Bryers to Goiânia and Brasília – to get them started. Later, He would let me "see" Curitiba." From this, it is clear that the Foreign Department was pushing the "Brasília strategy."

The final meeting of January 1964 with the Mission leadership in Curitiba did not go well. Sam later described it as being a "blast of [his] dream of a co-operating Argentine contingency." Paul Bryers, who did not accompany Barnes on his survey trips, describes what he recalls of the long-ago encounter: "There was some sort of disagreement [between Barnes and Rev. Constance]. One day I got a message to go to the Brasília Airport and pick up the Willys. [The Barneses] had left." More than a half century after the fact, it is difficult to understand why this imbroglio occurred. Sam and Vera Barnes had been commissioned to open the field and chose the area of concentration; however, their recommendation was overruled by the mission leadership. As a result, they suddenly left the field on February 6, 1964. Sam had been in Brazil for about 16 months and Vera about 14. They returned to their home in Greenville, SC, and some years later they planted an Alliance Church.

As a result of their sudden departure, Bryers writes: "The surprise news regarding the vehicle and everyone's departure left me up in the air. I was really a rookie with no experience and now I was the [Board] representative of the Board of Managers in New York. No one sat down with me and helped me work out a strategy, or even how to organize things. I set out to do my best." Working with a local lawyer, Paul was able to draw up the first mission documents, the "Estatutos" or constitution and by-laws, incorporating it as a foreign mission by mid-1964. Setting up the mission's bookkeeping was another new task for Paul. Now he was in charge of the two couples in Campinas, and later in July of that same year, the Bryers received a veteran missionary couple, Alwyn and Edythe Rees and their two children, Dilys and Dylan. They had served for more than 20 years in the Belgian Congo and the Portuguese-speaking protectorate of Cabinda just north of the Congo River. Al and Edythe arrived in Goiânia and took up residence, while their children went to school in the nearby town of *Leopoldo Bulhões* where they studied at the Unevangelized Fields Mission School for missionary kids. Al and Edythe were assigned to work with Paul and Claudia at the Alliance gospel hall in Goiânia.

Soon another new couple, Emmit and Sandra Young arrived on August 7, 1964. They began language study in Campinas. It was at this point that Paul and Claudia moved to Brasília to pursue the Brasília strategy, the legal registration of the mission, acquisition of a lot in the Pilot Plan and the establishment of the Alliance work there. John and Beverly Nicholson were assigned to Brasília following graduation from

Edythe, Dylan, Al, and Dilys Rees

Language School, while Dave and Marilyn Sundeen were sent to Goiânia where they worked with Al and Edythe Rees. Without the seasoned leadership of the Barneses, difficulties arose in the mission. Paul Bryers was about the same age of the newcomer missionaries, except for the Reeses, 20 years his senior; yet he was specifically maintained as the Board Representative. His was not a comfortable position in which to be. In Brasília, Paul set out to secure land from *TERRACAP*, the government-run real estate company. He worked with Mr. Hélio Krahenbühl, the Treasurer of the Federal District, whose knowledge of the in-workings of Brazilian bureaucracy were a great help.

The story of the Krahenbühl family is interesting. "Dr. Hélio," as he was called, had gone to Detroit, Michigan and earned his Master's degree in public administration at Wayne State University. His wife, Dona Celí, began to attend the Detroit Central Alliance Church pastored by Rev. T. E. Thompson,; it was very close to the Wayne State Campus. She became born again while there and developed a great love for the Alliance. She and her husband returned to Brazil and her husband eventually became the treasurer of the Federal District of Brasília. As a matter of record, the Krahenbühls were the first couple to work with the Alliance in the "Plano Pilôto" (Pilot Plan).

Thus, the surge of Alliance mission interest in Brazil, born first in Japan in the hearts of Miss Ninomiya and Missionary Mabel Francis in 1958, and stirred up that same year in Argentina by the sexagenarian missionary Sam Barnes, and shared with his Argentine colleagues, speaks of God's Spirit at work on each side of the globe in sister Alliance national churches. Likely because of this attention given by sister churches of the C&MA, the North American Alliance began to take another look at the "waking giant" to the south. The first steps, although faltering, showed a definite commitment in that six Alliance missionary couples were sent out in less than three years. In addition, another Alliance national church in Colombia was sensing God's call to send out their own missionaries, as a result of the testimony of Rev. Sam and Vera Barnes, two farsighted missionary pioneers who would eventually see their vision of the "southern strategy" based in Curitiba take shape. Better yet, their daughter, Ann and son-in-law, James Hemminger, would be a part of that pioneer initiative.

Lessons Learned

In closing this chapter, the question, "what can be learned from this chronicle?" demands an answer or maybe several. First of all, it is apparent that God had a plan for the Alliance and Brazil. The year, 1958, was critical in that God began to touch lives in Japan and Argentina, with no human coordination. The long-felt burden that Sam and Vera Barnes had sensed, even the invitation made by Rev. Dinwiddie back in the 1920s to enter Brazil, only confirmed what they had first felt before leaving for missionary service in Argentina. Despite the lack of agreement which eventually surfaced as to where the C&MA Mission should center their efforts, God was saying, "The time has arrived; go!" History has confirmed that mandate.

Another thing that this "rediscovery chapter" makes

clear is that mission leadership should trust veteran missionaries who have prayed long and planned well a strategy for entering a new field. Sam and Vera Barnes were proven veterans who had more than four decades of successful service in the very difficult field of Argentina. They were called and commissioned to open the mission in Brazil, choose the area for missionary occupation and prepare the ground for the young missionaries to follow. They set out to do this but the competing vision of Foreign Department leadership eventually brought the lack of agreement to a head, resulting in the premature departure of the veteran Board Representative. The result was a leadership vacuum. Barnes sudden departure thrust Paul Bryers, a young and inexperienced first-term missionary, into the leadership role with other new missionaries of similar age and experience. Making matters more complicated, a four-term couple from the Congo arrived on the field to work under a first-term Board Representative. This trying experience put the Bryers in an uncomfortable position with their colleagues. The old adage, responsibility without authority breeds frustration and futility, continues to be true.

Yet even at this end of the first difficult years, a glimmer of "prophetic" light appeared on the horizon. In *The C&MA Missionary Atlas of 1964*, the next to the last paragraph summarizing the still-new field of Brazil stated: "It is expected that the Alliance area of operation will embrace the federal district (Brasília) and the states of Goiás and Paraná." The vision of Sam and Vera Barnes wasn't dead, yet.

CHAPTER FOUR
MOVING FORWARD

Following the difficult and eventful first years of Alliance presence in Brazil, the good seed began to take root. From it, several branches soon sprang forth, demonstrating the spiritual DNA that originated in A. B. Simpson. The branches came from several parts of the Alliance world and all took root about the same time in the mid 1960s.

Manaus

In 1964 in Colombia, a young Alliance couple, Pastor Hernan and Edilma Osorio, began to sense God's call on their lives. "Don Hernán" had attended the Second Latin American Conference in Temuco, Chile in March 1963. While there, "he had heard Rev. and Mrs. Samuel G. Barnes tell of the tremendous need as well as the lack of workers in Brazil. . . . At the close, Don Hernán was the first up front to offer himself for missionary service in Brazil." As is often the case with an "ice-breaker," many of the Osorio's Alliance pastoral colleagues thought the idea was foolish, for him and "Mamita" to go to Brazil as missionaries, when so much need was evident in Colombia. However, they pressed into God and pushed on toward their goal. At the annual Colombian Alliance convention later that year, the delegates came to the realization that the Great Commission was binding on all churches everywhere,

Hernan and Edilma Osorio

regardless of size or situation. As a result, twenty-eight persons responded to the call for consecration, and a missionary offering of 330 pesos was given for sending out the Osorios. Eventually, Hernán and Mamita and their little daughter, Judith, arrived in Manaus, the capital city of the state of Amazonas, in the heart of the Amazon rain forest in 1966.

Despite meager financial support, the Osorios worked hard and prayed harder. By dint of constant visitation, prayer for their pagan neighbors, and evangelistic meetings, a congregation was raised in the "Santo Antônio" neighborhood and a second later in the area called "Compensa," where a plywood factory employed the local population. Soon Pastor Hernán became well known in the local evangelical community. He even worked with the pastor of the Central Presbyterian Church, Rev, Caio Fabio d'Araujo, father of the famed preacher, Caio Fábio. Pastor Osorio led the Central Presbyterian's youth ministry for a time while in Manaus. Many years later, they moved south to the city of Curitiba where they pastored the Capão de Imbuia Alliance Church. Rev. Osorio was a gifted preacher and teacher, and he was president of ACEMBRAS in 1980 and 1981.

Rudge Ramos

In another part of the world, during the same year of 1964, God was calling another worker to Brazil. Some years after Miss Ninomiya was sent out, the president of the Japan

Alliance, Rev. Suteichi Oye met a leader of the U.S. Alliance at an Asian Alliance conference. There, Rev. Oye received a word of encouragement and a challenge: "The Alliance of Japan has shown to the Alliance churches of the Orient a fine example by sending out Miss Ninomiya. However, she is alone in that great country and there is much to do. Perhaps God has someone ready to send to Brazil from your church? "

Rev. Oye took these words seriously, and upon returning to Japan, he challenged his son. Pastor Hiroto Oye, a university graduate, as well as from the Hiroshima Bible Institute, and an official of the local Family Court in Hiroshima. He took the challenge to heart and rose to the occasion. Thus Rev. Suteichi Oye's son was sent out as the second missionary of the Japan Alliance to Brazil. In 1964, Japan was hosting the Olympics, and in the November 11 *Alliance Witness,* the article entitled, "The Sacred Flame" states: "[Rev. Suteichi Oye] likened missionary interest to the Olympic torch and speculated about what would happen to the flame if the rain of disinterest or prayerlessness should fall. Those who stay at home, like the men on the truck [who accompanied the Olympic torch bearer] have the less glamorous but important task of tending and feeding the flame. . . . Today a large group of Christians gathered on the Hiroshima train platform to wave farewell as Mr. [Hiroto] Oye left for the port of Kobe. We sang the traditional, 'God Be with You Till We Meet Again," followed by a prayer of blessing. Then, as the train pulled out, there was a completely Japanese touch – three rousing *'Banzai* cheers for the messenger of the cross."

Arriving at the port of Santos, he was met by future Rudge Ramos elder, Toshiaki Fukuura, a member of the Fukuyama Alliance Church who had gone to Brazil some years before. With his wife, Asae, he received the Japan Alliance's second missionary to work in the industrial city of São Bernardo do Campo in São Paulo. The Fukuuras were founding members of what came to be the Rudge Ramos Alliance Church.

1965 was an important year for Hiroto as he studied Portuguese at the School of Portuguese and Orientation in Campinas, São Paulo. That same year, Pastor Oye met Miss Kazue Nomura, daughter of a Holiness Church pastor and leader. Not long after, in 1965, they married and began to minister to the large Nikkei population located in Rudge Ramos, a "bairro" of São Bernardo.

First Service

As recorded in "*Memória em Movimento* (Memory in Movement)," a book commemorating the 50th anniversary of the Rudge Ramos Church (Konno, p. 23): "In 1965, the Christian and Missionary Alliance of Japan authorized the beginning of an evangelistic preaching point [in Rudge Ramos] and, on January 2, 1966, the first official church service of the Rudge Ramos Christian and Missionary Alliance Church was held in the living room of Pastor Oye and his wife, along with Toshiaki and Asae Fukuura, Nagayoshi and Masue Shimizu, Fukou and Misao Kajiwara, Seiji and Sakae Inoue, Kazuo and Toshiko Yamauchi and Hideo and Eiko Yamamoto."

First group of attendees at Rudge Ramos.

From that humble beginning, Rev. Oye led the little band of believers that same year to reach out to compatriots living in the nearby town of *Atibaia*, as well as another Japanese "colônia" in *Pilar do Sul*. From the beginning, Oye felt that the mission of the Rudge Ramos ministry was to reach both the Nikkei expat community as well as the Brazilian population that had received the immigrants from Japan. In another few years, 1969, a third preaching point was opened in downtown São Paulo in the neighborhood of *Liberdade*, where a large contingent of Chinese and Japanese immigrants lived and worked. From this group, which grew out of a band of sushi lovers, the future Rev. Hideo Tokuue and his wife, Hiroko, came to know Christ as Lord and Savior.

By 1976, the Liberdade group began to attend the services at the Rudge Ramos Alliance Church. One of the ways that this new band of believers from downtown São Paulo integrated into the Rudge Ramos congregation came about through the institution of a communal meal served after the Sunday morning service. This *Koinonia* meal prepared and served to one and all had the same kind of effect on the church as did the original common meals of the early church. God's hand of favor was on the growing body of Christ. Eventually, newcomers to the church included not only those of Japanese background but also Brazilians. Like the Antioch Church, Rudge was becoming a multi-ethnic, multi-cultural and multi-generational church.

Due to the gradual but continual growth of church members, a property was purchased in 1970 on Rua Dourados, 164, the present site of their temple. In April of 1971, Rev. Oye returned to Japan with his wife for a well-earned furlough. Shortly thereafter, he was asked by his father, Rev. Suteichi Oye, who was pastor of the Hiroshima Alliance Church, to become part of the pastoral staff. Subsequently, Rev. Hiroto Oye became the senior pastor following his father's retirement. In his absence, other missionary pastors from Japan came to the Rudge Ramos' aid by training and equipping the lay leadership so that the church continued its forward movement. In addition, Rev. Oye's absence meant that the church had to find another home. Not long after, in 1974, the church moved to a member's garage while they awaited the construction of a "first unit" on the newly purchased property. A small two-story house was built which enabled the church to have its own "home."

Rudge Ramos Independent

After waiting till the end of 1973 for the return of Rev. Oye or the sending of another pastor, it became apparent that the Rudge Ramos congregation was going to have to "go it alone." Providentially, there were several Nikkei pastors in the São Bernardo area who took turns ministering to the members. With no prospect of having their own Alliance pastor from Japan, the Rudge Ramos Church officially withdrew from the Japan Alliance and became an independent Nikkei evangelical church while maintaining good relations with the home church in Japan. They received visits of several Japan Alliance pastors over the next years, including a return visit by Rev. Oye in 1982 when the new temple was dedicated at Rudge Ramos. That year saw the beginning of the annual "Ashram," or spiritual retreat that the church holds each year at Carnaval weekend. The next year, 1983, Rev. Akinori Izumi was sent to Rudge Ramos by the Japan Alliance to pastor the church. For the next four years, he and his wife Yoshie, with their two small children, ministered to the growing congregation. Many of the leaders that later were to arise from the still-small congregation were nurtured and mentored by the gentle leadership of Rev. Izumi, who had visited Brazil in the 1960s while a seminary student in Japan.

It was also at this time that God called the first of Rudge

Ramos's youth to the ministry in the person of Eduardo Toshiaki "Toshi" Yassui. He had been invited to the church by school mate, Hélio Kimura, to attend a service at the church, which contrasted sharply from his nominal Buddhist upbringing. Yet the message of Christ and the warm reception by the members drew him closer till he received Christ as Lord and Savior in 1978 while helping to care for the kids at a church Couples Retreat. Soon after, while attending a youth camp at the Holiness Church campgrounds in Panorama, São Paulo, Toshi sensed God's call on his life to enter the pastoral ministry. Consequently, Toshi began an arduous five-year routine at the Baptist Seminary in the *Perdizes* "bairro" of São Paulo. Long days and short nights of sleep while studying under professors like Drs. Russell Shedd, Carl Lachler, Richard Sturz and others were rewarded when he received his diploma in 1985. The now "Pastor" Yassui assisted Pastor Izumi till his return to Japan in 1986 and the church's own "son," Toshi, became lead pastor till 1991.

Desiring to be ordained, Pastor Yassui eventually was mentored and coached by the US Alliance missionary, Pastor James Medin, who had just arrived in São Paulo in 1985 to lead the church-planting team that was being formed by the arrival of several new missionary couples over the next several years. Thus at the age of 27 years, Reverend Eduardo Toshiaki Yassui became the first ordained Brazilian pastor of the still-young *Aliança Cristã e Missionária Brasileira (ACEMBRAS)*. In 1991, he and his wife, Hiroko, returned to Japan due to Hiroko's visa problems and remained in Matsuyama, where they worked as pastor-interns with Rev. Eichi Fujika, pastor of the large Alliance Church. While in Japan, Pastor Yassui perfected his command of Japanese and gained valuable experience in ministry with the people of his land of origin. The Alliance

Church in Matsuyama was the home sending-church of Japan Alliance's first missionary, Mutsuko Ninomiya. Upon their return to Brazil in 1993, after two years of ministry experience in Matsuyama, Toshi and Hiroko were invited to work with Miss Ninomiya at the Alliance Church in Núcleo Bandeirante in the Federal District of Brasília.

In 1991, the same year that the Yassuis went to Japan, Pastor Jurandir Yanagihara and his wife, Masumi, returned to Brazil after completing his studies at the Yokohama National University and Covenant Seminary. While in Japan, this Rudge couple found time to begin the *Salt and Light Community*, which ministered to the descendants of Japanese immigrants, the *dekasseguis,* who returned to Japan for work during the devastating economic crisis in Brazil. Thus upon their arrival, they pastored the Rudge Ramos Church. During their next ten years of ministry at the "mother church, a large number of called-ones obeyed God, entered seminary, graduated and today are missionaries, pastors and involved workers in Rudge Ramos, São Paulo and other Brazil Alliance Churches.

Curitiba

Following the early return to the United States by Sam and Vera Barnes in 1964, it seemed that the vision for the "southern strategy," using Curitiba, capital of Paraná as the base, had died an untimely death. However, God has a way of resurrecting the dreams of the old through the vision He passes on to the young. Such was the case with the Alliance entry into Curitiba, as a new "branch" rooted in Southern Brazil.

Tom and Mary Kyle were part of the "first wave" of missionaries that came to Brazil after the U.S. Alliance entered in 1962. The Kyles studied at St. Paul Bible College, now Crown College. Following graduation in 1960, they pastored the

Alliance Church in the town of Milaca, Minnesota. After four years of ministry, the church had grown, a new building erected, and Tom had become a dynamic, "stand-up" preacher. The Kyles, C&MA missionary candidates, sold their "stuff" and followed God's leading for their lives. When asked if they felt a special call to any specific country, Tom said, "Anywhere it's NOT hot!" God showed His sense of humor by guiding the Kyles, with their two young daughters, Lynette and Laurie, to Brazil on August 27, 1965. Their year in language school in Campinas turned out to be Tom's trial by fire since he despaired of ever learning the tricky conjugations of Portuguese. Though he shed no blood, he certainly poured out much sweat and tears seeking to master the beautiful language of Camões.

God Writes Straight with Crooked Lines

While studying in Campinas, the question of where they would work was heavy on their hearts, as well as those of the field leadership. Some months before their language school graduation in August 1966, the field leader, John Nicholson, asked Tom to go with him to visit three different cities, one of which was *Uberaba*, one of the large cities in state of Minas Gerais. While not in the Federal District of Brasília, it was part of the Central Brazilian highlands. Uberaba numbered more than 200,000 and was surrounded by cattle ranches and meat processing plants. Dutifully, Tom met John and traveled to Uberaba to spy out the land, only to discover that it was one of the hottest cities in central Brazil. In the summer, the thermometer stayed in the high 80s and 90s for months, and the "winter months" saw the mercury "drop" to the 70's. For Tom, this was a major problem since he was a big man, tall and broad, not built for hot climes since his internal cooling system

The Kyle Family

was designed for cooler weather. His fame as a "perspiring preacher" eventually became known far and wide. The weekend spent in Uberaba was typically hot, and Tom's "radiator" overheated constantly with torrents of sweat pouring off his brow. "There's no way I can survive here," Tom thought. "There has to be a cooler place in Brazil." That was his thought upon returning to language school.

Mary Kyle wrote up the Kyle story for a retired pastor's publication, and she tells about the critical decision that was to be made regarding their placement. "After a year of language study, Dr. L. L. King wrote George Constance, the South American director, that we should go to a city (Uberaba) in central Brazil and look at the possibility of living there and doing evangelism. George never received the letter and wrote us on a post card saying that we should go to Curitiba and look for a house to rent. God works in mysterious ways for His will to be accomplished, and for our good!"

Apparently before receiving the post card, Tom had already decided to act. In answer to his question as to where the coolest city in Brazil was located, the director of the language school said, "Oh that's easy, Curitiba, south of here." So Tom and Mary traveled down to Curitiba during the next school break to visit the beautiful city with its European architecture and large Northern European population. At that time, it was undergoing a huge growth spurt of migrant workers from Parana's interior. Since the Kyles visited Curitiba in the "winter," June or July of 1966, it was cool, even downright cold in the evenings. As they prayed, they felt, "This is the place where God wants us to work; we won't die of heat prostration here!" So Tom began to lobby the mission and field leadership, writing about the city, its growth to more than 500,000, the dearth of evangelical churches and missions, and the spiritual needs of the migrant population that was moving into the growing neighborhoods on the city's edge. Here was a place with serious need and relatively meager evangelistic resources. Little did Tom know that this very city was the same one that Sam and Vera Barnes had visited years before and had chosen as the ideal location for the start of the Brazil Mission of the C&MA. Truly, God's mysterious ways and will were working out with this Midwest couple who were to make a lasting mark on Brazil.

Soon after their year's study at the Campinas language school in August 1966, George Constance's postcard arrived and the decision was made: The Kyles were assigned to church planting in Curitiba, as envisioned by Sam Barnes back in the early 1960s. After moving there, Tom began to pray and dream. He met an independent Pentecostal missionary, Rev. Lesley Dickerson, who worked in tent campaign evangelism. He discovered that Tom was a gifted evangelist who preached for decisions, and he invited Tom to speak at a tent campaign in one of the outlying "bairros" of Curitiba. Tom later said, "I only had a few sermons that I had worked on while in language school, so I couldn't preach for more than five nights." But preach he did, simple, straightforward and easy to understand. God's Spirit rested on him and souls were saved nightly. An added attraction was the fact that Tom and Mary were excellent trumpet players, and nightly they played their horns to call the folks to the service. In a guitar-loving country like Brazil, trumpets were a fascinating novelty. Due to his energy and enthusiasm as he preached, beads of perspiration poured off Tom's brow as he spoke, and he carried a stack of white hankies to wipe away the sweat. Eventually his preaching performance was gauged by the number of sodden hankies thrown down on the pulpit.

Holy Oil

One night, Pastor Les told the crowd, "Tonight, Pastor Tomás will be praying for the sick at the end of the service and will anoint with holy oil." The only problem was that Tom had no "holy oil." As the service ended and folks came streaming forward, Tom's prayed: "Lord, help; what can I do? I have no oil." Suddenly he had a moment of inspiration: "In the trumpet case, there's valve oil. That will work." So Tom Kyle prayed for the crowd using his "holy" Holton Valve Oil, anointing the brow of all who came in obedience to James 5. God's Spirit heals, not man's prayer, or any special blend of oil, and many were healed through the simple faith of those who sought prayer. Prayer for the sick and miraculous healings became part of the early days in Curitiba as God confirmed the gospel message.

After working with his missionary friend, Tom began to dream a big dream, of a one-hundred day evangelistic campaign in a "big top" circus tent. Pastor Les worked with a former circus roustabout who made tents in Campo Mourão in Northern Paraná. With the approval of Alliance "headquarters," Tom drove to the interior town and purchased the heavy canvas tent. Then he and his helper hoisted the bulky bundle onto the top of his DKV station wagon. Driving back the several hundred kilometers on Parana's rough roads left permanent "stress marks" on the roof of Tom's long-suffering vehicle.

In the meantime, Paul and Claudia Bryers had returned to Brazil following their furlough; they were assigned to Curitiba and joined Tom and Mary to form the first U.S. led church-planting

Gospel "Big Top"
on Avenida Paraná in Curritiba

missionary team in Brazil. It was decided that the inaugural evangelistic campaign would be held on *Avenida Paraná*, a major thoroughfare on the northern side of the city. As reported in the April 10, 1968 issue of the *Alliance Witness*, "Faith and Work Rewarded," the plan for the campaign was explained: "Carry on a 100-day tent campaign (beginning November [1967]) in an unchurched area – preach the gospel nightly, distribute literature as widely as possible, start Sunday school, hold a vacation Bible school, utilize radio. In short, [use] every means possible to make Christ known and persuade men to receive Him as Saviour and Lord." Thus the Kyles and Bryers began the extended evangelistic campaign with no contacts or converts. One Brazilian worker, João França, an excellent singer and preacher "lent" to Tom by Pastor Les was their only outside help. He worked with Tom on a daily radio program on *Rádio Colombo* that aired just before the 6 p.m. Catholic mass, which proved to be a great timeslot.

The *Alliance Witness* article asked the question: "*What was the result?* Services were well attended and there was almost immediate response. In all, about 100 persons professed faith in Christ. Some were radically transformed, including one whole family, and a number were healed. One young man is now seeking God to determine if he should become a pastor himself." Nine converts were baptized in February, 1968, regular services were being held in the Big Top and a fund-raising campaign was begun to purchase property in order to build a permanent church home. This first campaign was the seed plant of the Boa Vista Alliance Church located a few blocks away from the original Avenida Paraná site.

Mary Kyle's account describes the results of the first few nights: "The 100-day campaign in Curitiba . . . opened with about 150 in attendance. Most were unchurched and came of curiosity to see what these Americans were doing. Two adults, five teenagers and several children went forward to make decisions for Christ the first evening. The following night over 200 filled every seat in the tent. It was an exciting time!"

Paul Bryers leading a Bible class.

Paul and Claudia's Christmas prayer letter of 1966 gives the words of *Maria Edite*, a lady who attended the tent meetings and met God: "Just to think that I had to come to this humble place to find peace! And how humble it is! Simple hard, unpainted benches, sawdust floor and crude poles that support some streaky looking canvas over our heads. To me it looks like a circus tent, but they call it a 'House of God.'" This lady, who had been a practicing, lifelong Roman Catholic, found Christ and peace of heart, as well as her sister and son who followed her to the front of the tent to receive salvation and forgiveness and new life in Christ.

A Christian builder began attending the meetings and

became a faithful follower. After almost two years under the canvas, it became obvious that the big top had so many holes that it forced the congregation to dodge the raindrops during heavy rains. Nearby property was

Boa Vista—First church building.

sought and found a few blocks off of *Avenida Paraná*, and construction began on what became the first Alliance Church in Curitiba, in the *Boa Vista* (Good Vista) neighborhood. As a result, the simple wooden building with brick façade and big concrete cross in the front yard was soon completed and occupied. Missionary Paul Bryers with his wife, Claudia, pastored the growing congregation. Soon Tom was thinking about the second church-planting campaign to be held in another part of town. In 1968, because of the obvious gift for evangelistic preaching that Tom displayed, he was invited with wife Mary and the girls to hold evangelistic meetings in the Alliance works in Gama and Taguatinga in the Federal District of Brasília, as well as in Goiânia, capital of Goiás. The Kyles returned to Curitiba where first Tom, and then Mary, ended up in the hospital suffering from hepatitis. This forced rest gave them time to think and plan for the second evangelistic campaign in Curitiba. Yet, before this could happen, a major change of mission focus and strategy had to happen.

CHAPTER FIVE
BACK TO THE FUTURE

The still young Brazil field was only five years old and was found to be seriously understaffed. The C&MA Foreign Department set out to build up the mission team and expand the work. As a result, a new couple was sent in Brazil in 1967. David and Judy Jones, with one-year old son, Tommy, both graduated from Nyack Missionary College (now Nyack College) in 1964. They met while studying together in the missions' course. Married one week following graduation, they finished up their graduate studies and home service and flew to Brazil on August 12, 1967. Their Varig flight aboard a Boeing 707 jet was their first international flight, and they were thrilled to be arriving in the country that they had studied and dreamed about for the past few years. Just a week before they arrived on the field, Dave and Marilyn Sundeen, who had worked in Goiânia and Gama, returned to the United States on an early furlough due to ongoing health problems with their son, Leslie. The Joneses inherited some of their furniture and household items.

Like their colleagues, they studied Portuguese in Campinas, SP and had a thoroughly enjoyable year. Riding the open-sided "*bondes*," the ancient trolleys made by Baldwin Locomotive works years before, was all part of their learning experience. Like the other missionaries while in language

David and Judy Jones
With their son Tommy

school, they were anxious to learn where they would be assigned. Eventually they received word of their deployment to the Federal District of Brasília to take over the work begun by Emmit and Sandra Young in the satellite city of *Taguatinga.* Following their graduation from language school in August 1968, they left the next day for the long drive north to the Central Highlands.

Proud possessors of a used, but useful 1963 blue VW Beetle, they drove up the busy, pot-holed major north-south highway, the *Via Anhanguera.* They followed in the footsteps of Brazil's *"Bandeirantes,"* the intrepid explorers who entered the wild interior of Brazil hundreds of years before. Leaving the lush red-soil cane fields of São Paulo behind, they drove through long miles of scrub-trees in Minas Gerais, with its vast fields of cattle, hundreds more miles in barren Goiás, and finally arriving in the Federal District. Son Tommy enjoyed seeing all of the cattle trucks and brush fires set by the farmers. At last they arrived in the Federal District and took up residence in Taguatinga. One week after graduation from language school, Dave was installed as the pastor of the Taguatinga church plant.

What Dave and Judy found was a ground-floor hall made from two-store fronts, with a second floor. Metal roll-down doors opened on the "sanctuary," and upstairs was a small office, a Sunday school room and an open area with a ping pong table. This ministry had opened more than a year before and had a promising beginning with evangelistic meetings held by Tom and Mary Kyle, but by the time the "new kids on the block" arrived, few were attending. One of the big problems was the location, in the heart of the town's business district, several blocks away from the residential neighborhoods. The most faithful attendees were the shoe-shine boys

Tom Kyle & Emmit Young, Taguatinga

who worked in the "praça" right in front of the chapel and the occasional drunk who would stumble in the door. They held Sunday school and evening evangelistic services, Vacation Bible Schools, did home visitation jumping across trash-filled open ditches, wept and prayed. Despite their best efforts, the little church plant seemed to be going nowhere. In fact, there was a general sense of discouragement among the missionaries working in Brasília and Goiânia. After seven years of effort, the Mission decided to close the work in Goiânia, and Al and Edythe Rees were reassigned to work in the Federal District with Japan Alliance missionary, Mutsuko Ninomiya.

In 1968, Paul and Claudia Bryers returned to North America for their first furlough, and John and Beverly Nicholson, with their children, did the same. Due to continued health issues, the Nicholsons did not return to Brazil and soon resigned from the Alliance Mission. About that same time after years of bureaucratic red tape, the Brazil Alliance Mission received property from the government in a "residential super-block" for the construction of a church in the still-new capital city of Brasília. An architect was commissioned to draw up plans which were finally approved by the Federal District government. A mockup of the futuristic design was prepared and plans were made to begin construction in 1969. At an earlier Alliance General Council in the U.S., an amazing special missionary offering totaling $50,000 had been raised for the construction in Brasília and was finally about to be invested. And it was just this development that caused a serious disagreement between the missionaries.

The issue which had divided opinions had to do with "building or body." The matter in question dealt with the fact that despite the missionaries' best efforts, there was no body of believers in the capital city. Notwithstanding Bible studies, English classes, doing door-to-door visitation in the super-blocks, and pursuing friendship evangelism, there was no viable "body-of-Christ" group of believers that considered themselves as being "Alliance." When the new capital was inaugurated in 1961, all of the major evangelical churches and missions working in Brazil obtained property and began to build. As soon as they had a building up, they had ready-made congregations that had moved to the capital from Rio, the former capital, São Paulo and other major cities. When the Alliance Mission arrived in 1962, they had no ready-made body of believers, no church identity, no proven church-planting strategy and no experienced missionaries. There was only one lady, Dona Cely Krahenbühl, who lived in the capital and welcomed the new Alliance missionaries. She, who had become a believer while in Detroit, Michigan in the 1950s, returned to Brazil hoping that one day "her church" would come to Brazil. Her husband was now head administrator at a local brewery.

Sensing the disagreement between the missionaries and their growing discouragement after seven years in Brasília, the

Foreign Department made the decision to close the work in the Federal District and move the staff south. As reported in the *Brazil Bulletin*, Vol. IV, 1969, No. 1:

> In light of the high cost of building, lack of response to missionary efforts and the great number of other evangelical works already established there, it was decided by the Foreign Department that the Alliance's efforts should be exerted in an area which is not so heavily worked and has a more realistic promise of God's blessing.

Southward Bound

Thus, the mission headquarters was moved south to Curitiba. The Youngs and Rees family were soon to furlough, and Dave and Judy Jones packed their furniture and boxes on a moving van and made the long, two-day drive south to Curitiba. Young Tommy got to see many more cows, cane fields, brush fires and much more in their jam-packed VW bug.

Suddenly, the Joneses were thrust into the exciting ministry in Curitiba and assigned to work with Tom and Mary Kyle, who were then preparing for a second 100-day evangelistic campaign. It soon became apparent that the enemy was not happy with what was happening in Curitiba following the successful tent campaign and the first church planted in Boa Vista. Mary Kyle writes:

> During one of Tom's trips to Brasília . . , he ate at a Brazilian home and contracted hepatitis B. Can you imagine . . . they put him in the maternity section of the hospital?! A few weeks

later, we both were trying to recover [from hepatitis]. I was seven months pregnant.

Fortunately, they both recovered and baby daughter, Tami, was born healthy with no ill effects. About that same time, Tom Kyle faced another serious health issue: his voice. Due to fatigued vocal chords from constant preaching, Tom was ordered by a specialist to not speak for at least three months. As a result, prayer was raised and Tom rested his throat while getting ready for the next campaign.

One important decision was made following the first campaign on Avenida Paraná. Due to the poor quality canvas used, and the less-than waterproof treatment, the "big top" after a year or so became porous as cheese cloth and useless in a rain storm. Consequently, Tom envisioned a portable structure, simple and economical, that could be put up, used, taken down and then moved to new location for another campaign. Having seen A-frames used for vacation homes in America, Tom believed that a big A-frame would be the answer in Brazil. So construction was begun on a 21-foot tall frame building, clad in galvanized metal sheets, with the floor covered in crushed rock. It was designed to hold about 250 people seated on hard wooden benches. However, it was discovered that with the double doors and windows opened, and people sitting in the aisles, another hundred or so could be shoe-horned in.

Capão da Imbuia

Having no power tools, the missionaries worked with a local builder, sawing by hand and drilling with brace and bit the heavy beams used in the frame. The benches and platform were all done by the same method. After about two months of work, the double-corner lot, originally intended for a gas station, was ready for the kickoff campaign, and the neighborhood was buzzing with curiosity. Local kids asked those working, "What is this building going to be?" Since it was a long and tall hall, a rumor began that it was to be a

If you build it, they will come!

"cinema." The missionaries did nothing to combat it. They felt a little mystery would build up anticipation for the strange building.

The campaign kickoff weekend saw the tabernacle filled to overflowing, with at least an extra hundred people jamming any spare space. Lending credence to the "cinema" tale, the first film shown was *Apollo 11*, a film produced by NASA highlighting the first moonwalk by Neil Armstrong and Buzz Aldrin. When questioned about using a U.S. propaganda film, Tom said, "For sure, it will draw a crowd and I'll use it as a lead -in for the message." The packed hall made his prophecy came true. Following a rousing, rowdy song-service, the crowd watched entranced as the space saga unfolded, featuring Armstrong's famous quote. "That's one small step for man, one giant leap for mankind." As the projector dimmed, Tom sprang into action and began to talk about the feats of modern science. "Man has gone to the moon

Opening night with Apollo 11 and the Gospel

and back. Medicine has eliminated many diseases. Surgeons have even performed a heart transplant." Then after a dramatic pause, he said, "But only God can change the heart of man!" With that, he preached a strong evangelistic message on God's power to save and transform the sinner.

At the close, he invited all who wanted to receive Jesus as Savior to come to the front of the hall, and a few started forward. When he said: "And Pastor David will help you pray and he will give you something," meaning a gospel portion and decision card. But the offer to "get something' caused a mass move to the front, and chaos broke out. The rookie missionary hardly knew what to do as he gave out the literature, the decision cards and pencils. It was mass confusion as he tried to instruct them to write their names and follow-up information. In the midst of the mess, he cried out in his heart: "Oh God, please save someone despite all of this craziness!" When the crowd filed out, Dave wondered if anyone had really met God. The next night, evangelist Kyle asked if anyone wanted to tell what God had done in their lives. Without hesitation, a tall, thin middle-aged man stood and said,

> All my life, I have gone to church weekly, done confession, taken mass and tried to be a good Catholic. And I have never felt forgiven or close to God. I knew I was a sinner and didn't know what to do. Last night, I heard Pastor Tomás say that God can change a man's heart. When he said we could come forward for prayer to receive forgiveness for our sins and to receive a new heart, I came and prayed with Pastor David. For the first time in my life, I felt that God heard me and forgave me and saved me. I feel like a new

man."

As he sat there in the crowded tabernacle, the young missionary whispered a prayer of thanks to a Savior who can bring the lost one home even in the midst of a mob scene. That tall, middle-aged man, *André Poloi*, proved to be a column in the church being planted in this growing lower-class neighborhood. He devoured the Word of God, became a man of prayer and was often called upon at night to pray for the sick in the "bairro." During the almost four months of six nights-a-week that the campaign went on, hundreds of decisions for Christ were made.

Those early days of this second church plant were educational for the new missionaries as they dealt with demonized individuals, prayed for the sick, counseled the broken hearted, discipled and baptized the new believers. God's power was demonstrated with some dramatic healings as well as deliverance of those held captive by demonic forces. Within a year, construction began on the permanent building for the Capão church. The church was formally organized on July 7, 1970 with eighteen charter members. Average attendance was 70 and 264 decisions had been recorded since the campaign had begun the previous October. At the corner-stone laying service a few months later on October 18, 1970, two hundred people attended.

Mission staff was increased with the arrival of James and Ann Hemminger, with their daughter Lori, in 1969. Due to a communications breakdown between the field staff and Alliance field headquarters, the Hemmingers arrived at Viracopos Airport in Campinas, São Paulo with $25.00 in their pocket, and no one from the Brazil Mission to meet them! Pastor "Jaime," as Jim was called, said, "If I had had a ticket, I

**Rev. and Mrs. J.W. Hemminger
With their daughter, Lori**

would have flown right back to the States!" However, they didn't have a return ticket, and Ann was a veteran MK, having been raised in Argentina as daughter of Sam and Vera Barnes, the same missionary couple that had been sent out in 1962 to open the Brazil Field. Fluent in Spanish, Ann was able to get them to the language school with the help of another American missionary. From there, they were taken to the house that the mission had rented and Tom Kyle received a phone call that "your missionaries are here in Campinas." That news required a trip up from Curitiba to Campinas, traveling more than eight hours on the "road of death," as the infamous BR 116 was called. Eventually reaching Campinas, they belatedly greeted their new colleagues.

Their year in language school was difficult as Ann was expecting their second child, Debbie, who was born while they were still in language school. Due to Jim's being very sick with fluid on his lungs and in a great deal of pain, they were not able to buy presents for their first Christmas in Brazil. Ann determined that they were going to "have Christmas" and she set out with two-year old Lori and Debbie, only nine days old to buy a dog. And after a long taxi ride, "Fluffy" came home for Christmas "and Jim even perked up some when he saw the puppy." Emmit and Sandra Young returned to the field for their second term and he took over as the field leader, "Board Representative," and the Kyles left for the States. After a month's delay due to visa problems, another new couple, Darrel and Jan Smith arrived in Campinas with their two and a half year old daughter, Lisa, and began language school.

These were exciting and encouraging days in Curitiba after so many years of struggle and frustration in Brasília and Goiânia. Sam and Vera Barnes' vision to begin the new Alliance field in the thriving city of Curitiba was unfolding and their own son-in-law and daughter were part of this move. The construction of the Capão da Imbuia Alliance was finished and the building dedicated in 1971. Built for a little more than $5,000, the brick building seated 250 "in a pinch," with two rooms for Sunday school and a baptistery. The portable "tin tabernacle" was then taken down and moved to another site to begin another church-planting campaign.

Following their language study, the Hemmingers moved to Curitiba and soon began pastoring the Boa Vista Alliance Church. Sometime after beginning there, the *Custódio Reis* family, members of the Boa Vista church, moved out to a neighborhood six miles north of town in *Colombo*, where home meetings were held for several months in the Reis home, little more than a temporary shack. When it rained, it poured inside and out, requiring Jim to use an umbrella at times when Ann was telling Bible stories. With the completion of the Capão construction, the tabernacle was moved to a lot in Colombo purchased near the Reis home and the "Chapel at the Foot of the Cross" was officially begun. The land was purchased by the Boa Vista "mother church." Following the kickoff campaign with Tom Kyle, the Hemmingers led both the mother and daughter churches.

Hallelujah Valley

With three Alliance churches in operation, it became apparent that national help was needed in order to grow the ministry. Thus the missionaries began to train teenagers and adults to lead Vacation Bible Schools, to teach in the church Sunday schools and do personal evangelism. Extension courses offered by the Maringa Bible Institute of the Missionary Church Mission were held in Boa Vista and the Capão. Youth retreats were held over the long *Carnaval* weekends, and it soon became apparent that the youth camps and retreats were fertile ground for seeing God call young men and women into ministry. Following a time of prayer, God provided a gift from a medical doctor in the United States that made possible the purchase of a 120-acre woodland site. "Situated just 18 miles north of Curitiba, less than two miles off the busy BR 116 highway that runs to São Paulo and Rio, are over 120 acres of land covered by a variety of native and imported species of trees and plants dozens of different kinds of wild flowers and ferns as well as hardy orchids." (*Brazil Bulletin*, Vol. IV, 1973, No.7).

Thus, the Hallelujah Valley Camp, so named for the beautiful, purple and white flowery "Aleluia" trees, was purchased in October 1973 and became the camp and conference center for the C&MA churches of Brazil. Eventually, busloads of youth would come from Brasília, São José dos Campos and Porto Alegre to take part in the Carnaval Camps held forty days before Easter. For many years, the majority of the youth who entered the Alliance Bible Institute received their first call to ministry while at Hallelujah Valley, paralleling the experience of 90% of the Brazil field missionary staff. In just a few years, the transplanted missionary staff saw God's blessing on their ministry as people were being brought into the Kingdom, lives transformed, churches planted, and converts discipled, baptized and trained for ministry. A beautiful campsite was made operational through the hard work of missionaries and nationals, as well as work teams from Alliance Churches in the

Eastern PA District.

The Alliance Training Center

The next big step forward was the opening of "The *Alliance Training Center*. With ten students registered, [it] opened as of the second week in March [1974]. Offering a Mini-Bible Institute Course to be concluded in two years, the Training Center will provide practical training and classroom theory for Alliance Youth and adults that wish to serve the Lord more adequately. Operating in the recently opened Central Church of the C&MA on one of the busiest downtown street in Curitiba, the Center offers programmed -learning courses, plus classroom lectures in Introduction to the Bible, Homiletics I and Theology I. Operating three evenings a week so that the students can continue at their normal day-time employment, those that study at the Center are being used in the local Alliance churches where they apply practically what they are learning in the classroom." (*Brazil Bulletin*, Vol. XI, 1974, No. 8)

Through contacts made with a missionary couple sent out by the Argentine C&MA, Adolfo and Anna Barria, another facet of the Barnes southern strategy began to be set in motion. In 1973, a young Uruguayan, Nelber Nuñez, who had studied for a few years at the Buenos Aires Bible Institute, was sent to Curitiba by Pastor Barria to work with the US missionaries. Since he was fluent in Portuguese and Spanish, an accomplished guitar player and experienced in working with youth, he began to work with Jim and Ann Hemminger. In another year, several members of the Rivera Church's "Shalom" musical group came to Curitiba and ministered in various churches. Their ministry included leading a VBS with more than 250 children attending—and many found Christ as Savior as a result of their labor.

CHAPTER SIX
MORE ROOTS
AND BRANCHES

As the original Barnes vision for Curitiba became a reality, another piece began to fall into place. In 1971, an Alliance pastor working in Rivera, Uruguay on the border of Rio Grande do Sul, attended a *World Vision Pastors Conference* held in Gramado, RS. Chilean-born Pastor Adolfo Barria had married an Argentine C&MA young lady that he met at the Alliance's *Bible Institute of Buenos Aires*. Part of Barnes' dream saw the C&MA of Argentina becoming a missionary church. Part of that strategy included planting churches on the border with Brazil and to reach across to plant churches. So one of the first missionary initiatives of the Argentine Alliance was to plant what became a thriving church in Rivera, literally across the border from the town of Santana do Livramento, RS.

Another attendee of the World Vision Conference was first-term worker David Jones. Immediately the two Alliance missionaries became fast friends. Soon a mutually beneficial exchange between the churches in Curitiba and Rivera developed. Tom and Mary Kyle held evangelistic meetings in Rivera since the border town populous were bi-lingual.

Sam and Vera Barnes had visited their daughter, Ann,

and son-in-law, Jim, in January 1972 and shared their vision with the mission team at their first field retreat. He laid out his early strategy of moving south down the BR 116 highway all the way to Porto Alegre, capital of Rio Grande do Sul. To the missionaries, it seemed the logical goal. Several believers from the Rivera Alliance Church had moved to Porto Alegre, and Pastor Barria requested that the U.S. mission send missionaries to pastor the little group and lay a foundation for a church planting campaign. Thus this request determined the next outreach venture of the Brazil Mission, with an assist from the Argentine-planted Alliance Church in Rivera.

Emmit and Sandra Young returned to Brazil after furlough in July of 1970. They moved south from Brasília to Curitiba and began to work at the Boa Vista and the Capão churches. Emmit also became board representative when the Kyles returned to the U. S. In 1972, Emmit was hit head on in a near-fatal accident with a "playboy" driving on the wrong side of the street. Following a long hospital stay, he went home to convalesce, but had to return to the hospital a short time later due to hepatitis contracted from a transfusion of infected blood. More long weeks of hospitalization were required before returning home. He had further corrective surgery in late 1972 before finally achieving full recovery. It was decided that Emmit and Sandra and sons, would move to Porto Alegre and begin a new work with the goal of planting an Alliance church in the city, Brazil's largest city south of São Paulo.

B
R
A
Z
I
L

EMMIT, SANDRA, TIM
MIKE and STEVE YOUNG

Moving South

In early 1973, Tom Kyle and Dave Jones drove

down to Porto Alegre and met Pastor Adolfo Barria of Rivera, who invited the Rivera group for a meeting. Eleven adults attended the first meeting, made up of professionals with backgrounds in banking, the military, railroad, education, a medical student and others. As a result of this survey visit and good response, the American C&MA mission decided to open the first initiative targeting middle-upper class Brazilians. Once Emmit and Sandy arrived in this city of one million a few months later, they began to gather with the little band of believers from the Rivera Alliance Church. The work progressed slowly as they held Sunday services and led Bible studies in apartments. By late 1973, they needed more room and began looking for a suitable downtown location to begin a more aggressive church-planting venture. Eventually they rented a small ground-floor meeting hall seating up to 70 and a room for Sunday school and bathroom facilities. *The Alliance Bible Center*, as it was called, was in the heart of town on *Avenida Borges de Medeiros*, and was located in a tall apartment block surrounded by other apartment buildings. It was there that the small band of believers moved just before the Youngs furloughed in 1974. David and Judy Jones were reassigned to take over the work and begin a new phase of evangelistic initiatives.

Downtown Porto Alegre

Evangelistic meetings were held as soon as possible after their move in June 1974. The meetings held in late August saw fourteen decisions for Christ recorded in the kickoff campaign held with Tom and Mary Kyle. One of those decisions was made by a sixty-five year old Italian-Brazilian lady, Dona Albina, who said: "Tonight I felt a great weight lift from my heart. For so long I have been a stray sheep, yet even though I am old, it is not too late to find the Lord." A musical group came from Rivera for the opening with Pastor Barria. Sunday school began with 22 adults and children, an encouraging sign. A young Alliance couple from Rivera with musical talent became part of the congregation. Veteran Alliance pastor and evangelist, Dr. Richard Harvey, spent a week in November, nightly preaching memorable illustrated sermons that captivated the audiences and saw many saved. All told, every month through the end of 1974, evangelistic meetings were held and many decisions were made. Much plowing and planting occupied those first months.

For the next year, the Joneses worked to build the little congregation, disciple the new believers and reach the surrounding neighborhood through literature and visitation. Sunday school, Vacation Bible schools and evangelistic meetings continued but results were sparse. Some who were from the Rivera/Livramento area moved back home while others stopped attending when the Bible-study group transitioned to church-

**Alliance Bible Center
Porto Alegre**

planting in the center. Some of the original group had Spiritist beliefs that they refused to abandon and they stopped attending. Eventually the Alliance Bible Center, which had been so promising, dwindled down to the Jones family and three elderly ladies, who had been genuinely saved, baptized and faithfully attended. The hall's rent went up by 25%; the two-year mission rental subsidy had come to an end and offerings fell far short of the monthly payment. Eventually in February

1976, it was decided to close the downtown work on Borges de Medeiros and concentrate church-planting efforts in a "bairro" in the "South Zone" of Porto Alegre, not far from the Jones' home. As a result, the downtown center was closed.

During the difficult, "desert" months of 1975, God began to open another door. Dave met a young man of Baptist background at a weekly prayer meeting at the CLC book store in downtown Porto Alegre. This young man, Sergio Moraes Pinto, had been touched by the growing charismatic movement in Porto Alegre. It was called the *"Seara Latina,"* or "Latin Harvest." This move of the Spirit deeply impacted almost all of the major denominations in Porto Alegre. A strong Christian who had sensed a call to ministry at age 18, Sergio worked for the state highway administration. Yet he hungered for the deeper things of God and sensed that He had plans for his life. With his wife, Regina, they had begun a Sunday school some time before in the neighborhood where they lived. Eventually the Joneses began to work with them in the *Jardim das Palmeiras*, helping with the teaching. Dave played his trumpet to draw a crowd, and they shared the gospel with a lot of wild kids and their unchurched families. In due course, the Pintos moved to another bairro, but the Sunday school continued, led by Dave and Judy.

Jardim das Palmeiras

With the closing of the downtown Alliance Center in early 1976, it was decided to transition from a Sunday school to a church-planting effort in the Jardim das Palmeiras. Thus permission was given to build in the backyard of the home where Sergio and Regina had lived. The owner, Grandma Alfrida, led to the Lord by the Pintos, permitted the Mission to build a portable frame chapel. The "plywood cathedral," 25 by

40 feet and seating up to 150, was erected by Dave Jones and Jim Hemminger and became the site of spiritual warfare. As soon as the building was up, evangelistic meetings were held with Tom Kyle and other of the mission staff. People were saved and healed. Spiritist neighbors complained because their "spirit guides" would no longer appear at their Spiritist sessions in their homes. On occasions, the simple chapel was "rocked" by neighborhood boys, but the work moved forward. Despite their moving to another neighborhood, the Pintos worked with the Joneses each weekend. Sergio's gifts in singing, leading services and preaching were evident. Since the Joneses were looking at furlough in mid-1977, they began to pray that God would provide leadership to continue the work. While they were praying, God was speaking to Sergio and Regina. Thus when Dave approached Sergio about leading the Jardim das Palmeiras work when furlough arrived, the Pintos sensed this as the confirmation of God's call on their lives. Thus began the ministry of one of the pioneer leaders of the Brazilian Alliance.

Meanwhile, in February 1976, Dr. L. L. King and Rev. David Volstad, Vice President and South America Regional Director of the Alliance Mission, visited the field and spent time surveying the work in Brazil. Dave wrote in another letter home: "We had mission meetings [with Dr. King], planning sessions, reading of the Field Report, etc. I think it was good for the new missionaries to see what had been accomplished over the past several years, and see what is projected for the future." And one of the major

Pinto Family: Sérgio, Regina, Rangel, a neighbor and Marta.

future projects was the organization of the national church in Brazil. Dave was put in charge of the five-person "Pro-Tem Committee" with the responsibility of formally and officially launching the Brazilian C&MA. Thus for the next year and a half, he met regularly with Rev. João Costa and other Brazilian committee members to draw up a constitution and by-laws. This was done by obtaining copies of the organizational documents of Alliance churches in South America, and a few other countries. Starting with the principle that the best founding document is the simplest and most straightforward, the committee was able to prepare for consideration the necessary founding documents before the Joneses returned to the United States in mid-1977 for furlough.

For the next year, while the Joneses furloughed, the Pintos carried on the work in Porto Alegre with occasional visits from missionaries who came down from Curitiba to encourage and assist. At the same time, another new missionary couple had arrived on the field in early 1977, Dick and Marilyn LaFountain, with their daughter, Aimée and son, Andrew. Like their other colleagues, they studied Portuguese in Campinas. At the end of their year's study, they were assigned to Porto Alegre since the Joneses returned in mid 1978 and were assigned once again to work in Curitiba at the Alliance Bible Institute and a new church plant in *Vila Camargo*. Dick and Marilyn LaFountain's ministry would have a profound effect on the progress of the work in Porto Alegre. The following is an account of the work in Porto Alegre by Richard LaFountain and Steve Renicks.

<u>Richard and Marilyn LaFountain</u>

In the spring 1976 I finished my studies at Alliance Theological Seminary, and we were appointed as missionaries to Brazil. We waited for our visas to arrive for almost 8 months. While we waited, we communicated with the Brazil mission staff asking a myriad of questions about what to expect, what to bring, what not to bring, what could be purchased there, what kind of clothing we would need to bring. In January 1977 we were granted our visas to enter the country and traveled to Brazil on the eleventh of the month, arriving in Curitiba where the Alliance headquarters was located.

We arrived in the middle of summer and it was very hot; we perspired a lot. I'll never forget the first encounter with Dave Jones; he greeted us heartily and asked me, "Well, what can you do?" I replied: well I teach, I preach, I disciple, I evangelize. Dave replied "No, I mean what can you do with your hands? What expertise do you have? Do you do carpentry work? Are you a plumber or are you an electrician?" That took me by surprise. I didn't come to Brazil to build buildings. I didn't come to Brazil to do physical labor. I came to Brazil to preach Christ, to win the lost, and plant churches. Little did I know that there was a lot more waiting for us then just preaching teaching and evangelizing.

We arrived in time to attend the Alliance Churches' second Congress held in Curitiba. We remember how daunting it was to be suddenly surrounded by Brazilian Portuguese with no English. Except for a few missionaries who would whisper the jist of what was being said. I had taken Spanish in high school so I had a basis in Latin languages. I could

Andrew, Marilyn, Angélica, Dick and Aimée LaFountain

decipher about a third to half of what was being spoken in a sermon, but normal conversations were way beyond my ability to understand.

Despite the language barrier I was able to strike up a few friendships, especially with the younger pastors and lay leaders, by playing games. With sign language and a few Portuguese words that I knew, I could understand what was being said. I remember playing a game on the ground which resembled checkers called "*trilha*."

After the Congress, we went to Campinas for language study, an entire year for eight hours a day, five days a week. It was tough, though we enjoyed learning languages. This was different; we were treated as children who knew nothing. We had to learn the basics of the language and pronunciation, being interrupted and corrected in every attempt to speak a simple sentence. There were hours and hours of repeating phrases, pronouncing and re-pronouncing words, memorizing dialogues, doing assignments, and watching teacher's tongues as they attempted to show us what was happening in their mouths when certain sounds were made. We were glad to have John and Loraine Todd in Campinas with us. They preceded us by six months. John was a tremendous help in buying furniture, negotiating deals, exchanging money, and getting around the city.

After a year we finished language study and passed the final exam. We were then assigned to go to the city of Porto Alegre. Other missionaries had attempted to plant churches in Porto Alegre but were not successful. We were now being asked to go there and try our hand at church planting.

Dave Jones had most recently spent time in Porto Alegre, built good relationships and had constructed a little wooden chapel in a backyard in a poor community, Jardim das

Palmeiras. Dave had assigned a young lay pastor, Sergio Pinto, to shepherd the little congregation. We were told to not pastor the church but to seek to plant churches elsewhere. But for the first year we attended that church and assisted the pastor as best we could.

While attending the chapel in the backyard and completing our language studies with tutors, we met *Delfino*, who was Sergio's brother-in-law. Delfino was a gregarious layperson partially invalid from a birth defect. He was a great help to us, encouraging us and our language skills, helping us to understand the culture, assisting us in finding a house to rent, and ultimately assisting us in planting our first church.

We decided to settle on the north side of town but the little church was on the southern side of town. At that time, we were without a car, without telephone and had to transport ourselves by way of several buses to get to the chapel. While we spent time traveling by bus we observed the city, all the while praying and analyzing where would be the best place to plant a church.

While doing this, we surveyed many of the neighborhoods and found that the northern part of the city was the growth area. Many new developments were occurring with high-rise apartments being commonplace. And the main road through the north part of the city showed signs of becoming a main thoroughfare for a new development. Although we were told to plant a church, we were also told that the mission had no money to rent a building or for construction, and little money for evangelism and outreach.

Vila Elsa

At this time, Delfino told us of a little village outside of the city where he lived. He wanted to establish a church in that community and asked us if we would consider planting a church in *Vila Elsa*. We consented on the condition that Delfino would be mentored to be the pastor of that church. We knew that village was not a place where we wanted to establish a strong vibrant church but would be a start.

For the first year, not having a car, our whole family traveled by bus to visit Vila Elsa for evangelism and church services. At first we met in Delfino's little house. When I say little house I mean a very small house. It was a house measuring 24' x 24' and divided into four small rooms. Gradually we met people, led people to Christ and established a small congregation in his home. We looked for land to build a small chapel. But the mission informed us they had no money for us to build. At the same time, the little church in Jardim das Palmeiras was struggling to grow. They had a chapel more than sufficient for their needs.

Our little church planting team of one missionary and two lay pastors struggled as we prayed through what to do and how to establish a new church. At the same time the little chapel in Jardim das Palmeiras needed to move off the property where it was located. The mission was able to obtain financing to purchase property on the main road in the Jardim das Palmeiras. The property was cheap and we found out why. It was basically a swamp, a drainage area for the surrounding houses. We had to pay for many truckloads of earth to be hauled in to fill in and firm up the property.

In one of our planning meetings, we talked honestly: "We have no money to build another chapel; it might be a good idea to divide the chapel in half . . . take one half to Vila Elsa and leave the other half in Jardim das Palmeiras." We consulted with Thomas Kyle, the mission leader, and after much thought he said "OK, let's do it." As a result, we were able to purchase a small lot in Vila Elsa on time payments with little or nothing down on which to build a chapel.

Now we had two small chapels in two small neighborhoods outside the city of Porto Alegre. God blessed; people were saved and baptized, and a church was born. But I wasn't satisfied with that. God had not called us to plant tiny churches in isolated *bairros*. God wanted to reach the entire city a POA.

By this time we had purchased a car and were able to drive the 20 miles to Villa Elsa. That trip took us through the northern part of the city on a major thoroughfare where high-rise apartment buildings were being built and middle-class housing was springing up everywhere. My heart cried out this was where we ought to plant a church.

The house we were renting wasn't central to our work and ministry. So we began looking for another home to rent within the growing northern suburbs, but there were no rentals in the area where we wanted to plant a new church. They only had houses to buy, newly constructed homes which were well out of the reach of our missions' finances. As we prayed and walked through this area, we saw a house that looked appropriate for us, but it was for sale, not to rent. We investigated the possibilities, received the estimates of what it would cost, what the down payment would be, and how long we would make payments on this house.

Chapel and Tent in Vila Ema

Then we approached the mission with the proposal of buying the house, which would cost us essentially the same monthly payments we were making to rent a house. Time was of the essence. So we talked with Tom Kyle. After much prayer and consultation with the national office, Tom made and the decision to go ahead and buy the house. He said, "It's of God, and it's easier to ask the mission for forgiveness than to wait for permission." In the space of time it took to negotiate the house, gather the down payment, and complete the deal, the Brazilian economy tanked. The Brazilian *cruzeiro* was devalued against the dollar so that in the end the house cost us one third of the original cost! All this happened days before finalizing the purchase of the home. God had plans for the northern part of the city.

By this time Marilyn was pregnant with our third child and the ride from the northern part of the city to Vila Elsa was very difficult over rough, dusty, dirty, potholed roads. It was very uncomfortable for her to travel to this little church. About this same time, Delfino decided he didn't want to Pastor the little church; so he resigned leaving me solely responsible for the little congregation.

What's In Your Hand, Dick?

As I struggled in prayer with what to do, how to do it and how to make a larger impact on Porto Alegre, I attended another Alliance Congress, this time at the rustic camp of Vale de Aleluia near Curitiba. Tom Kyle was preaching on Moses' call and his insecurities and inability to do what God was asking him to do. Tom kept repeating the question God had posed to Moses, "What's in your hand?" Over and over Tom hammered that question throughout the sermon. God was speaking to my heart. "*What's in your hand Dick?*" "What have I given you to use that you are not surrendering to me?" I knew immediately what He meant.

Back in the United States in my first church, I had challenged my congregation that gifts were first motivations and desires God puts on our hearts. I asked each of the participants in that evening service what God had put in their hearts as a desire to do that they never tried. Several volunteered secret motivations, and we immediately challenged them to step out on faith and do it. An elderly gentleman turned the question back to me. "Pastor, what secret motivation or desire is in your heart that you never did." Good question. For me, watching *Sesame Street* with my children, I was intrigued with puppetry and animation. So, I answered, "I've always wanted to try puppets. I think I'd be good at it." Immediately the Sunday School superintendent said, "Great pastor, we've got Vacation Bible School in a month. I want you to do a puppet presentation every night of VBS." I consented half-heartedly. Having no puppet and no money to buy one, I took one of my daughter's stuffed animals, a turtle, and tore it apart making the head and neck a puppet. Then each night of VBS I did a puppet skit with my wife being the "straight man" to dialog with the puppet. It was a great success! The kids loved *Milton* the puppet. But I didn't want to be permanent puppeteer, so on the last weeknight I had Milton die and go to heaven. Parents were upset. Their kids were crying. I got dozens of calls to resurrect Milton during the Sunday night program, which I did, to everyone's delight.

The last thing to go in my suitcase as I packed for Brazil was Milton. I didn't want to take him; after all, he couldn't speak Portuguese. But as the Lord suggested, maybe someone else could use him I relinquished my stubbornness and threw him into my suitcase. Now years later, God was asking me to take what was in my hand and surrender it to God. That night in tears I knelt at the altar weeping and telling the Lord I didn't like the idea but Milton was His to use as He wished. Upon returning home and praying much, I laid out a vision and a plan to reach the northern part of the city where we now lived. We would use a mobile outdoor theater we called "Noah's Ark" to first reach children, and then through them gain access to the hearts of their parents.

Actually the Lord led me to write up a proposal for the mission, a ten year plan for church planting using Noah's Ark. We needed help to do this, so I proposed that Steve and Diane Renicks be assigned to work with us as a team. This had never been done before. Up to that time, every missionary was a church planter. They were spread out to get the most "bang for our buck." Traditionally, two missionary couples did not work in the same church plant, although it had happened in Curitiba. In the end, our South American regional director, David Volstad, heard all the arguments and came down with a decision. "We will do Dick's plan. It has never been done before but it's worth a try."

And so it began. Steve and Diane were assigned to work together with us on this church plant. I knew Steve from college. We had worked together on outreach at Nyack College. His gifts complemented mine. I was the crazy entrepreneur, evangelist, daredevil, and risk taker while he was the musician, people person, discipler and teacher. Give Steve and Diane credit. They took the risk with us, crazy as it sounded; they would work with us on the outdoor puppet theater and

Marilyn and Noah's Ark

be our supporters. We built the ark, a big box on a motorcycle trailer, painted with bright colors, with a window for the puppet theater in the side. We mounted speakers on top and drove through neighborhoods announcing Noah's Ark and inviting kids to the "*praça*," the neighborhood Central Park and playground found in every neighborhood.

Parque Santa Fe and Leopoldina

I remember our first big outdoor program scheduled for the biggest neighborhood, *Parque Santa Fe* and *Leopoldina*. We rented a flatbed trailer as a portable stage, borrowed musicians and vocalists with Steve at the piano, a young Brazilian evangelist, *Vitalino*, preached, and of course the main attraction, "Noah's Ark." We had no idea how it would go over but it was worth a try. My neighbor, a pilot and businessman, promised to attend. We were all frightened and nervous. But we plunged in believing God for a miracle.

The Gospel was presented and the Gospel of John with a Bible study handed out. The female soloist, *Carmélia Borba*, was so good that traffic stopped dead in the street. And of course there was "Noah's Ark," Milton and a new puppet, *Mrs. Noah*. I returned home after that long day, excited but nervous to hear the response from Brazilians. My neighbor came over and quizzed me on what we did. He said the vocalist was amazing and the puppets were hilarious. Then he popped the question I dreaded, "Who did the puppets?" Sheepishly and half ashamed I admitted I did. He responded incredulously, "Ricardo, it couldn't have been you. You speak with an American accent, all Americans do. But Mrs. Noah speaks perfect street Portuguese with no accent at all!"

And so Noah's Ark ministry was born and became one of the most successful evangelistic tools we have ever used. Not only were children coming to Christ, but adults as well responded to the simple message of salvation. It became a key ingredient to all our church planting endeavors. Today it is being repeated and replicated in many countries around the world.

As Steve and I prayed and continued to plan to reach out to this growing part of the city, we would take days to walk and pray over the hills and valleys where we felt God wanted us to plant a strong regional

Open Air Meeting at Parque Sta. Fé

church. On one of those prayer walks, God gave me a vision of the church as it was to be. I saw it standing on the corner of the main bus stop on the main thoroughfare where thousands passed by every day. I wrote down my vision and even drew it in my journal. Years later, long after I had left Brazil and the church had been planted and entrusted to a Brazilian pastor, I returned to visit. Steve Renicks drove me from the airport to Santa Fe. He stopped in front of the church. It was on the corner where I had envisioned it being so long ago. It was on that same corner where our 12 year old daughter was hit by a car and died many years before. I was shocked and started to weep. That building is exactly the church I saw down to the brick and mortar; even the windows were what I saw in my vision.

It was on that same visit that the assistant pastor introduced himself to me by asking if I remembered him. I didn't. Then he told me he was that whiny irritating kid who followed the Ark each week. He got saved and now is in full time service. Then, as he introduced me to preach that evening, he asked the crowd of 250 to stand if they had attended Noah's Ark as a child or came to Christ through the efforts of the Noah's Ark ministry. A good 2/3 of the congregation stood. I stood there amazed at the work of God and laughed within myself, "Who has despised the day of small things?" "But God has chosen, not the wise of this world, but the foolish, to confound the wise. It is through the foolishness of preaching He chose to save some." So, I ask the next generation: "What's in your hand?"

Steve and Diane Renicks

Diane and I arrived in Brazil on August 9, 1979 to begin Portuguese language study in Campinas, São Paulo. Getting to Brazil was rather circuitous. We had been assigned to Brazil in 1972, applied for our permanent visas in 1977 and waited and waited. In the beginning of 1979, we were told that our visas would not be approved because of the political environment in Brazil. We were then reassigned to Chile and began Spanish language study in Costa Rica in May, 1979. However, there was a caveat. If we received our visas to Brazil during the first unit of Spanish language, we would be sent to Brazil rather than Chile. Two weeks before the end of the unit we received word that our visas had been approved.

When we arrived in Brazil we discovered that David Jones had gone to the government offices in Brasília responsible for granting visas and found our applications in a filing cabinet. They had been approved and archived lacking only the signature of the supervisor of that department. God's hand was on our going to Brazil and that became evident when we received a letter from a member of an Alliance church in New Zealand. In 1978, I took a group of young people from the church where we were completing our home service to Ecuador.

We were featured on a program on HCJB, the Christian radio station in Quito that broadcasts the Gospel around the world. During the program I had asked for prayer concerning our visas. When we opened

STEVE DIANE PAUL & TIMMY RENICKS

the letter from New Zealand we read these words, "One evening I was listening to HCJB and heard you ask for prayer concerning your visas for Brazil. I just read in the *Alliance Life* that you had arrived in Brazil. I wanted you to know that I had prayed for you every day after hearing your prayer request on HCJB."

Towards the end of our year of language study we were asked to visit Porto Alegre, the capital city of the southernmost state of Brazil. Dick and Marilyn LaFountain were already there and were requesting another couple to team up with them in a new church planting project. As we talked with them, they shared their vision for planting a church in a new area of the city that was just developing. There were a few apartment buildings and some houses but it was mostly open land. They had talked to the developers and discovered that when completed there would be tens of thousands of people living there. The vision was to plant a church located on the main avenue and near a bus stop, a location that would be highly visible and easily accessible.

Diane and I returned to Campinas and after a period of prayer we accepted the invitation to join the LaFountains. We moved to Porto Alegre in late July, 1980. We hit the ground running ready to make contacts with people living in the area. Dick had prepared a short study of John 3:16 to be distributed door to door. With the help a group *Alliance Youth Corp* college students, 6,000 studies were distributed. If the person completed the study and sent it back in by mail, they would receive a New Testament. Approximately sixty studies were sent back. We visited each home that had responded and gave them the New Testament. As we talked with them everyone expressed excitement about having a church in the area.

Parque Santa Fé

However, we did not have a meeting place. The area was so new that there were no schools and no storefronts to rent. Two ideal lots located in *Parque Santa Fé* had been placed on sale. They were on the main avenue with a bus stop in front. Dick wanted to buy them but there was no money available for the purchase. The rented house where we lived had a large enclosed area in the back of the property which could be used as a meeting place; so we decided to invite all these contacts to our place for a Brazilian style cookout. We set the day and time and went back to each of our contacts. Many of them responded positively to the invitation and so we made our plans. We bought forty pounds of meat and prepared all the accompanying salads and desserts. With everything prepared we waited and waited. None of the contacts came. Discouraged, we prayed for God's guidance.

One morning Dick came to our house telling us that the Lord had showed him how we were to proceed. He said that during his prayer time he heard the Lord tell him. "Use what is in your hand." He remembered that in the States they had used puppets in their church ministry and they had brought the puppets with them. He outlined his vision for a puppet ministry that would be called "Noah's Ark." We purchased a small trailer and built a box on top. Noah's Ark was painted on the side and an opening was cut out of the side for a stage. We had Mr. and Mrs. Noah and various animal puppets such as Miss Piggy and Kermit the Frog, all given appropriate Brazilian names. All served as the basis for biblically-based skits and stories. With a portable amplifier and speaker, we would drive around the cobble-stone streets announcing "Noah's Ark is coming." Then we would stop on a street corner or at a playground where we would sing, tell Bible stories and share the Gospel. However, when people would ask "Where is your church located?", we would have to answer that we did not have a meeting place. However, we were compiling a growing list of contacts. We had no idea at that time the important role that the Ark ministry would play in planting the church.

Parque dos Maias

Parque dos Maias was one of the neighborhoods that was very receptive to the Noah's Ark ministry. However, it was about two miles from Parque Santa Fé where we believed that the mother church should be located. Nevertheless, we needed to start somewhere. One afternoon, Dick and I were driving around the Parque dos Maias neighborhood when we saw a for-sale sign on an open lot. We called the number on the sign and discovered that we could purchase the lot without a down payment with 60 months to pay for it. That was workable and we were given permission to make the purchase in 1980.

We cleared the land and borrowing the old Big Top that Tom Kyle had used for evangelistic campaigns in Curitiba, we began in 1981 to hold weekend services. Families from the community started to come and many received Christ as Savior. There were other believers that came telling us that they had been praying for a church to come to their neighborhood. Soon we had a solid core of believers.

Parque dos Maias Chapel

The two sons of the family that lived next door to our property started attending Sunday school. As we talked to their parents, we discovered that they both came from a Christian background but were no longer attending church. We also found out that the father, Thomas, was a contractor. We needed a more permanent meeting place. So, Thomas began building at the back of the property while we still met in the tent. It was large enough for about sixty people. We had a core group of about forty people and continually shared with them our vision of having the large central church located in Parque Santa Fé. The building was completed and dedicated in 1981. I shared with Thomas our vision of having the central church and told him when we were ready to build we wanted him to be the contractor.

Parque Santa Fé

It would take several years before our full attention could be given to starting the central church in Parque Santa Fé. In mid-1981, the LaFountains returned to the United States for their furlough year. Diane and I concentrated on pastoring and discipling the Parque dos Maias congregation.

Shortly after their return in July 1982, the LaFountains suffered a personal tragedy. Their 12 year old daughter, Aimée, was struck by a car as she was crossing a street and died a few days later. Her death impacted all that knew her and we all focused on ministering to the LaFountain family as they grieved the loss of their daughter. It was a dark day as we struggled to know how to move forward. Ministry was limited to the Noah's Ark program and leading the Parque dos Maias congregation.

Then, in early October, two months after Aimée's death, we received a telephone call from Thomas. He told us that he was building a warehouse for a man and that he did not have enough money to complete the construction. Thomas said, "He keeps saying that he has two lots in Parque Santa Fé and that he might have to sell them in order to finish the warehouse. I think the lots might be located where you want to have the central church. I will call you when he runs out of money."

During this time, we had received $25,000 from the Alliance Women's annual missionary offering that was designated for the Porto Alegre church planting project. So we waited and prayed. A couple of months later, Thomas called again and said, "He has run out of money and needs to sell the lots in Parque Santa Fé. Come right away." Dick and I drove to the construction site and introduced ourselves to the gentleman. He was very nervous and bluntly told us that if we could not pay in cash he did not want to talk with us. We asked, "What is the selling price?" When we calculated the value in dollars it was exactly $25,000! We replied. "We have the money but it depends on the location of the lots." We had a map of the Parque Santa Fé area with all the lot numbers. When we looked at the deed and compared the lot numbers with their location on the map, we discovered that they were the exact two lots that Dick had previously wanted to buy on the main avenue with the bus stop in front of it.

When we purchased the two lots and signed the deed, we marveled at how the Lord had orchestrated this. The lots had been purchased by a man who would use Thomas as his builder, who was our neighbor, and who knew of our vision for a church in Parque Santa Fé. This was a sign that the Lord was directing this project, not us.

Diane and I furloughed from July 1983 returning in July 1984. Before our return to Porto Alegre, Dick and Marilyn had returned to the United States in order to recover from the strain of grief resulting from Aimée's death. We were struggling to make sense of all that was happening. We believed that the Lord was in all that had happened. That had been confirmed with the success of the Noah's Ark ministry and the miraculous provision of the two lots. Now the team had been decimated with no promise of reinforcements.

Then another confirmation came in October, 1984. As we studied the zoning codes it became evident that the two lots we had purchased were not sufficient for accommodating what would be needed for a central church. There were two empty lots adjacent to the lots that we had. We were aware that they belonged to the construction firm responsible for developing the whole area. Everyone knew that "Guerino does not sell; they only buy." Yet the Lord impressed on us that we should pursue the purchase of those lots. I went to talk to a real estate agent and he reaffirmed that the firm would not sell. I finally convinced him to go talk to the owners. Later that day, he came to our house. When I answered the door he is shaking his head and said, "They have agreed to sell the lots only to you. The sale price is $14,000 and it must be paid and the papers must be signed by October 31st." There was one minor problem. We did not have $14,000. We didn't even have $100! I called our field director and he called Rev. David Voltad, the C&MA Regional Director for Latin America. We were told that he was out of the office and would not be back until October 30th, allowing 24 hours for the whole transaction. So I called him as soon as he was back in his office; he approved the purchase and we were able to sign the purchase contract and pay the $14,000 by the deadline. Forty five days later I went to the legal office to pick up the title deed. The officer called me over and said, "You are one lucky man." I told him that I didn't understand and he explained, "The construction firm that owned those lots just filed bankruptcy and all its assets are frozen. If you had waited another month it would have been impossible to make the purchase. Here is the deed in the name of The Christian and Missionary Alliance."

We rejoiced in God's faithfulness and all doubt was erased. The vision for the central church in Parque Santa Fé was not of human invention. It was God's vision, and He was in control of each step. So in 1985, we decided to take steps to begin a preaching point in Parque Santa Fé. The Noah's Ark ministry had been very successful in the *Dona Leopoldina* neighborhood which was located across the street from the Parque Santa Fé property. New apartment buildings and houses were under construction and there were thousands of people within walking distance.

There was only one storefront in the area that had adequate space for a church, and it was located just 100 yards from our property. A night club that had been using that space closed and a FOR RENT sign was posted. When I went to the realtor, I was told that someone else had already rented the storefront. We watched as renovations were made by the new tenants. We continued to pray believing that the Lord would make a way. Suddenly the FOR RENT sign went back up! This time we were able to rent the building. God amazed us; the storefront had been painted and was ready for us to move in. We were curious about what had happened. Several months later, a Christian doctor and his wife joined our new congregation. Over lunch one day, he told me that he and several other Christian doctors had decided to open a clinic in the storefront. As they were renovating the space they found a better location and decided not to rent it. Once again we experienced how the Lord was working behind the scenes and granting us His favor.

Sanford and Wendie Hashimoto and Brenda Kurtz had joined our team, and the Hashimotos were leading the Parque dos Maias congregation while we led the group in Parque Santa Fé. The work in Parque Santa Fé was struggling to get started while we had a solid core of believers and leaders in the Parque dos Maias congregation. In 1986, we approached the Parque dos Maias congregation and asked them to join the Parque Santa Fé group uniting the two congregations. They agreed unanimously. This decision gave us a group of sixty people adding a new dynamic to the Parque Santa Fé work. It is important to note that Thomas was one of those Parque dos Maias members. Both he and his wife had given their lives to the Lord and were active in the church.

During 1986, architectural plans were approved to build a sanctuary for 400 and a three story educational building that would house offices, a fellowship hall, classrooms and an apartment. We had received a $35,000 grant from the C&MA and with these funds we began construction of the educational building. Thomas was our builder, and his practical wisdom was invaluable. He explained that he could build the first floor where the offices, restrooms and fellowship hall were located in such a way that we could move into the building while he continued working on the other two floors.

Step Into the Water

We began construction in 1987 and soon we arrived at a crossroads. The $35,000 was gone and all we had to show for it was the foundation rebar rods that were protruding from the ground. Unlike in the U.S., it was impossible to obtain a loan.

Construction would continue only as we had money and Thomas had contracted twenty men that he was obligated to pay or lay off.

I knew that I had to give Thomas an answer concerning what we would do. It was a Tuesday morning and in my devotional time I read these words from Joshua 3 that recounts the Israelites crossing the Jordan River to enter into the Promised Land. The priests had to step into the water first before the river stopped flowing. The message was clear – we were to move ahead believing that the Lord would provide. Thomas came to my office later that morning to hear our decision. I said, "Thomas, we have no more money to buy materials or to pay your workers. However, I believe that the Lord wants to keep building." I waited for his response. With a smile he replied, "It's about time you came to that conclusion. I had already decided that if there is no money to pay my workers, I will pay them with my own money." I thought back to when we had first met Thomas in Parque dos Maias before he became a Christian. The Lord had placed the right man in our lives.

Two days later, the owner of a lumberyard stopped by the construction site and donated lumber for the building. The next day, we received a letter advising us of a $2,000 gift for the building. We never stopped building for lack of funds. After the completion of the educational wing, we began construction of the sanctuary in 1992. When it was dedicated in 1995, over $600,000 had been given towards the construction of the two buildings. They are a testimony to the Lord's faithfulness and provision.

Thomas did more than build the physical structures. He wanted to be a true testimony for the Lord. We met with the workers every morning and prayed for their safety. All the construction was done by manual labor. Not even the concrete was purchased ready mixed. So there was a lot of danger for work-related injuries. Thomas made sure that God received the

glory when he reminded the men that there had been no injuries throughout the construction. Thomas hired José to be the guard for the construction site as well as one of his workers. I remember the day when we

**Parque Santa Fé Alliance Church –
Porto Alegre**

were preparing the baptistery and José was in the hole laying brick. We joked that he better be careful or he would be one of the first to be baptized there. He just smiled. José later accepted the Lord and was among the first group to be baptized in the new baptistery.

Not only were we erecting buildings, we were also building a team. It would be the combination of giftedness that would allow us to provide a solid foundation for the new church. In 1987, *Jeff and Jo Kiel* came after completing language study and the church called Brazilian Pastor, Sérgio Pinto. Those were exciting times. Sanford Hashimoto started *Evangelism Explosion* training and visitation; as his teams went out, many people received Christ as Savior. In one year there were more than 200 conversions. Jeff and Jo headed up the discipleship training program and initiated the Bible Academy with courses that prepared the church members to understand their faith and to be leaders in the church. *Brenda Kurtz* headed up the youth ministry from which emerged a group of youth that would later become pastors, pastors' wives, and missionaries.

We all worked together with the Noah's Ark ministry

that continued to be the church's flagship for making contacts. *The Santa Fé Alliance Church* was better known as the *Noah's Ark Church*. We used the Noah's Ark in three different neighborhoods, but the most effective location was Dona Leopoldina, the neighborhood across the street from the church. More than 150 children and parents would attend the Sunday afternoon presentation. During the summer months at nighttime, we would drive to the main park and there would be over 500 people present. It was so gratifying to see young people from the church comfortably leading the singing, telling the Bible stories and presenting the Gospel to hundreds of people. One evening Sanford and Wendie Hashimoto visited an Ark contact and when they arrived at the apartment the living room was filled with other children and families. Sanford seized the opportunity. There was a beach chair that had all the colors of the Wordless Book. Using the chair, he presented the Gospel and several prayed to receive Christ.

Only in heaven will we witness the tremendous impact of the Noah's Ark ministry. One day I took my car to a mechanic and while talking to the receptionist she told me her story: "When I was eight years old, my aunt took me to see "Noah's Ark." I am now a baptized believer but I want you to know that it was at the Ark that I first heard about Jesus." We heard of three sisters that had visited another church. During the visit they mentioned that they had grown up in Dona Leopoldina and mentioned that they had gone to "Noah's Ark." They proceeded to sing the songs that they had learned there.

Over the years other missionary couples as well as other Brazilian workers joined the team that provided more stability and leadership especially during the furlough years. We were able to keep the ministries at full strength. David and Sue Manske arrived in 1990, Dwayne and Rhonda Buhler in 1991 and Brian and Vickie Joyce in 1998. This integrated work resulted in having a congregation of over 200 members by 1996. There was an active governing board, a group of deacons and deaconesses and several young people who were studying for fulltime ministry.

The goal was to have Brazilian leadership in the church so that the missionaries could concentrate in other areas. However, this transition was not easy. The Brazilian Alliance did not have many pastors at the time so there was a small pool to draw from. Pastor Sérgio Pinto and his family left in 1990 to assume the pastoral leadership of another Alliance church in São José dos Campos, São Paulo. It was not until 1999 that the church called Dari and Regina Pereira to lead the Parque Santa Fé church. Pastor Dari had been a part of the church since its beginning, had pastored in Brasília, the nation's capital, and now had returned to his home church as its leader.

A Full-Circle Church

Another goal was to establish a "full-circle church" meaning that it had the same missionary vision as the churches that had sent us and supported us. Shortly after moving into the fellowship hall for our services we held a missionary conference where several of our young people dedicated their lives to the Lord to serve Him in full time ministry. In 1989, we held a church retreat in the interior of the state, near an Indian reservation, where a *New Tribes* missionary couple had a retreat center. They were working among the *Kaingang Indians*, who lived in a similar setting as the American plains Indians. We held a joint service with the Kaingang believers. At the end of the service, one of the Kaingang church leaders stood up and said, "We are so grateful for the missionaries who have come from so far away to tell us about Jesus. But I have a question.

You live right here. Why didn't you come to tell us of Jesus?" Strong conviction fell on our congregation and we returned to Porto Alegre determined to become a missionary supporting and sending church.

In 1999, André Sousa, one of the young people present at that retreat, and his family moved to the Amazon to work among the *Wai-Wai* Indians there. Today he oversees more than seventy Brazilian missionaries working among a variety of tribes in the Amazon jungle and lectures at various missionary training institutes preparing other Brazilian missionaries. In 2012, Simone, another person attending that retreat, and her husband Sílvio, moved to the Amazon and are living in a *Yanomami* Indian village. They gave up a successful dentistry practice in Porto Alegre to serve the Lord among the unreached tribes in Brazil. The church had come full circle.

Since the year 2000, the focus of children's ministry has been reaching out to "children at risk." With financial cooperation from the city of Porto Alegre, the Santa Fé church has provided homes with church families being foster parents, overseen a triage center helping place children back in relatives' homes, in adoption homes, or the foster homes.

Morada Do Vale

In 1992, four couples from the Santa Fé church had moved to *Morada do Vale*, a housing project in a nearby city about 12 miles from the Parque Santa Fé church. It is interesting that Morada do Vale was one of the areas being studied by the LaFountains as a possible church planting site. We began to hold home Bible studies during the week and the couples continued to attend the Santa Fé church on the weekends. It soon became evident that we had a solid core group to launch a church plant in that area. A small storefront was rented for public services. Once again the Noah's Ark was instrumental for making contacts and inviting people to the services. Weekend evangelistic campaigns provided opportunities for the core members to invite friends and neighbors to hear the Gospel.

There was a bus drivers' strike the week of one our campaigns and hundreds of people were left without transportation. One of the church members, *Angela*, had a car and as she left her home one morning she asked the Lord to direct her to someone who needed a ride. As she drove down the street she felt led by the Lord to offer a ride to a woman standing at a bus stop. When *Godiva* got in the car, she explained that she had a doctor's appointment that she needed to keep. During the ride Angela witnessed to her and invited her to the evangelistic services that would be held that weekend. Angela came that Saturday night. She responded to the invitation given at the end of the message and gave her life to the Lord. She asked us to pray for her husband who had been heavily involved in the occult. She said she was going to ask him to come to the Sunday night service, and on Sunday night she was back with her husband. We gathered before the service and specifically prayed for his salvation and deliverance. At the end of the service, he went forward and received Christ as his Savior and was miraculously delivered from the demonic influences in his life. Within a month their daughter and son-in-law, *Cristina* and *Damião*, had also given their lives to the Lord. Once again, the Lord was way ahead of us. Damião was an independent builder and led the construction of the Morada do Vale church.

The congregation was growing and we began to pray for a permanent location. A main avenue led into the heart of the neighborhood where there were empty lots zoned for business; however, nothing was for sale. The same construction company that had filed bankruptcy and from whom we had purchased the two lots in Parque Santa Fé owned all this property as well. These lots were part of the company's frozen assets. In early 1995, we learned that the lots along the avenue were now available for sale. We were able to purchase two lots with no down payment and with 60 monthly installments. The Parque dos Maias property in Porto Alegre was still being rented. The rent received from the property was sufficient to pay the monthly installments for the Morada do Vale property.

Once again, we did not have money for the construction. One day in 1996 we were informed by the C&MA Director for Latin America, David Volstad, that an Alliance Chinese foundation led by Phillip Teng had designated $15,000 for the construction project. We immediately contracted Damião and construction began that year. Once again God provided and construction did not stop for lack of funds. The sanctuary was dedicated on March 10, 2001. Missionaries Sanford and Wendie Hashimoto and Jim and Ann Hemminger were instrumental in providing direction and mentoring the Brazilian pastors that were called to lead the church.

Petrópolis

In 1999, a decision was made to focus in a major upper middle class/upper class area of the city. Dwayne and Rhonda Buhler had made some contacts who attended the Parque Santa Fé church. However, the Canadian C&MA reassigned Dwayne and Rhonda to Mexico. Thus following their return from home assignment, Steve and Diane Renicks were asked to spearhead this church plant initiative. An area of the city called *Petrópolis* was chosen. It was an upper middle class/ upper class neighborhood plus Petrópolis Avenue provided bus access from almost all other parts of the city.

It was decided to use a church-in-cells approach for the church plant, and a cell group was established in the home of a family who lived in the area while still attending Parque Santa Fé church. In the beginning the members of that cell group attended the Parque Santa Fé church for Sunday services. As the group grew, plans were made to rent a store front on Petrópolis Avenue and begin services. However, a larger core group was necessary for that step. Dari Pereira, pastor of the Parque Santa Fé church, commissioned several families from his congregation to help provide leadership to the new group. A store front was rented and renovated; public services began in the fall of 2001. Bryan and Vickie Joyce, Brenda Kurtz and Charlotte Hisle joined the church planting team. The growth of the group had its ups and downs. The storefront was located in an upper-middle/upper-class neighborhood. Despite many efforts, this neighborhood was not open to the Gospel message.

In 2004, it was necessary to move out of the storefront because of increased rental costs and the group began meeting in the conference room of a local hotel. Brenda Kurtz began English classes, and this became an important outreach tool for the surrounding community and provided many contacts for the church. In 2007, the decision was made to move from the hotel to another storefront where the congregation grew to more than 60 members. Although, there was always the hope of having a permanent location, purchase and building costs were prohibitively expensive.

In May of 2008, the decision was made by the Alliance leadership in the U.S. to transition the Brazil Alliance mission staff out of country within the next five years for redeployment in the United States or other fields. In mid-2008, Bryan and Vickie Joyce were reassigned to Eastern Europe; Steve and Diane Renicks returned to the United States in December of that year. Sanford and Wendie Hashimoto returned to the United States, and Charlotte Hisle transitioned to the new Alliance field of Portugal in 2011. Brenda Kurtz remained in Porto Alegre supporting herself by teaching English where she passed away in 2013.

Two Brazilian couples continued to lead the Petrópolis congregation. However, Marcos and Lilian "Lily" Bacarel moved to Chile to work with the Alliance in that country, and Sílvio and Simone Albuquerque became missionaries and moved to the Amazon to work among the Yanomami. As a result, the congregation disbanded. On paper, it may seem that this last church planting effort was a failure. However, dozens of lives were transformed by the power of the Gospel and are actively serving the Lord in congregations spread out over the city. One couple stands out in particular. *Luis* and *Elisandra* started to attend the first cell group in 1999 where they both accepted the Lord. They had little direction in their lives; as they grew spiritually, they also were blessed in their personal lives. They both enrolled in a Seventh Day Adventist college. Luis is now the head of the maintenance department at that college and Elisandra is employed by the city of Porto Alegre where she works with the "children at risk" program.

The Legacy

As missionaries our goal is to preach the Gospel, baptize the new believers, train local pastoral and church leadership, and turn self-propagating and self-sustaining churches over to that local leadership. In the 35 years of Alliance missionary presence in Porto Alegre, thousands have responded to the Gospel message and had their lives transformed by Jesus Christ. For example, when the Parque dos Maias property was rented out and the congregation moved to help start the

Parque Santa Fé church, the renter had contact with the missionaries where he heard the Gospel. Over twenty years later, he came to the Parque Santa Fé church, introduced himself and shared how he had become a Christian and attributed his conversion to the times twenty years earlier we had shared the Gospel with him.

Both the Parque Santa Fé congregation and the Morada do Vale congregation received church buildings and parsonages for their pastors debt-free because of the faithful giving of Alliance people. They are able to support their pastors and carry on their ministries without worrying about where they will meet or how they will meet their financial obligations. These congregations have also produced Christian workers, pastors, and missionaries that continue to serve the Lord and work for His Kingdom. To God be the glory.

CHAPTER SEVEN
DEEP ROOTS RUN FAR

As the story of the Alliance in Brazil progresses, it is amazing to see new roots surface from distant and unexpected corners of the globe. Such is the case with the thriving city of São José dos Campos, located on the *Via Dutra* highway connecting São Paulo with Rio de Janeiro, about 220 miles to the northeast. São José has a long and rich history as an important commercial center. By the second half of the 20th century, the city of São Paulo was congested, polluted and increasingly seen as an unattractive location for new businesses. The city and state leadership decided to decentralize and open new industrial poles in the state of São Paulo to alleviate the urban crush and pollution.

As a result, many industrial giants looked at the interior town of São José dos Campos as an attractive place to relocate or open new industrial installations. Johnson & Johnson, General Motors, Ericson, Philips, Fuji, Panasonic, Kodak and other multi-national companies took advantage of the cheap land, abundant water, clean air, government incentives and a less frantic pace than São Paulo. The city of São José became a major center for aerospace and scientific research. Consequently, the courageous and ambitious risked moving there in search of better jobs and a better quality of life for their families.

Across the continent, the coup that occurred in Chile in 1973 resulted in the death of leftist president, Salvador Allende, and the establishment of a military government led by General Augusto Pinochet. It sought to restore the country's fractured society and depressed economy to some semblance of order. Unemployment, labor unrest and a deep recession followed, and many skilled workers left their homeland to seek their fortunes elsewhere. Such was the case with a middle-aged couple with deep Alliance roots when *Andrés Barria Aburto* and his wife, *Margarita*, with their three young daughters, arrived in São José in 1975. Andrés was a skilled electrician and soon got a good job at the nearby General Motors plant. As soon as they settled into their home, the Aburtos began reaching out to their neighbors. Since their Chilean Spanish was not easily understood by their Brazilian neighbors, they often found it difficult to share their faith. However they persisted and began weekly services in their home. Andrés also openly evangelized his colleagues at the GM plant.

Meanwhile back in Porto Alegre, Dave and Judy Jones continued plowing away at the hard ground downtown. In addition, they had begun working with a young Brazilian couple who had started a Sunday school class in their neighborhood. It was idyllically called "The Garden of the Palms," where in reality there was neither garden nor palms. Sérgio and Regina Moraes Pinto were just coming onto the Alliance horizon in those days. With the Kyles' return to the United States for furlough, Dave was appointed Board Representative. Despite his mission leadership responsibility, he did not live in Curitiba where the field office was located. Dave's good friend and colleague, Jim Hemminger, field treasurer, lived in the "mission house," which had the only mission telephone. Those were the "good old days" of *TELEBRAS*, the government telephone monopoly which required people to invest thousands of dollars to "buy a line" and then sometimes wait for years before receiving a phone. Accordingly, any time Dave needed to care for mission business, he had to go to the "telephone post" downtown and wait in line to use an available phone. In some cases, calls could be made to Dave's neighbor's house and they would yell over the fence and let him know that a call was on their line.

São José dos Campos

Thus one afternoon in August 1975, Dave's neighbor shouted over the fence: "Pastor David, you have a call from Curitiba." So Dave went next door and took the call. He heard the voice of Jim Hemminger as he described a strange visitor at his home. "Dave, we were visited by a Chilean guy who lives up in São José dos Campos. He works at the GM plant there and says that he is a member of the Chilean Alliance. He says that he knows David Volstad (C&MA regional director for South America and former missionary to Chile) and a lot of the other missionaries. His name is Andrés Barria Aburto, and he wants to know if it's OK for him to start holding meetings in his home in the name of the Alliance. What do you think?"

"Wow, Jim," Dave replied, "that's about the strangest thing I've heard in a long time. Before we say 'yes or no,' let me write to Volstad and ask him if he knows this man, Andrés Barria Aburto. In the meantime, he can hold

Andrés and Margarita Aburto and daughters

meetings and we'll get back to him. Make sure he knows that we have no money or personnel to send up there, but we will pray for him and his family. And be sure he realizes that this is not 'official permission.'" That unusual call was the first sign of one more Alliance root seeking good soil to work in, and the first chapter of an amazing story.

Thus a letter immediately went off to C&MA headquarters in Nyack, New York. Due to previous unfortunate experiences, the Brazil C&MA staff was reluctant to accept at face value the stories of people who claimed to be from other Alliance fields like Argentina, Chile or Peru. So we checked to make sure. In a few weeks, a reply came from David Volstad's office affirming that he knew Andrés Aburto and his wife. He confirmed that they were active Alliance church members from the Santiago region, had helped plant churches there and were to be trusted and encouraged as the field was able.

In a letter dated September 24, 1975, Dave wrote home to his parents: "Jim and I will be driving up to São José dos Campos, a city north of São Paulo, where an Alliance man from Chile has moved and is working at a General Motors factory. He wants to start an Alliance work there. So, we are going up to visit with him and hold a service in his home. Pray that this work will grow and prosper. The city is very prosperous and this is a tremendous opportunity." A more prophetic statement would be hard to make.

Thus a trip was planned to visit their new Alliance friends from Chile. Dave took the night bus up to Curitiba, and then he and Jim drove the 500 mile trip up the always dangerous BR 116, passing crowded São Paulo and on to São José. Arriving in town, they located the Aburto Family in their rented home. When they entered the house, they noticed that the furniture had been moved in the living room, shoved against the wall. It was set up like a small meeting hall with plastic chairs. Following their effusive greetings, Andres said, "We are having a service tonight; we have invited friends and neighbors and one of you will preach."

Following a delicious evening meal, the missionaries and their new-found Chilean friends waited for people to arrive. Dave had noticed the little table in the front of the room that served as a pulpit. There was an open Bible on it and a flag – a Chilean flag. "Hmm," he thought, "this could be interesting." During the mealtime, Andrés and his family explained why they had come to Brazil and told about God's provision of a good job at the GM plant and other material blessings. But it was also obvious the family was struggling with culture shock. The girls had encountered difficulty in school with the language and different educational system. Andrés' wife felt that the Brazilian women were not friendly, and she didn't like the potatoes she found in the stores (Chileans love their potatoes). The missionaries explained the Brazilians were really very warm and friendly, and that they were not big potato eaters but loved their beans and rice. Dave and Jim used the mealtime to help them understand some of the cultural adjustment issues they were facing.

It was then that the Chilean flag came up. "I see that you have the Chilean flag on your little table." "Yes," Andrés said. "In Chile, we always have a Chilean flag in the front of the church along with the Christian flag. We don't have a Christian flag here but we do have the Chilean flag. We really love it; it's so beautiful and reminds us of home." The missionaries mentioned that the Brazilians loved their flag also, and the girls replied that they thought it was rather garish and unattractive. "All of that blue, green and yellow is so gaudy." The missionaries tried to help them understand that "flag beauty" is to the eye of the beholder. "Each country's citizens love their flag and think it's lovely; those of us from another country really can't judge another country's flag simply because it looks different." That was when the light went on in Andres' eyes: "Oh, so you think it might be better if we didn't have our flag on the table?" The missionaries agreed that it would probably be better to remove the flag and just leave the Bible. That way, no Brazilian will think that the gospel message being preached is somehow associated with the Chilean flag. And that night, a good group of people showed up, songs were sung, Scripture was read, a message preached and seed was sown and the Bible was the only thing on the little table. That first visit showed the potential that was there in São José.

Vista Verde

On the last day of their visit, Andres took them to a huge new housing project just under development a bit north of the town center called *Vista Verde* (Green View). It was a massive undertaking by IBECASA BRASILEIRA, a non-profit multi-national venture financed by the Rockefeller Foundation. This multi-million dollar undertaking was being built on the site of a large ranch. Heavy machinery tore up the red soil, carving out house sites, streets and parks. Laborers covered the land like worker ants, laying brick, pouring concrete, paving streets and sidewalks. The houses went up in a matter of days rather than weeks. This vast undertaking was unlike anything seen previously in those parts. Before the more than 3,500 houses were built, the water, sewage and electricity were all installed. The entire infrastructure for the thousands of projected houses was done before anyone moved in. This was a pioneer "turn-key project," which meant that the buyers moved into well-built homes, built to high standards and financed by a foundation with plenty of much-needed capital.

Andrés pointed out the Catholic Church under construction and said, "They are building a church for the Catholics and giving it to them, for free. And we are going to get one too." One of the missionaries asked, "By we, do you mean us, the Alliance?" He nodded his head. "God put this place on my heart and told me we are going to have a church here." He then went on to mention that the head of the foundation, Mr. David Rockefeller, would be visiting the enterprise in the near future and he wanted Pastor David to talk with him. When it was explained that the Rockefellers and the Joneses were not mutual acquaintances, that fact did not seem to faze the faith-filled Chilean. "Before he comes to São José, I will let you know; then you can come up and meet with him." No amount of explanation seemed to dissuade the brother. Every four weeks for the next few months, one of the mission staff would go up to São José to hold services in the Aburto home, and soon there were several new believers meeting regularly with them. The group grew to twenty-five or thirty people meeting weekly with the Aburto family.

In March 1976, another call came over the fence came from Andres for Dave. "David Rockefeller will be here in a few weeks, and you need to come up and talk with him." The man's faith was mountain-moving, while my faith was mole-hill-size." However, in order to at least try and satisfy Andrés, I took the long bus trip from Porto Alegre to São José dos Campos, via São Paulo. Sure enough, David Rockefeller and his entourage were there to inspect the housing project where people were already moving in. And sure enough, I couldn't get past the burly Rockefeller security guards. Eventually I managed to talk with Rockefeller's son-in-law and present our request. I explained that I represented the evangelicals of São José dos

Campos (even though I lived hundreds of miles away) and was asking for a piece of land, the construction of a building and a gift from IBECASA.

The young man looked at me rather strangely and asked that I repeat my request again. Then he asked, "Are there any evangelicals here?" I assured him there were thousands in the growing city and that they should receive the same treatment that the Catholic Church had received. He explained that they gifted the Catholics with a church as a PR measure. However, In order to get rid of me, he suggested I send a "memo" to the São Paulo office with a written request. Relieved and believing that I was off the hook, I left him and explained what had transpired to Andres. And he was elated: "See, all you have to do is write a letter." I didn't tell him that I had been given a kind but cold shoulder. For the next few months, I wrote one letter after another with no response from the São Paulo office. So after some time Andrés said, "Next time you come up to visit, stop by the office in São Paulo and talk with the head of IBECASA." I agreed to do so in order to get the issue settled. His dream what just that – a dream.

So once again, I took the bus to São Paulo, cleaned up at the bus station and took a cab to the *Conjunto Nacional*, at that time, one of the most prestigious office buildings in the whole country. I took the elevator up to the IBECASA suite and saw that their offices occupied the whole floor. "Wow," I thought, "this is a big outfit!" I went into the office, saw the receptionist and asked her if I could see the project engineer, Mr. Harvey Weeks. She asked coolly, "Do you have an appointment?" "An appointment?" I thought, "nobody makes appointments in Brazil. Oh no, he's not Brazilian; he's a gringo and they make appointments!" I could have kicked myself but didn't show my chagrin to the young lady. I simply explained that I had come up from Porto Alegre and wanted to see Mr. Weeks as a follow up to the letters I had sent to him. She said, "He is very busy with no time open today. Come back tomorrow." I explained that I was going to São José that same night and really needed to see him. She said," Alright, if you want to wait, you may wait, but no promises." I waited and waited. During the next few hours, I read all of the magazines in the office, drank many cups of *cafezinho* and prayed that God would open the door. And amazingly, He did and I got into Mr. Week's office. The following excerpt from another Jones letter tells the story:

> Here's a tremendous praise report. You know about the work in São José dos Campos with the Chilean family. Well, we were trying to get property for them in a housing development [Vista Verde]. Well, the company was giving us the run around. So, I went to São Paulo and spoke with the president of the company, an Episcopal. I explained who we were and what we wanted. And God moved in. The man is giving us a good sized lot 400 sq. meters, will build the church at cost, and contribute $5,000 to the building cost. Wow, I could hardly believe my ears! Needless to say, the folks in São José are thrilled. So pray that we can raise the other $15,000 needed. . . . God is really moving there. Four families are already attending regularly with the Chilean family.

What was most fascinating about the meeting with Harvey Weeks is the way that God broke down his barrier of disinterest. He didn't believe there were many "Protestants" in

Brazil, and I assured him that there were millions, which surprised him. He then asked who I represented, and I asked a question back. "You worked previously for the Rockefeller Foundation in Lima, Peru, right?" I had just seen that fact in a magazine article that I read while waiting outside his office. He admitted that he had lived and worked in Lima. I asked him if he had ever seen the *Lima al Encuentro con Dios* church built on *Avenida Lince*. He said, "Yes, I've seen it, big and beautiful. I hear those are good people." I then said, "That's who we are, the *Alianza Cristiana y Misionera*, only we're called the *Aliança Cristã e Missionária* here in Brazil." Like water turned into wine, his attitude changed. Within a few minutes made the offer that launched the Vista Verde church. Another Alliance root connection surfaced in Brazil.

While I, the missionary, was astounded at the response of Mr. Weeks, the president of IBECASA BRASILEIRA, Andrés was not. "I told you that God told me we were going to have a church. You just needed to believe." That exercise of "risky-faith" was a new and important lesson to learn. By August 1976, Jim and Ann Hemminger had moved into one of the new Vista Verde homes. They began to work with the Aburtos to build the little congregation. For a while, they met in a small building that had been the first police station in Vista Verde.

**Jim and Ann Hemminger
Vista Verde Alliance Church**

Evangelistic meetings were held, people were saved and Jim and Ann became well known all over the neighborhood. Up and down the dozens of streets, they walked, drove, prayed and visited. Good seed was planted and the "root" that had come all the way over to Brazil from Chile, with an assist from Peru, sank deeply into the brick-red soil of São Paulo, producing much fruit.

The old police station was soon overcrowded with 35 to 40 attending regularly. Besides the Vista Verde work, another 35 or so were meeting regularly in the Barria Aburto home. After much delay and a lack of enthusiasm shown by the Bolivian engineer in charge, a Marxist who said that the building would never be filled, ground was broken in 1977. The church was dedicated later that same year—and it was full.

Campinas, São Paulo

The story of the Alliance in the city of Campinas, Sao Paulo began with Pastor Koon Tu Shuen and his wife, Lucy. While touring the Western District in November 1975 in preparation for departure for the field, John and Loraine met Paul Bartel and his wife, Ina, retired missionaries from China, in Colorado Springs, CO. Rev. Bartel had baptized the young Koon (pronounced Kwan) at Rennie's Mill refugee camp in Hong Kong many years before and had become his teacher and mentor there at the Alliance Bible School where Pastor Koon was ordained. As a young man, Pastor Koon, had been an apprentice of a famous calligrapher/painter with whom he trained for many years. Eventually in the late 1930s/early 1940s, Koon was drafted into a local warlord's army and fought against the Japanese, as well as Mao Tse Tung's forces, during World War II. After the communist takeover of China in 1949, Koon fled to Hong Kong and took up a new life at Rennie's Mills camp on a deserted hillside on the backside of Hong Kong. It was there that Koon met his wife, Lucy, and there they were led to Christ and discipled by Paul Bartel.

Sensing that life in a refugee camp was not a good

Koon Family: Ana, Paulo, Pastor Koon and Lucy

prospect for their soon-to-be born baby, they decided to begin a new life and took the long Dutch freighter voyage to Brazil. While onboard, their son, Koon Yan Sang, known as "Paulo", arrived. Being born on the "high seas," he had no legal passport or papers other than a birth certificate supplied by the captain. However, the family disembarked in Santos and began their new life. Rev. Pastor Koon worked in Sao Paulo for several years as a restaurant cook before moving to Campinas. Before the Todds arrived in Brazil, Rev. Bartel requested that they look up the Koons. Thus they soon became acquainted with the Koons after arriving in Campinas July, 1976 for their year of language study.

The Todds began to study Portuguese in August 1976, and eventually became acquainted with a neighbor family and in September began a Bible study on Monday nights in their home. These studies resulted in several conversions. Other opportunities, such as teaching a Sunday school class for youth at the Baptist Church their family was attending, and visits to the new church plant in São José dos Campos, were very profitable for language learning. It also helped them become acquainted with the region. Meeting regularly with the group already gathered at the Koon's home was a joy as the singing was done in four languages: Chinese, Portuguese, Japanese and English!

The annual mission meeting held in Curitiba in January 1977 gave John Todd opportunity to present a vision proposal for beginning a work in Campinas. This proposal was mentioned in an *Alliance Witness* article dated October 1977, "Brazil Overview." Called the "apostolic team approach," it envisioned "the training of Brazilian leaders who in turn will begin congregations in various sectors of Campinas. Mr. Todd in effect will be a pastor to the pastors." The proposal was approved by the field committee and at New York headquarters. Todds were appointed to Campinas to put the plan into action.

In April, the Todds and Koons began meetings twice monthly in one home, and then the other. At the Koon home, preaching was done in Chinese then translated into Portuguese by Ana Koon, Paulo's younger sister. On June 24 1977, the Todds graduated from language school and began the required second year of individual study with tutors. They began meeting in a downtown hall in the city center on July 10th. Pastor Koon began holding Chinese services on Saturday evenings. Agostino, a Portuguese immigrant and early friend and brother, joined them and became a co-worker.

Serving with the Koons was a privilege. In September John went with Pastor Koon for the ordination of three Chinese pastors in São Paulo with the service held in two Chinese dialects and Portuguese. On October 2, the Koons and Todds attended the dedication of the new church building in São José dos Campos. The year, 1977, ended with a youth camp outside of São José, final language exam and the start of a home Bible study on Wednesday in the bairro Santa Monica – the beginning of the work there.

In January 1978, a Vacation Bible School (VBS) was held there with sixty present for the closing program. Later in January, Richard and Marilyn LaFountain arrived with their two children to begin language study, and they were able to

The TODD'S — David. Thomas, John, Loraine Diana, Philip

take part in this new venture even while learning the language. The next month, Todds and Koons began Sunday school in the Center. On Holy Week in March, special meetings were held downtown with Jim Hemminger and John Todd as evangelists. The attendance was low, but good contacts were made. Despite this modest beginning and the mission's counsel to not tackle too much too soon, the Todds began to develop and expand the ministry at a breakneck pace.

Two months later in May, a corner lot was purchased for the *Santa Monica* chapel and a VBS was held in June with the help of the Alliance Youth Corp (AYC). Sunday evening meetings were begun as well as children's Sunday school classes. Also in June, Friday night youth services began in the downtown hall with an assist by the Alliance Youth Corp college students. That same month in another part of town, *Parque Taquaral*, a corner lot with a building and another smaller structure with a classroom and bathrooms was rented. Fresh paint and repairs made it useable, and the main service was moved there from the downtown hall. Two ladies were saved through a Bible study with Loraine. *Geni* and *Maria*, both neighbors, became great helpers with the children and women groups. The ladies' study continued to grow, and several more women made professions of faith. Several ladies became members, attending with their families. Two men, *Agostino da Conceição* and *João Silva*, a gardener from Santa Monica, were faithful men and helped the ministry. As is usually the case, the husbands were more difficult to reach.

Soon a third evangelistic endeavor began in *Jardim Santana*, the bairro where the Koons lived and the church plant met in their converted garage. Thus, in less than six months after the mission began work in Campinas, there were two church plants initiated by the Todds as well as the Chinese work led by Pastor Koon. With a mix of Bible studies, Vacation Bible Schools and evangelistic meetings, the ministry progressed. A baptistry was built at Parque Taquaral in November and three ladies inaugurated it. Weekly services averaged twenty in attendance. A lay preacher, *Percival Santos*, joined John's apostolic team. This kickoff year, 1978, closed with Christmas programs at all three locations: Santa Monica, Parque Taquaral and Jardim Santana.

The summer of 1979 began with Loraine and ladies from the churches holding Vacation Bible Schools in January. Daily, Bible stories recounted the truth of God's Word to dozens of children. Special evangelistic meetings were regularly held

in the three chapels using different preachers from the Mission and Alliance churches. Easter services at Parque Taquaral resulted in five new believers.

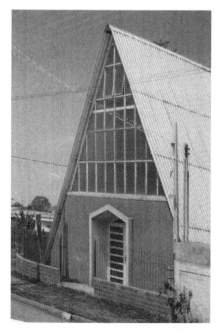

From February through June, construction of the A-frame in Santana Monica was an exciting time with many helping, both from the bairro as well as from Parque Taquaral. They pitched in with the painting, building the frame and erecting the metal roof.

Construction ended in late September. The August highlight saw Pastor Koon commissioned as a pastor; The Brazil Alliance President, Hernan Osorio, led the service. Before the end of the year, another four had been baptized at the Parque Taquaral chapel. About that same time *Steve and Diane Renicks* arrived with two sons. They were a great help with music while in language school. Todds, as the knowledgeable locals, located a house for them and helped them get settled as they did with other new missionary couples as they arrived.

In November, the first Sunday morning service was held in Parque Taquaral. Agostino attended after being absent for almost 2 years because his wife, *Idalina*, had become ill and struggled with cancer until September 1980. He spent much time at her bedside and continued to encourage the Todds even in his grief. Ministering to him and Idalina gave the Todds many opportunities to spend time with their large extended Portuguese family. On December 1, the three chapels held a joint baptism and communion service, thus ending their first very full year of ministry as Alliance missionaries in Campinas.

With the coming of the new year, 1980, *Sanford and Wendy Hashimoto* arrived for language school in late January. A second VBS was held in Parque Taquaral. Friday evening services were begun in the Santa Mônica chapel. Also, in Parque Taquaral, a Bible memory program was started with 8 people. Four more participated at the Santa Mônica chapel. Nine received all the awards finishing the course in time to receive special recognition from President Hernan Osorio in June.

The first extended evangelistic campaign was held in Santa Monica in May during the Easter season with fifty present nightly. The Renicks, now in their second semester of language studies, Jim Medin, who was leading the Vista Verde church in São José dos Campos, Pastor Alcides (a new worker in

Parque Taquaral) and John Todd shared speaking responsibilities. There were 13 decisions, including 4 adults and several teenage girls. A highlight of the campaign was the participation on the last Saturday by a group of young adults from São José dos Campos. They did visitation during the day holding several home services, then took charge of the evening service. Many needs were met and their initiative encouraged the workers in Campinas.

Jardim Santana also held an evangelistic campaign in May. Gospel tracts and invitations provided were given out in the community. Pastor Hernan Osorio, ACEMBRAS President, came to Campinas while touring the Alliance churches. He participated in the June 6-18 evangelistic meetings at Parque Taquaral. New missionary, Richard LaFountain, completed the preaching responsibilities. By September, the paperwork was complete for the purchase of the building in Parque Taquaral. Further improvements on the property could now go forward including an attractive wall around the property.

A second evangelistic campaign was held in Santa Monica with David Jones, Jim Hemminger, and John Todd as preachers. Two decisions for Christ were made; one was a teenager who led Loraine Todd back to her home where the mother was ready to receive the gospel. She was not allowed to attend services but Loraine and *Aurelina* held weekly studies in her home.

The first Alliance Youth Congress was held in November at São José dos Campos. Four youth from Campinas were able to attend. Pastor Koon's son, Paulo, was elected second-secretary for the national youth organization. November ended with a joint communion and baptismal service at Parque Taquaral with six baptized, representing all three chapels. The year ended with thirty baptized believers in the

Alliance of Campinas.

1981 began with a big responsibility for the three small chapels. Campinas was the host city for the *Fourth Annual Council of ACEMBRAS* led by Rev. Hernan Osorio, president. The meetings were held at the *Independent Baptist Seminary*. The facility included everything necessary for council. Under the banner, "*To the Regions Beyond,*" encouraging reports on the ministry activities underway in Brazil were given by nationals and missionaries. The 29 voting members included pastors, missionaries and 11 delegates from 13 church congregations. Six new workers were licensed. The first Annual Banquet of the *União Feminina Missionária* was held. Following the ACEMBRAS Council, the ANNUAL mission retreat was held at the *Solar das Andorinhas* outside Campinas with the purpose of officially organizing the Brazil field with its own elected leadership rather than being administered as an "unorganized field" directly by the North American leadership. The first mission banquet was held at the conclusion of five productive days.

In February, Campinas sent six youth to the Carnival Camp in Curitiba. In March the weekly Saturday night services grew in attendance with MK, Philip Todd, leading the singing with guitar. New national church president, Rev. João Costa, and Richard LaFountain preached for Easter week meditations in April 9-19 at Parque Taquaral. While doing visitations in Santa Mônica, Richard gave the gospel to a man that had been prayed for and ministered to for weeks. The following month of May, *José Nilson*, the National Youth president, spoke to the youth of the three chapels. The Winter 1980 edition of the *BRAZIL BULLETIN* reported: "In this city of almost one million, we have three infant groups. These are small, being carved out of nothing and the work is very difficult. However we feel that we do have a 'toehold.'" Despite the hard work, investment of time, talent and treasure, the spiritual soil in Campinas was proving to be rocky and resistant.

As the Todd's first term was coming to an end, the first part of June 1981 was spent preparing the chapels for the handoff to the Jenks Family, with the Todd family leaving for furlough on June 27, 1981. Upon arrival, the Jenks found that there were no men attending the churches. During that year, *Lawrence and Ida Jenks*, with their two daughters, *Ruth and Christie*, carried on the responsibility of the work in Campinas, joining forces with the Koon Family. During that year, Pastor Koon's work formally came into the Alliance fold. Together they worked to build up the work in Campinas. Pastor Koon had been ill since late 1979 and was hospitalized in August of 1980. The Jenks and the older Koon children continued the work in Jardim Santana aided by their father as able. In August, 1980 Pastor Koon suffered a serious stroke and his recovery was difficult.

Upon the Todds return to the field in July 1982, the two chapels, Santa Mônica and Parque Taquaral, were down to one service a week. José Nilson of São José dos Campos spoke at Parque Taquaral as part of an evangelistic effort. The combined communion service for the two chapels in October counted thirteen present with twelve baptized membership. Eliete Cardoso, a young lady from the Capão de Imbuia church in Curitiba spent several weeks with Loraine in visitation and assisting in the Sunday school. She returned other times to work in the Campinas chapels. The rest of the year was spent working to strengthen believers and the ten faithful families at both chapels. Thus the year, 1982 ended with one adult member at Santa Monica and averaging twenty in Sunday school. Parque Taquaral had three adult members. Because of these meager results, Todd consulted the Field Chairman about the possibility of closing one of the chapels in order to be able to concentrate the effort in only one area.

At the 1983 National Council, Loraine was the delegate for the Campinas field. At the annual missionary conference, John was elected to the mission Executive Committee. Loraine became editor of the field paper- *The Brazil Bulletin*. Miss Regina Bartel arrived for language study in January; following language school she became the field secretary/bookkeeper. The Todds helped her get settled in a home and registered with the government in São Paulo as they also did with the second single worker, Rebecca Otero from Puerto Rico, who arrived late June.

Work continued in all three chapels but a consistent effort was increasingly difficult. Meetings with Alliance leaders and the field Executive Committee concerning the future for Campinas were held. A plan for the work presented by John Todd was accepted with the recommendation that one more year of intensive initiative be given before a final decision be made. Another church group the Todds had worked with in the bairro showed interest in the Santa Monica property; thus, *Brasil para Cristo* began to rent the building in mid 1983.

Pastor Koon died from a second major stroke in October 1983, a huge blow to his family, the Chinese church group, as well as the Alliance ministry in the city. He had been an integral part of the Campinas work from the very beginning. His gentle nature and sweet smile could always be counted on even in times of difficulty. His vision for Campinas carried on through his wife, Lucy, and children. Paulo Koon continued to labor in the Jardim Santana chapel with the help of several young men.

Beginning in 1984, the Todds faced a time of difficult decision making. At the annual mission conference held in

January, the decision made by the field mission staff was to close the work in Campinas. Inasmuch as no alternative position was available to the Todds, David Volstad and David Moore from the Alliance headquarters met with the Todds in February and their work with the Alliance was terminated. Until their return to the United States, the Todds continued to minister to those under their ministry in Campinas to prepare them for transition. Volstad and Moore asked John to survey the São Paulo metro area for a possible location for a new church-planting initiative in the great city. The results of that excellent survey became part of the strategy for establishing the new thrust by the Alliance into Brazil's greatest city.

In conclusion, the vision for Campinas given to both Pastor Koon and the Todds has been fulfilled in that both Santa Monica and Parque Taquaral chapels are being used by the Lord. The buildings have been enlarged and as of August, 2015, both were under being used by evangelical groups. *The Church of the Nazarene* ministers at the Parque Taquaral chapel while *Brasil para Cristo* continues to reach the Santa Mônica neighborhood. Paulo Koon had continued his father's ministry with the help of others and just recently, to the joy of all those who labored with Pastor Koon, Paulo, and the family, Paulo announced on July 30, 2016 the registration and inauguration of the Christian and Missionary Alliance Church of Campinas, located about three blocks from the first hall downtown where his father Pastor Koon Tu Sheun and John Todd began the work back in 1977. All to the Glory and perfect timing of God!!

Other Roots in the Amazon

The "Brazil Overview" article by Judy Jones found in the *Alliance Witness*, October 5, 1977, gives a panoramic

picture of the amazing expansion of the Alliance work in Brazil in less than twenty years. From the first roots planted in Brasília by the Japan Alliance, to those planted in Curitiba and Porto Alegre by the North American Alliance mission with an assist from the Argentine Alliance, the next tendril took root in São José dos Campos and produced the Vista Verde Church. In addition to the "Chinese" root planted by Pastor Koon, another penetrated the humid soil of *Amazonas*, planted by Pastor *Hernan Osorio Gomes and his wife, Edilma*, better known as "Mamita."

This veteran Alliance couple from Colombia had been originally challenged to go to Brazil as missionaries while attending a missions conference in Temuco, Chile in 1963, where Rev. Samuel Barnes gave an impassioned "Macedonian Cry" for help from other South American Alliance Churches. Thus sensing a call from God, they went to Brazil, living largely by faith with meager support and were able to plant two churches on the outskirts of *Manaus*, capital of the state of Amazonas. In 1977, the Osorios were called to pastor the Alliance Church in *Iquitos, Peru*, far up the Amazon from Manaus. The two churches in the bairros of *Santo Antonio* e *Compensa* requested affiliation with the Brazil Alliance.

Just a few years later, another Colombian Alliance missionary, *Daniel Tovar*, working deep in the heart of the Amazon on the border of Brazil, Colombia and Peru, invited David Jones to visit the Alliance churches that he had established in the three countries. He especially asked for help in Benjamin Constant, on the Brazilian side of the Solimões

River. The relationship had begun when the students of the *Instituto Bíblico Aliança* in Curitiba had raised money for the purchase of a canoe. Jones won the privilege of riding in the long canoe loaded to the gunnels with believers, riverbank dwellers, from Peru, Colombia and Brazil. The Sunday afternoon service was held on the banks of the mighty Solimões River in a big room built on pilings over the river's edge; it was unforgettable. These simple forest people had heard the message of Christ and their singing and worship was joyful and authentic. Thus this little congregation came to be counted as part of the Alliance work in Brazil.

To quote the *BRAZIL BULLETIN* – Summer 1980 edition: "GROWING, GROWING, GROWING . . ."

> What is it? Is it a weed, a fungus, a cancer? No!
> It's the Christian and Missionary Alliance in
> Brazil. We praise God for His abundant blessings
> upon the efforts of Alliance missionaries in
> Brazil. They planted a precious Seed in the early
> 1960's. With God's Son shining brightly, and
> showers of blessing, that Seed has taken root, in
> the garden of Brazil. Beginning from scratch in
> 1962, our garden has sprouted 17 churches in the
> intervening years which are located from
> Manaus in the extreme north 3,000 south to the
> Brazil-Uruguay border. Our gardeners number
> 10 missionary couples from the United States,
> one Colombian pastor, one Chinese pastor, and 4
> Brazilian pastors. . . . Following is a résumé of
> our 'fields'. Please pray for all as you can that our
> fruit will be further multiplied by the grace of
> God. *Benjamin Constant, Manaus, Brasília, São*

José dos Campos, Campinas, Curitiba, Porto Alegre, and *Santana do Livramento.*

The last few paragraphs of the "Brazil Overview" lay out the steps soon to be taken to organize these mission-led churches into an autonomous national church:

"Meanwhile, Brazilian leadership is flowering. Early next year [1978], the first annual Council of the Brazilian Christian and Missionary Alliance is scheduled to be held in Brasília, the city where it all started nineteen years ago. . . . The delegates will elect an executive committee, adopt a constitution and formally organize themselves as a national church within the fellowship of The Christian and Missionary Alliance.

Organization of the Christian and Missionary Alliance in Brazil—ACEMBRAS

Thus the next year, January 6-8, 1978, the First Annual Council of The Aliança Cristã e Missionária (ACEMBRAS) was held in the Federal District of Brasília, at the Gama Alliance Church planted back in the early 1960s by Japan Alliance missionary, Mutsuko Ninomiya. During those days, the meetings were presided over by Rev. Thomas Kyle, veteran Alliance missionary leader of the Brazil Field. Alliance church delegates arrived for the three days of meetings from Porto Alegre, Curitiba, São José dos Campos, Campinas and Brasília. The name, *Aliança Cristã e Missionária Brasileira (ACEMBRAS)*, was adopted as was the constitution and bylaws previously drawn up by the Pro-Tem Committee. The first national executive committee was elected, composed of:

President—Rev. João Alves da Costa (Gama)
Vice President—Pastor Sérgio Moraes Pinto (Porto Alegre)
Secretary—Sr. Noriyuki Kaji (Nûcleo Bandeirante)
Treasurer—Sr. Juan Nelber Nuñez (Curitiba)
Member at Large—Sr. Breno Bittencourt (Curitiba).

The executive committee was formally installed on Sunday, January 8, 1978, receiving prayer and the encouragement of those present. As described in an Alliance Witness note in the July 26, 1978 issue: "It was a precious scene to those who had poured out long years of prayer, work and tears. . . . The business sessions were a delightful balance of delegates, young and old, who together wrestled with the heavy issues facing a newly formed national church."

Thus ends this chapter which portrays the proliferation of roots and branches that sprang up in Brazil since the first steps made by the courageous missionary from Japan, Mutsuko Ninomiya, followed by the vision of veteran missionary Samuel Barnes, the innovative leadership of Tom Kyle and the cooperation of a brand-new missionary staff in a recently-opened mission field. The roots came from Simpson's original seed message of "the whole gospel for the whole man for the whole world," and the branches springing up all over Brazil came from that good seed.

CHAPTER EIGHT
BRASÍLIA AGAIN

Following the Brazil Mission's departure from Brasília in 1969, Japan Alliance missionary, Mutsuko Ninomiya, pressed on alone in the Federal District (FD). She continued to work in the two churches that she had planted. One was the largely Japanese congregation in Núcleo Bandeirante, and the other, a Brazilian congregation located in Gama. Pastor João Alves da Costa with his wife, Elsa, had been working with her for several years pastoring the Gama church. Both churches were growing and the Alliance work in the Federal District was gradually increasing; help was needed. So a request was sent to the Brazil Mission in the late 1970s to send a couple to help with the existing churches as well as expanding the ministry in the FD.

Consideration was given to the request and it was decided that despite being short-handed in southern Brazil, the growing ministry in the Center-West region merited attention. This decision was made in accordance with the recommendations from Mission leadership in North America, which specified that Brasília and Porto Alegre receive support in the areas of theological education, evangelism and church planting. As a result, following their furlough in mid-1979, Bob and Shirley Kallem were reassigned from Curitiba, where they had spent a positive first term shepherding the Capão da Imbuia Alliance Church. While there, they led the congregation in building a two-story Christian education wing with much-needed Sunday school room and additional office space. Now a new challenge lay before them, moving their family from the cool climate of Curitiba to the dry highlands of Central Brazil.

Gama FD Alliance Church

With their children, Brad and Bretta, they moved to Brazil's capital where they served for two terms. They went to work with the Gama Church, which was about to begin construction on a larger property some distance from the original lot where the first wooden meeting hall stood. The city government had condemned the old run-down church hall since it had been built in a residential zone. The church had obtained a large lot and was putting up a temporary structure. Bob's call to Brasília was providential for them since he was a builder and could greatly help in that area. The Kallems arrived in August 1979 and immediately began their new ministry. By September, they had thirty students from the Gama and Nûcleo Bandeirante churches enrolled in the Theological Education by Extension (TEE) program.

In March 1980, after the usual back and forth dealings with the local government, plans for the new building in Gama were approved and the cornerstone was laid, as well as the dedication of the portable structure where they held services till the permanent church was completed. By May 1981, the Brasília TEE Theological Education program had almost fifty students. In January 1982, the Fifth annual Council of ACEMBRAS was held in the new Gama building. The Council was a blessing to the church members in the Federal District. The business sessions accomplished all of the Council's agenda and the evening services saw the altar full of people seeking God. Historically, this was one of the most positive early Councils of ACEMBRAS, just before a time of testing began in church and mission.

After a year and a half in Brasília, the Kallem's "Station Report" for December 1980 indicated that they were in the FD (Federal District) to serve "all of the FD [Alliance] churches. We envision a move to a centralized location on the Asa Sul (South Wing) and setting up a 'district office'. This would be a service, not an authority." The report went on to describe the "center" as a location for the TEE ministry, a library for students and pastors, weekly Bible studies for Plano Pilôto contacts, providing a place for counseling and meetings. The Kallems recommended that a house be bought in the 703-705 blocks of the South Wing. The report and recommendation were ambitious but proved to be amazingly prescient and were largely realized in just a few years.

Taguatinga One More Time

In the meantime, with encouragement from Pastor João Costa of Gama and Missionary Ninomiya, an evangelistic outreach was launched in Taguatinga in 1982. This was the same satellite city where Emmit and Sandra Young had worked before David and Judy Jones arrived following language school in 1968. Due to the high rents, difficulties in obtaining property for a permanent building and the lack of fruit after several years of Alliance mission work in the FD, the Brasília staff had been moved south to Curitiba. Now, ten years later, the Lord seemed to be calling the mission to go back to the same place where it had previously struggled. In September 1979, the first Vacation Bible School was held in Taguatinga. This new initiative came about from another Alliance transplant.

Due to the continued economic difficulties in their homeland, another "Chilean root" took hold in Brazil. Francisco and Elba Pinilla, longtime Chilean Alliance members, moved to the FD in the early 1980s for the same reasons that Andrés Aburto and his family had moved to São José dos Campos. Francisco was a skilled carpenter and furniture maker and Elba worked in tourism. Kallems trained and encouraged them to prepare for ministry in their adopted land. Church planting seemed to be in the bones of Chilean Alliance folks. So in the latter part of 1982, *the Brazil Bulletin* announced that "Francisco and Elba [Pinilla], lay workers, have assumed the leadership of the congregation in [Taguatinga]. At the present time, they are meeting in a school house, but they need to find a more permanent home." For the next few years, the Kallems worked closely with the Pinillas in this church-planting project.

Plano Pilôto Project

Following their third furlough, David and Judy Jones, with their three sons (Thomas, Randy and Phil) were reassigned to Brasília and given the challenge of planting an Alliance Church in "The Pilot Plan" of downtown Brasília. The city plan, resembling a swept-wing jet airplane, was designed by Brazilian architect and urban planner, Lúcio Costa, back in the mid-1950s, when President Kubitschek's administration built the new capital city. The major Federal Government buildings located in the Plano Pilôto were designed by famed architect, Oscar Niemeyer. The overall city plan laid out distinct sectors for the big apartment blocks, banking, commerce, schools, churches, clubs and other associations. The capital city, Brasília, was and still is, populated by a middle-upper and upper class population. Most lower-level government workers live in the satellite cities and work in the capital. The whole Federal District

Randy, Phil, Dave, Judy and Tom Jones

is slightly larger than the US state of Rhode Island.

With no Alliance members in the Plano Pilôto, the Joneses began to plow on their knees before beginning to plant any seed. In consultation with pastors of other denominations in the capital, it was obvious that there were tens of thousands of unchurched *Brasilienses*. Over the next several months, they began to do "soil testing" to determine which, if any, affinity groups were proving to be responsive to the gospel. As a result, the Joneses, with an assist from the Kallems, hosted evangelistic dinners for distinct professional groups. In November 1983, Mr. Mike Feather, Vice President for Finance of the US Alliance, was the speaker at an event held at the *Hotel Nacional* attended by thirteen couples made up of bank managers and their wives. Feather gave his testimony as former president of a Florida bank; he told how God had called him to leave his lucrative position to serve God and the Alliance. No decisions were recorded but the feedback was very positive. In March 1984, Dr. John Eagan, then president of St Paul Bible College (now Crown College) in Minnesota, came to Brasília and twenty-six university professors, administrators and students attended. As was the case with Mr. Feather, Eagan's testimony and strong evangelistic message impacted the target audience. However, follow up visits were difficult to arrange and no lasting fruit resulted from the dinner meetings.

In the meantime, an important meeting between the ACEMBRAS Executive Directory was held with the Brazil Mission's Executive Committee, beginning March 5 1983. As stated in the Brazil Bulletin of May/June 1983:

> [The meeting] was time to consider a new 'Memorandum of Cooperation' between Mission and National Church. Rev. David Moore and Rev. David Volstad, representing the sending churches in the U.S. were on hand to participate. The National church leadership presented a survey of the Alliance Church in Brazil, sharing their burden that we had indeed reached a critical hour in the development of the Brazilian Alliance Church. In order to emphasize the crisis, the National Church made requests of the Mission which could not be granted. How we praise God for your intercession! Just when it appeared that no agreement could be reached, He met our need and provided divine wisdom. A new working agreement was not signed. However, Rev. Moore offered to create an international study team to evaluate the work in Brazil. The offer was unanimously received with joy. An official 'Study Agreement' was drawn up and signed by the twelve representatives of the Brazilian church and the Brazil Mission.

The five-man Study Commission, led by Dr. Arnold Cook, Vice-President for Overseas Ministries in Canada, was in Brazil from November 26 to December 12, visiting all of the mission stations where they interviewed missionaries and national workers, as well as meeting with other evangelical mission and church leaders. "The result of the study commission that came down in November and December has been a big bomb! The field is being changed back to the status of an unorganized field, with a Board Representative. (Jones letter – Jan. 11, 1984)" Thus just three short years after attaining to "Organized" field status with an elected field chairman and executive committee with relative autonomy, the Brazil Mission was once again under the direct administration of the Regional Director for South America for the North American C&MA.

Other decisions made by the Study Team's recommendations called for measures to resolve the tension between Mission and National Church, that "a field strategy for urban church growth" be developed to plant strong central churches in Porto Alegre and São Paulo, and that "current ministries" elsewhere in Brazil be maintained. Thus, by the absence of mention, it was apparent that the Brasília church-planting project was not eliminated but also would not receive any additional personnel or support. The overall effect of the Study Team's findings was to take initiative from the field missionaries and return it to the Division of Overseas Ministries of the U.S. C&MA. The general feeling among the missionary staff was discouragement.

At the next Council of ACEMBRAS held in Curitiba, early January 1984, a new executive directory was elected and the former national church president resigned from ACEMBRAS. The council was on edge at times and reflected the impasse that had occurred when the Mission and ACEMBRAS leadership were unable to agree on a new working agreement earlier in 1983. However, the final Council results were positive and a marked improvement over the last two years.

These were difficult days for the Brazil Alliance Churches well as the Mission, which held its Field Conference in Curitiba from January 22 to 25. Like ACEMBRAS's Council that had just ended, the conference was tense where clear differences of mission philosophy, ministry practice and field placement were dealt with. The conference decisions led to the eventual resignation of John and Loraine Todd after two terms of service with the Brazil Mission and the closing of mission ministry in Campinas. The Chinese Alliance work begun by the Koon Family continued and eventually was given strong assistance by the Chinese Alliance Church of Suriname.

Immediately after the Mission Field Conference, Bob Kallem had a major medical crisis with severe bleeding ulcers that required two surgeries and multiple transfusions. Due to his serious health condition and long recovery, the Kallems received an early health furlough. Consequently, the Jones assumed responsibility for the Centro Bíblico Aliança (CBA) and the Theological Extension (TEE) program. In June 1984, Miss Rebecca Otero of Puerto Rico finished language school and was assigned to Brasília to work with the TEE program as well as assisting the Pinillas in Taguatinga.

Bob and Shirley Kallem
Brasília FD

After the better part of a year, the "Brasília nut" had not yet been cracked open and the future of the church-planting project seemed to be in limbo following the Study Commission's report. Yet

God providentially broke through. Years before, on August 1972, the night before the Joneses were to return to the U.S. for their first furlough, a young man from the Capão da Imbuia Church alleged that he had been "robbed," and had lost a large sum of a jewelry store's money. Jones had unwisely co-signed a note as guarantor so that the young man could get a job. Now, Jones was going to have to come up with the money before traveling the next day. No, don't panic! Missionary colleague, Darrell Smith, introduced Jones to a lawyer friend. And in a matter of a few hours, the lawyer, Dr. Luis Dotto, had revealed that the "robbery" was a scam and he resolved the problem. The Joneses breathed a sigh of relief and took off for the United States with their boys. Ten years later, that one-time relationship was about to be renewed.

A Divine Coincidence

The Joneses were at a local supermarket. On their mind was the question, "How do we reach this target group of the professionals of Brasília?" Dave followed Judy around the store, when suddenly a shout, "Pastor David!" woke him from his reverie. "Pastor David, what are you doing here?" And amazingly, on the other side of the supermarket was Dr. Luis Dotto, the lawyer, now a Federal District judge. He came over and gave the Joneses a big hug and asked again, "What are you doing here in Brasília?" "We live here," was their reply. Dotto then asked what they were doing. "We're trying to reach the middle-upper class professionals of Brasília and plant a church." Dotto's eyes gleamed, "God has sent you here!" Then he proceeded to tell about a Bible study that he had begun in his apartment for professionals, university law school students and friends. This was the exact target group that the Jones were trying to reach. Dotto said, "I have been teaching them, trying to share the gospel with them, and have kind of run dry. You need to come to my apartment this week and speak to them." Thus in early March 1984, God began to crack the tough Brasília nut.

The August 2, 1984 Jones prayer letter reads:

> Through a chance encounter with a Christian Federal Judge [Dr. Dotto], we were invited to [speak] to a group of people that he had invited to his home . . . army colonels, lawyers, teachers, university students were among those that made up this group. Beginning in April, we met with these people preaching and teaching the Word; and since that time, seven people have been born again: some lawyers, a school teacher, a university student and the judge's son. Several have been delivered from occult and Spiritist beliefs and practices. God is blessing and we request your prayer. Four people have asked to be baptized, and our first baptismal will be held in later September.

After Dotto invited him to speak to the group, Jones had a few days to think and pray about what to say. As he began to actually consider it, fear came into his heart. Here at last were the people that they were trying to meet and a whole apartment would be filled with them. "Intellectuals, professionals, university students – these are all educated people. I've got to say something . . . what?" Then the Lord spoke quietly. "David, tell them what you know that they don't. Tell them about Jesus. He's the One they need to know." That's always good advice to follow.

That Friday night, after a short word of introduction by Judge Dotto, Jones opened his Bible and invited those that had one to do the same. Since he had brought a box of Bibles along, everyone had a copy. He gave the page number and directed them to John 3 and read the story of Nicodemus the rich, well-educated Jewish religious leader. At night, embarrassed and maybe a bit ashamed, he came to Jesus to ask Him a vital question. As Jones told the story the listeners quickly forget that here was an American pastor in a Brazilian judge's apartment telling them about a Jewish carpenter rabbi who lived two thousand years before.

Jones told how Jesus answered Nicodemus' question . He told him how he could enter God's kingdom by the "new birth" and receive eternal life. They walked through John 3 and arrived at verse 16 where they landed on the truth that God loved "the world" so much that "He gave His only son, Jesus, to live, die and resurrect from the dead to redeem us from our sin." The group was silent the whole time, no questions, no yawning. God had prepared the moment and His Spirit was speaking. At the end, Jones made no "invitation." He just told them that they would be back next week for more Bible study and closed in prayer. The Judge then invited everyone to drink some "suco de cajú" (Cashew juice) and we socialized.

Immediately, a tall, good-looking man came up to Dave and said, in perfect English with a slight British accent: "My, you speak Portuguese almost as well as I speak English.!" Jones was non-plussed and didn't know if that was a compliment or a wisecrack. So, he smiled and said, "Thanks." Then his wife and daughter came up and remarked, "Isn't it amazing that you spoke tonight from the very passage in the Bible that we had been puzzling over this week, about the new birth. Now we understand; it's so clear. Many thanks." And that was our introduction to Dr. Coreolano Fagundes, the director of the Ministry of Justice's Federal Bureau of Censorship. He and his wife, Marisa, and daughter, Monique, had been reading the Bible and reciting the Lord's Prayer nightly in their apartment after returning home from work for more than a year. They had been involved in a variety of esoteric, occult groups and Spiritist practices in their own home. Supernaturally, by the Spirit, they had been convinced that the Bible contained the answer to their questions and that "Jesus was the way."

For the next seven weeks, the Joneses returned to Judge Dotto's apartment and taught from the Word. Jones did not follow a sequence, and sometimes "jumped around" the Bible as the Lord guided. Amazingly, every week when the passage was announced, the Fagundes family would smile and point and whisper. Sometimes it was distracting. At the end, they would come up and say, "You did it again; you talked about what we were reading this week." This became a pattern and Jones felt pressure building up, like surfing on the crest of the wave and about to wipe out. But God was in charge and he didn't "wipe out." After two months of meetings, the Lord spoke clearly to Jones. "This week you are going to close the deal." "What do you mean, close the deal?" The Lord replied, "This week, you must give them a chance to receive salvation, to believe in Christ and be saved." "No Lord, it's too early." The answer came back, "No, this is the time." A struggle began because Jones was afraid to confront those dear new friends, afraid to tell them they needed to be saved, afraid that they might refuse and leave. "No, Lord, it's too early." God responded: "Now is the time. Do it."

That Friday, the day of the next Bible study, while Jones wrestled with the Lord, he read from Joshua 24, where Moses' successor challenged the children of Israel to choose whom they would serve, and God nudged him. "OK, Lord, I'll do it, but I still think it's too soon." So he prepared and went to the Judge's apartment. He gave the Scripture reference, Joshua 24, and once again, the Fagundes family pointed at the passage and smiled. Jones told the story of how God had freed Israel from Egypt, walked them through the Red Sea to Mount Sinai where He gave them the Ten Commandments, followed by thirty-nine years of wilderness wandering, the miraculous Jordan crossing, Jericho, and the conquest of the Promised Land. Most had never heard the epic story of God's awesome deliverance of His people, and listened intently. Then Joshua brought his story to a head. "You need to choose today whom you are going to serve, whether the gods which your forefathers served beyond the Euphrates in Abraham's time or the gods of the pagan peoples of this land. "But as for me and my house, we will serve the Lord."

Then Jones went on to explain that they had been reading and studying God's Word for two months, and it was clear that God was calling for a decision, just as Joshua did. Either to believe and receive and serve Him, or to continue in their old ways. Jones closed the study time with a "sinner's prayer" that they could follow in their hearts to give their lives totally to Christ. As soon as the "Amen" was pronounced, the Fagundes family came rushing over and said that God had spoken to them that very week; they had to decide between Him and Spiritism. They later explained that Monique had been a spiritist medium, and that she had "received spirits" many times. That night, they finally realized that these "spirits" were not from God but from Satan. Right there, Monique and her mother, Marisa, received Christ as Lord and Savior. Coreolano, was very supportive, but he had not bowed his knee to the Lord yet. That night began a new phase in the Brasília ministry.

About that same time, the Kallems left for their early

health furlough on May 24 1984, and by mid-June, the Bible study group had moved over to the Centro Bíblico Aliança (Alliance Bible Center) on 503 South Wing, the same place that the Kallems had opened believing that it would become a center of preaching and teaching in Brasília. The twenty or so new believers became the core group of the Alliance church in Brasília. Over the next several years this small congregation touched many hard-to-reach professionals. During this period, Brazil underwent the amazing transition from a military régime which ended peacefully in 1984 with the reestablishment on democratic government.

Former governor and federal senator from the state of Goiás, Dr. Osiris Teixeira and his wife, Dona Lídia, were saved through the prayer ministry of the Centro Bíblico Aliança. Dr. Osiris had been a state deputy in Goiás, then interim governor and federal senator, as well as the Grand Master of the Masons of Brazil. After meeting with him and together looking into Masonry's teaching, he realized that to be a follower of Jesus was to be a follower of the Bible alone and not other "sacred books" of the world's religions. Subsequently, he resigned from the Masons. Although he suffered professional and personal opposition, he remained faithful to Christ. Eventually following an abdominal aneurism and a botched surgery to repair it, he was left paralyzed and eventually died in October 1989. At his funeral in Brasília's major cemetery, D. Lídia and her family and members of the CBA were able to give testimony to the fact that Jesus Christ was the Lord of his life, and that his home in heaven came from Christ's good work, and not his acts of kindness and charity.

Following the move to the Centro, we began to face open opposition from one of the men who had previously attended the Bible studies at the judge's apartment. He called and visited those attending the Centro and discouraged them from doing so. Rumors were spread that the Joneses worked for the CIA and that they were "religious colonizers and spiritual imperialists." The attack definitely affected attendance. By the second half of 1985, attendance was limping along with less than ten attending the Thursday night and Sunday meeting. Yet, despite the small group, offerings were strong and the congregation was able to pay the rent on the Centro Bíblico after the mission rental subsidy was discontinued.

In December 1985, a special meeting was held with Rev. Caio Fábio D'Araujo, president of VINDE evangelistic association and Brazil's foremost emerging evangelical leader. As part of the Centro's ministry effort, CBA sponsored the national book signing event for his just-published book, "Abrindo o Jogo no Aborto," (Telling the Truth About Abortion). Through Dr. Teixeira's influence, the use of the Federal Senate's auditorium was secured where Caio Fábio spoke against the scourge of abortion in Brazil, and then signed books for the large crowd that had gathered. By having the Alliance sponsor this event they garnered a lot of good will, but brought no lasting results. For two years in a row, the CBA hosted an Alliance concert pianist from Illinois, Mr. Richard Diehl, who presented musical programs where he shared the Gospel through his testimony in shopping centers as well as the Centro Bíblico. Every kind of opportunity to spread the Gospel and call people's attention to the Alliance's ministry was attempted.

The "B-Team," the nickname adopted by the Brasília missionaries, was in a spiritual battle and used all of the weapons of spiritual warfare at their disposal with like-minded prayer partners. They prayer-walked, targeting the many Spiritist groups head-quartered in the nation's capital, and fought to break Satan's strongholds in the Federal District.

**The B Team: Dave and Judy Jones,
Dave and Sue Manske,
Bob and Shirley Kallem,
Tim and JoLee Bubna**

They also took a page from the Noah's Ark ministry in Porto Alegre and began to reach out to the families living in the residential superblocks that never darkened the door of the church. Crowds of children and parents weekly received the gospel through the antics of Juvina Donzela (lyric soprano who sang in the best opera houses of the interior of Goiás), as well as Mrs. Noah, Melo Camelo, Bicudo the Parrot and others. Lynette Kyle, daughter of missionary colleague, Tom Kyle, and teacher at the American School of Brasília, worked with the team and Ark ministry. She sang at many special events and dinners and was a welcome addition to the church worship team.

Despite dividing time between the church-planting ministry and teaching at the TEE center, the team had a small but committed core group. Well-known Christian counselor and psychologist, Dr. Esly Carvalho, became part of the CBA and brought many of her professional colleagues to the church services. She was an important contact person for the Centro till she moved to Ecuador.

At the same time, the Alliance church in Gama was in its new building and experiencing growth. In Taguatinga, the congregation had moved into their new building by mid-1985 and the work was progressing. The Pinillas continued leading Taguatinga until 1992 when they left, and Miss Denise de Oliveira, who had received her training at the Centro Bíblico's TEE extension school, was appointed leader of the congregation by the District leadership. She continued until Pastor Milton and Lídia Oliveira transferred from the Gama Alliance Church where they served with Pastor João Costa Junior. The Oliveiras led the Taguatinga Church for three years with the church enjoying a major growth spurt with more than 100 attending. During that period, they enlarged the facility to accommodate the growth. In 1996, the Oliveiras were called to return to Curitiba where they became pastors of the Capão da Imbuia Church.

In the meantime, the TEE extension center of the Instituto Bíblico Aliança of Curitiba, continued to serve the Alliance Churches of the Federal District, as well as those students who came from other evangelical churches. While small, the group was growing. Bob and Shirley Kallem returned to the field in May 1986 after an extended furlough in the United States due to Bob's slow recovery from surgery. Their return helped reinforce the Brasília Team. By 1987, Sunday attendance had grown to twenty-two weekly, a growth of 150%. Offerings were up and the congregation was paying half for the rent of the Centro Bíblico, with the rental for the IBA extension program covered by the Mission. The church was sending 25% of a minimum salary to the Alliance pastor in Manaus, supporting the Brasília Alliance Camp in Cocalzinho, Goiás, as well as supporting ACEMBRAS and other Christian ministries.

Celebration of the Centennial

With Alliance churches in Nûcleo Bandeirante, Gama and Taguatinga, as well as the church planting in progress in the Pilot Plan, there was a strong sense of identity as "The Alliance," which resulted in an important event in 1987, the centennial year of the foundation of The Christian and Missionary Alliance by Dr. A. B. Simpson. Thus in June of that year, a Centennial Celebration was held. More than 160 members and friends of the Alliance, from the four Churches of the Alliance of the Federal District participated in the Centennial Celebration on June 28, held in the beautiful auditorium of the "Juscelino Kubitschek Memorial." This special celebration featured a missionary parade with the flags of nations, a combined choir of the ACM Churches of the Federal District singing Alliance hymns, as well as other special music. "A full-sized oil painting of Simpson was done by D. Lídia Teixeira and was unveiled at the centennial program. The meeting was concluded by an powerful missionary challenge and a call for commitment made by international evangelist and former C&MA missionary to Brazil, Rev. Tom Kyle. We thank the Lord for the dozens who responded to the altar call and we trust that the ministry and the message of the Alliance will continue to grow in Brazil" (Jones Prayer Letter, January to March 1987).

ABA- The Brasília Alliance Camp

A major milestone of the Federal District of ACEMBRAS was the acquisition of a 100+ acre campsite in Cocalzinho, Goiás, truly another "God thing." Over the years the Alliance churches in the FD had followed the practice of other churches, holding youth retreats over the long Carnaval weekend to help the young Christians to grow in their faith and not be drawn back into the sinful practices that characterized Carnaval. After holding a few retreats at less-than-adequate facilities, the district leadership began to pray and ask God for an answer. Soon an excellent site was located outside the Federal District, about 100 kilometers out of town. The property was owned by a Wycliffe missionary who wanted to sell; his asking price was $5,000. Through gifts received from the Japan Alliance

Churches, Miss Ninomiya was able to donate the needed funds and the property was purchased in 1985. Groups from the FD churches worked on the scrub forest, clearing land for buildings and preparing for construction. A well was dug and camps were held

ABA—Brasilia Alliance Camp

under tarps and tents. Beginning in 1987 and continuing over the next several years, work teams from the Eastern District of the U. S. C&MA, led by Rev. Don Reitz of Watsontown PA, came down to help develop the camp. Most of the important structures was built by these hard-working Alliance men and women. Over the years, five teams led by Don Reitz blessed the camp with several buildings and important camp facilities. The Brasília Alliance Camp, *Acampamento Brasiliense Aliança*, continues to bless the churches of the Center-West District of the Alliance today.

The Joneses furloughed in mid 1988 and Kallems continued the ministry with the addition of a new missionary couple, Tim and JoLee Bubna and their three sons in January 1988, after finishing language school. When the Jones returned in mid 1989, they found the church struggling even though two new members had been added and the finances were still solid. An Evangelism Explosion ministry was begun to bring others to faith in Christ. Another missionary couple, Dave and Sue Manske, still in language school, was appointed to be part of the "B-Team," which was helpful since the Kallem's furlough was soon to arrive. Three evangelistic campaigns were held in 1989 with a total of eleven decisions for Christ.

The Brasília Church-Planting Report – 1989 - outlined the drop in attendance, a 450% increase in the rental costs for the Centro Bíblico Aliança while facing the galloping inflation that crushed Brazil's economy in the late 1980s. The last paragraph of the report stated: "In closing, this report has attempted to reflect the reality of a difficult year, but one that has not crushed us, nor taken away our hope." Thus the B-Team began the new decade of the 1990's with hope, which was soon tested.

After the first two months of 1990, when ACEMBRAS Concílio was held followed by the Mission Retreat, the B-Team began EE III training, the Alliance Women's Federation held their retreat in Brasília, and eight students received certificates for completing the "Pastoral Compendium" course. The Kallems furloughed on May 11 and the Manskes arrived by the 31st of the same month. Tim Bubna led the EE III ministry and saw two decisions for Christ made at local malls. An Alliance evangelistic musical group from Argentina, *Trio Mar del Plata*, ministered at the CBA from August 24 to 26 with excellent attendance and six persons praying for salvation. Then after these hopeful signs came the final blow.

> It was at this same time that our rental contract had its trimestral increase from CR$ 140.000,00 to CR$ 188.000,00 (US$ 2,200), bringing us to a financial crisis and crossroad. Since the negotiations of the new contract in May, which had an 826% increase over the previous year, the rent had [gone] beyond the combined efforts of the church and mission. From June through August, the rent had put the ministry in the "red." (Brasília Station Report – 1990.)

The Mission Advisory Committee met that same month of August 1990 and recommended that the CBA be moved to a more economical location and to give one more year to the Brasília project. Shortly thereafter the Field Director, Steve Renicks, discussed this recommendation with the B-Team and it was concluded "that the [advisory committee] recommendation would only prolong a decision that had to be made immediately. The rationale of the team was that if the church was not growing [while] located in a good area with good visibility, how would it grow if moved to a less-visible and accessible location? . . . So the painful decision was made to close the work."

Thus, the church members were notified at a special meeting in early September and the final service was held on September 23 with seventy-five people present. About half of the active members (13) had already found new church homes and were moving forward in their Christian walk. The sudden decision to close forced upon the B-Team by the crushing rental increase and the lack of growth and solidity after more than seven years of work on the Brasília church-planting project was difficult to understand. As a result of the decision, the Manskes were reassigned to move south and take up work with the Porto Alegre mission team. By year's end, the Bubnas had returned to North America for furlough, and the Joneses were reassigned to work with the São Paulo church-planting project in the South Zone of the city. In addition, they were sent to there to re-open the Instituto Bíblico Aliança, which had been closed in Curitiba.

CHAPTER NINE
SÃO PAULO
A NEW HORIZON

More than twenty years of ministry had passed since the U.S. Alliance mission entered Brazil. By 1983 there were a total of 13 national churches and 317 church members on the Brazil Alliance field. The numbers seemed small when compared to other missions who had arrived around the same time in Brazil, and to some of the other countries where the U.S. Alliance worked in South America. National pastors were few and there was only one ordained pastor. Morale was low among missionaries. Tensions existed concerning ministry strategies. Conflict also existed between national leaders and the mission. Some of the missionaries labeled the 80's as the "lost decade." However, it proved to be a watershed period in the history of the Brazil Alliance, between scattered ministries in smaller cities and concentrated efforts in large urban settings. During this decade a new direction dawned on a very broad horizon.

Due to these factors, a Study Team was sent by the U.S. Alliance national office to Brazil to look, listen and advise. In November 1983 the group arrived in Brazil; Franklin Irwin, missionary to the Philippines; Walter Perez, PhD, Argentine pastor; Rev. Humberto Lay from Peru; Samuel Wilson, PhD, former missionary to Peru and seminary professor; as well as Arnold Cook, PhD, former missionary and vice-president of personnel and missions of the Canadian Alliance. They spent two weeks and split up into two groups visiting all the cities where the Alliance had worked, except for Manaus in the north and Santana do Livramento in the south. One group traveled north to São José dos Campos, Campinas, Brasília and São Paulo. The other group spent time in Curitiba and went further south to Porto Alegre. São Paulo was the only city visited where the Alliance had no workers.

At this time, the largest city in Brazil in which Alliance missionaries had worked was Porto Alegre, the eighth largest city. São Paulo, the largest city in Brazil, and one of the largest cities in the world, seemed too big and expensive to know where or how to begin a church planting movement. It was believed that the meager finances and Alliance personnel were not great enough to make a viable presence in this mega-city of 9 million inhabitants at that time.

The 1983 study team made some evaluations that were painful to existing staff, but also gave concrete suggestions and visionary directives for existing works. The biggest change was that the mission was to establish a church planting movement in São Paulo, move the mission office and the "Alliance Bible Institute" from Curitiba to this city, making São Paulo a central hub for Alliance ministries in Brazil. By the end of the decade, a church had been started, the mission office moved and a Bible Institute was begun. In five years' time the basic suggestions for São Paulo had been put into action.

Entry into São Paulo

During the summer of 1984 Jim and Billie Jo Medin returned from their year's home assignment to the city of

Curitiba. A big change was about to happen in their lives; they had been recommended by the national office and the study team to spearhead the work in São Paulo and they were willing to go. In the face of this daunting task, Jim was encouraged by a quote: "Church planting is not a skill but an attitude." Jim's attitude propelled him into a period of studying the city in a tangible way, leaving Curitiba every month for the next nine months, staying 4-5 days each time in Sao Paulo, and visiting a total of 25 different church leaders. By March 1985, Jim and Billie took the plunge and moved to Cidade Dutra in southern São Paulo where they lived in the apartment complex of Green Village.

They started the church plant by leading two different Bible studies. One Bible study included two couples who lived in the southern zone of São Paulo, in the Jabaquara/ Campo Belo area. Sergio and Lidia Kamiyama,

Chácará Flora – São Paulo

the principal couple, were already Christians and had been part of the Vista Verde Alliance church in São José dos Campos, located an hour and a half northeast of the city of São Paulo before they moved to São Paulo. The Kamiyamas brought a couple who were their neighbors to the study. Jim and Billie Jo had previously worked in São José and had forged a friendship with the Kamiyamas.

The second Bible study was linked to Ricardo Lemos, a Brazilian of Presbyterian background who had attended the Alliance Theological Seminary in Nyack, NY. His presence in

Brazil was brought to the Medin's attention through the Alliance national office, with the hope of having national leadership from the beginning of the church plant. Ricardo participated in this second Bible study briefly before returning to the United States. He introduced a key couple to the Bible study, Carlos (Bebeto) and Deborah Bueno. Through Ricardo and the Buenos several younger couples were reached, some of these were from the Presbyterian Church in Lapa.

During this initial time the Medins hosted a Brazilian barbecue commemorating Jim's 40th birthday. Also, the two Bible study groups started meeting together for Sunday services at the Methodist Institute in Chácara Flora, a retreat center in the southern zone of São Paulo, where some international schools were located. It was a beautiful wooded area. At the one-year anniversary of the congregation there were 56 people present. During the Medins' three years in São Paulo a handful of people were baptized, a retreat was held, as well as Christmas and Valentine's dinners and a congregation was formed.

In January 1986, a second study team came to São Paulo with David Moore, Vice President for the Division of Overseas Ministries, David Volstad, regional director for Latin American, and David Peters the field director for Colombia and the strategic leader for Bogota "Encounter with God" (Encuentro con Dios) to see how the São Paulo project was progressing. At this time David and Arlene Peters, Canadian Alliance missionaries, were invited by David Moore to come to São Paulo as church planting project leaders. Their experience in Bogota, with the multiplication of churches and working with a church planting team, was desirable to have.

Encounter with God (Encontro com Deus) was a church planting strategy that was started by the Alliance in Lima, Peru

in the 1970s. It became a
powerful movement of the
Holy Spirit that grew to
reach   thousands   of
people, and plant many
churches. The principles
which were transferred to
some   other   Latin
American countries and
other churches outside of
the Alliance were these:

Dave and Arlene Peters

begin with fervent prayer; have a concentration of resources,
both human and financial; constant and dynamic evangelism;
systematic discipleship; development of leaders and pastors;
work in teams; have a vision for multiplication of churches; a
spirit of unity; church buildings located in strategic locations
and the expansion of missions to the ends of the earth.

Since part of the Encounter with God strategy was to
begin with adequate personnel resources, the U.S. national
office gave backing to the project and São Paulo began receiving
an influx of Alliance missionaries. In the second half of 1986,
Len and Diane Warden, Michael and Ruth Davis and Tim and
Jo Lee Bubna arrived. In 1987 Jeff and Jo Kiel, David and
Arlene Peters, Paul and Bev Clark arrived; and in early 1988,
Doug and Helen White arrived. Seven couples and a dozen
children were a huge boost to the missionary staff in Brazil.
Five of the couples remained in São Paulo after finishing their
language studies. The Kiels went to the south to Porto Alegre
and the Bubnas went north to Brasilia but returned to São
Paulo for their second term. In 1990 Charlotte Hisle arrived as
a new missionary, and David and Judy Jones transitioned from
Brasilia in 1991. Jim and Ann Hemminger came to São Paulo

from Curitiba in 1991 along with Regene Bartl. In later years more workers followed: Dave and Sue Manske, Alex and Julie Zell, Marshall and Teresa Erickson, James and Nikki Chung, Barbara Bradshaw, Ruth Strubbie, all of whom worked in São Paulo, and other families who then transitioned to the Porto Alegre team.

Brooklin Alliance Church Begins

On July 4, 1987, the second day after the Peters' arrival in São Paulo, Dave Peters and Len Warden were out walking the streets looking for a new place for the church to meet that would have more visibility than the chapel at Chácara Flora. High visibility on a main avenue is one of the Encounter with God principles. Several neighborhoods in the southern zone of the city were considered because of their rapid growth. Eventually, the Santo Amaro area was targeted. It had doubled in size from 1970-1980. Therefore, an ample storefront was found on 247 Princesa Isabel Street, in Brooklin. Church services started in this location on November 15, 1987. To facilitate having the building open and available to the public, plans were made to have a Christian bookstore in the front of the building. Initially Bethany Publications was present, connected to David Haase, a Bethany International missionary who was attending the Brooklin Alliance church. Later, Christian Literature Crusade used the space. It should be noted that both these publishers and Mundo Cristão (Christian World) had translated, published and were selling books by Alliance authors; A.B. Simpson, A.W. Tozer, Keith Bailey and Neill Foster. The presence of the bookstore not only kept the church doors open, but offered literature that paralleled the message people heard in services and Bible studies during the week.

Another "Encounter with God" strategy that was successful in Lima, Peru and Bogota, Colombia was to hold two week long evangelistic campaigns followed by two weeks of intense discipleship. Although similar campaigns were tried in São Paulo with people such as Tom Kyle, David Jones, Roy LeTourneau, Nazarene Pastor Aguiar from Campinas, the Trio Mar del Plata from Argentina and Companhia de Jesus, a Brazilian band out of Goiânia, the campaigns did not produce the same results as in other countries. Getting to church meetings every night of the week was difficult in the mega city of São Paulo; thus the campaigns were limited to weekends. However, the São Paulo church was made visible, evangelism and conversions did occur and there was a lot of joy in the hosting.

The two-pronged thrust of evangelism and discipleship were still important tenets of the São Paulo church planting movement. Arlene Peters' goal was to see that every person in the church be discipled. The "Be An Approved Workman" course, based on the Gospel of Matthew, was predominantly used for believers. This six volume, programmed-learning compendium has been used around the world to train leaders and pastors. It became a requirement for leaders in the Brooklin church, where, after completing the first two volumes of the course, the disciple needed to be involved in some sort of ministry or service. New believers were ushered into the Abundant Life course, or some type of new believer's class.

First Alliance Church – Princesa Isabel, Brooklin, São Paulo

Discipleship was especially important as almost every person who came to the church needed spiritual deliverance from the occult. This coincided with an observation made by the study team in 1983 that there was a need to have missionaries who had discernment and experience in dealing with the demonic.

In God's sovereignty, people were drawn to the church that gave influence and direction. Soccer players, particularly from the "Juventus Soccer Club" started attending. One of them was Marcelo Dorigo, now an Alliance pastor of the Taboão church in São Paulo. Another player was Claudinei Franzini who worked in the CLC bookstore in the Brooklin Church; he followed a career in Christian publishing and now is in educational administration. Another player, Tomaz Oliveira, came; prior to receiving Christ, he was known as "Indian" because of his wild lifestyle. Today he continues as a part of the Airport Alliance church, formerly named the Brooklin Alliance Church. They came wanting to be discipled, and they attracted the presence of other young people. In the same way, José Freitas, part of a ministry sports group, LEVAI, also started attending. Later, he became part of the staff and then head pastor of the Airport Church and has served as the national church president and missions director of the Brazil Alliance (ACEMBRAS).

From the church's inception, music and worship were important parts of the ministry and Sunday services. Gifted missionaries trained young people as keyboardists, guitar and bass players, as well as worship leaders. Teams of music ministers were eventually formed. Often, there were special Sundays when the entire service was dedicated to praise and worship music. At one Easter praise service, there was a time for anointing and prayer for healing. At that time a young couple, Joel and Andrea Konno, who later became ACEMBRAS pastors and missionaries, came forward to be anointed. Previously, a doctor had told them it would be difficult for them to be able to conceive and have children. That night, or soon after, a miracle took place and today they have two children. At times worship played a vital part in the deliverance ministry. Early on at the Princesa Isabel building, at a Wednesday evening prayer meeting, during the singing of the hymn "Holy, Holy, Holy", a demonized man jumped up and starting screaming "Stop," threw off his glasses, and ripped off his shirt with buttons popping in all directions. Dave Peters' wise counsel to the musician was "Just, keep singing." The man was dealt with on the side and praise to the living God continued front and center.

In a parallel vein, a musical group from church members in the São Paulo district was formed in the 1990's, with leaders Akira Fukuura, Glaucia Freitas and the Davises. The purpose of this group was two-pronged: to develop musicians in theory, practice and spiritually. As the group progressed they were called upon to sing at church anniversaries and missions conferences in the district. Quality musicians and leaders came through the group and their purpose was explained by their name "Jesus Only," exalting Jesus through music.

Another musician, Alícia Lauinger and family were transferred to São Paulo from Chile because of her husband's job with the German chemical company, BASF. They became part of the Brooklin Alliance church, having been members of the Alliance in Chile. Alícia played the piano and also wanted to see women's ministries develop. With the help of Arlene Peters, monthly ladies teas were started patterned after Campus Crusade for Christ's "Teas with a Purpose." It gave women an opportunity to know and serve one another. The existence of women's ministries in the Airport Alliance Church connected the São Paulo women to the national organization of Alliance women in Brazil. Alícia did everything first class to the point of renting tablecloths and matching dishes when the church had none.

In 1989, Josiane Lopez from Curitiba trained Ruth Davis in how to do Vacation Bible School the Brazilian way. 3,000 to 4,000 invitations were printed and distributed in mailboxes and about 80 children came. The Bible School was held in the afternoons for a week in July. Josiane said the school should begin daily with a march around the city block as an activity for the children and for publicity. That is what she had done in Curitiba. In São Paulo, the march only lasted for two days since the street behind Princesa Isabel was Avenida Santo Amaro, a main and busy artery of the city. It was potentially dangerous even on the sidewalk with so many children, and it stopped traffic.

In 1991 Dave and Judy Jones moved to São Paulo from Brasilia. Charlotte Hisle arrived as a new missionary. Dave and Judy restarted the "Instituto Bíblico Aliança" (IBA) that first met in the Princesa Isabel church building. Charlotte had a great impact on the Bible Institute as well as in discipleship ministries. Also in 1991 Jim and Ann Hemminger transferred from Curitiba after having closed the IBA and mission office, then moving all of the furniture and files to São Paulo. The office located in a building across the street from the Brooklin Alliance Church on Princesa Isabel during their first week in São Paulo. The building later doubled as IBA's home. This difficult move, which was well done, took a toll on Jim's health and the Hemmingers resigned in May 1991. However, they returned to Brazil in the next decade to work in southern Brazil.

During the early stages of the church plant still meeting

in the Brooklin area, there were those who attended who went on to become pastors and missionaries. Jorge Bazo, a Peruvian, who was studying at O Seminário Palavra da Vida (Word of Life Bible Seminary) in Atibaia, came with his wife Antonieta and family on weekends to work as an intern in the Brooklin church. They mainly worked with the youth group. Later the Bazo family went as independent missionaries to Spain. Abísaí Nunes, another student at Word of Life, originally from Brasília, visited the Warden family on weekends and came to church with them. Biza, as he is affectionately known, had come to Christ through Len Warden's ministry at a camp in Brasilia and they maintained contact. The Bubnas also knew him from their first year of working in Brasilia. As of this writing, Biza is the president of the Brazilian national church. Another man, Abiezer Avelino da Silva, who had read Tozer's books, contacted the editor to find out where the Christian & Missionary Alliance existed in Brazil, particularly in the São Paulo region. He felt that Tozer summed up his theology and doctrinal stance and wanted to find an Alliance church. He came about once a month from Itatiba, a forty-minute drive from São Paulo and completed the "Be An Approved Workmen" six-manual study program in record time.

Birth of the Itatiba Congregation

In the early 90's, Abiezer da Silva began holding meetings in his home in Itatiba. The Brazilian national church bylaws said that every new church birthed had to have a mother church, or be under another church. Because of this, and his relationship with both Len Warden and Doug White, the Itatiba church claimed the Vila Madalena Church as their mother after the Vila church was born. In this case, the church in Itatiba had come into existence before the Vila Madalena church was birthed. Often in jest, people said that the daughter church was older than the mother.

First Initiative in Bauru

Abiezer had a friend, Carlos Santana, from the city of Bauru. The two men participated in a Gospel radio program. Through an exchange of information, Carlos was introduced to the Alliance and became interested in the denomination. He began holding meetings with a small group of people with the intent of also becoming an Alliance congregation. Carlos had a theological degree from a Baptist seminary in Bauru. At certain points, Len Warden, Paul Clark and Pastor Toshiaki Yassui went to Bauru to give support to Carlos. At one Brazilian Alliance church council there was discussion about the inclusion of the Bauru group into the Brazilian Alliance. Two distinct leaders from this group besides Carlos came forward. Wanderlei, who worked for the post office and later asked to be transferred to Manaus to work with needy people there. The other leader was a young man, less than twenty years of age, named Fernando Pedro, originally from Curitiba, who soon came to São Paulo to study in IBA, which became known as the Seminário Bíblico Aliança (SEMIBA). Fernando was a talented young man who continues to serve the Lord today as a pastor of the Lagoa Santa Alliance Church in Minas Gerais. The Bauru group remained within the Alliance for two to three years before they withdrew.

Brooklin Alliance is Renamed the Airport Alliance Church

The Brooklin church grew and needed a larger meeting place. A warehouse was found on 113 Renascença Street, near the Congonhas Airport. The congregation moved there in 1993. The building needed a major renovation before it could house a church. With the help of Bebeto Bueno, a civil engineer who was part of the church, it took form and became an attractive building that could seat 300 people. During this time the Airport Alliance Church, which became the new name for the Brooklin Alliance Church, had reached an attendance of 270 people, counting all that attended the Sunday morning and evening services. According to statistics maintained during the first decade of this church, 1986 – 1996, the São Paulo church started with an average of 17 people and grew to over 260 attending. Between 1992 and 1996 there was a 70.1% increase in attendance. During the same five-year period of time there was an average of 133 conversions and 26 baptisms per year. It has been said that we overestimate what can be done in one year and underestimate what can be done in ten.

During the time the Airport Church was on Renascença Street, Werter Padilha and his wife, Claudia Cavalcante, started attending the São Paulo church, having come from the northeast of Brazil. They were passionate about missions, taking the Gospel to those who have never heard, which dovetailed with the C&MA heart. They had great influence when the first mission conference was held in the 90's, complete with workshops, special music and international dress. A vivid memory at one of the first mission conferences was a call to submit a faith promise card to give faithfully to the support of missions. People came forward, knelt, wept and placed their cards in the basket. Some came forward who were willing to be sent. Among those sent were Romário and Jaqueline Santos, members of the Airport church, who went to Peru in the late 90's as missionary interns. They spent two years and planted a church there. Subsequently, they returned to Brazil and later were sent to Calcutta, India. God's Spirit was not only moving and sending missionaries among the Alliance in Brazil at that

**Airport Alliance Church
São Paulo**

time but also from other Brazilian churches.

In 1994, the Airport church hosted its first church street party to make a connection with their neighborhood. They had permission to block off a section of a street near the church, set up a platform, serve food, lead the crowd in aerobic exercises and host the Brazilian Gospel heavy metal band, Oficina G-3. The party was well received and repeated in following years. Some people from the neighborhood even started attending the church because of this event and were baptized.

According to "Encounter with God" principles, a church should grow large and strong, perhaps to 500 or 1000 people, before initiating a daughter church. Even though the Airport Church has never reached that size, the missionary team was large, and there was a growing concern to see another church planted. Plus there was the presence of Pastor José Freitas, the part-time Brazilian pastor who had joined the staff in 1993. By this time Tim & Jo Lee Bubna had joined the Airport Alliance pastoral staff while also serving as field director for Brazil.

The Wardens and Whites were chosen to be the two couples to step out and plant a new church. The Airport pastoral team was to pray and confirm where the church was to be located. In 1993 these two couples met in the home of the Bebeto and Deborah Bueno to pray on Wednesday nights with others in the western area of the city. They were seeking God as to whether a church should be started, where and when.

The Vila Madalena Alliance Church Begins

As a result, the Vila Madalena church was birthed in May 1994, meeting first on Heitor Penteado Street, near the Vila Madalena metro station. Twenty-seven people launched from the Airport Church, and an Alliance Brazilian SEMIBA student, "Maggie" (Magnolia) Rodrigues. This group of people also represented about forty percent of the tithes and offerings at the Airport Church. It was a step of faith for everyone. Within six months the Airport church recovered from the birth experience, increasing their attendance beyond what it had been previously, while maintaining itself financially. To God be the glory!

Only a few months after Vila Madalena began holding Sunday services, Diane Warden experienced chronic migraine headaches and needed to return to the United States. A bit later, her husband Len and family joined her. She was miraculously healed during the year they were in the United States through the prayers of a couple people

Vila Madalena Alliance Church 10th Anniversary

in a church they were visiting. Two people unknown to each other in the service where the Wardens were ministering on home assignment, felt called to pray for Diane. The same word came to both of them separately, "Masonry." The headaches were a definite result of a spiritual attack on the Wardens since previously they had helped some members of the Vila Madalena church leave the unequal yoke of Masonry.

Because of this situation, the Whites stepped into

leadership in the Vila. In reality, they felt catapulted and unprepared. During this time, they had to depend on God to give them direction and they grew in their ability to minister. One highlight of this time was having a once a month, "Bring a friend Sunday," that included an evangelistic message and a meal following the service. Isabel Sanchez received an invitation to one of these Sundays as she was sitting at the hairdresser. She and her husband, Enéias, came and gave their lives to the Lord, becoming the first fruits in the Vila Madalena Church. They continue there today. Another strategy was that baptisms were made celebratory events at Vila, which included testimonies, cake and included the presence of many family members. Also, Vacation Bible School was started and continued every July.

From their first rented facility on Heitor Penteado, the Vila Madalena Alliance Church moved to three different buildings on Cerro Corá Avenue, the first one being quite close to the Pious XI Catholic Church. Len Warden became friends with the priest of that diocese. The priest came to the inaugural service, vested in his robes and gave the Vila congregation a greeting. Sometimes he attended the Sunday evening service, as did some of his parishioners. Unfortunately, the priest was transferred to another diocese.

"Maggie" initiated the youth group at the Vila Madalena church, made up mostly of young men. Not only did she work with these youth, but she discipled them using the "Be An Approved Workman" series. Out of this group came Wilson Ferrante, now pastor at Vista Verde Alliance Church in São José dos Campos. Later, Fernando Pedro or "Fernandão" (Big Fernando) came on at Vila Madalena as an intern and also led the youth group after "Maggie" left. He trained these young men musically and formed a great worship group for the Vila church.

Another young man André Aéneas from the group has become a Baptist pastor. And Fernando Moraes finished the theological course at SEMIBA and is a leader in his church.

Church Plant Attempt in São Roque

Around the same time as the Vila Madalena church was being birthed, another opportunity appeared for the Airport Church to start a ministry in São Roque, a town 70 kilometers away. Everardo and Celia Albuquerque were attending the Airport Church with their family. Their daughter and son-in-law lived in São Roque. This young couple had a vision to start a church and asked for help. Their friend, Carlos Vieira, who owned a super market chain, became thoroughly saved through a Bible study ministry there. On Friday evenings, in 1993-94, the Joneses went to São Roque to lead the study with the hope that this group would grow into a church. When the Joneses returned to the United States in 1994, leadership of the group was given to Tomaz and Bia Oliveira, members of the Airport church and seminary students. However, due to various difficulties the ministry ended.

In late 1995 the Vila Madalena church plateaued. Doug and Helen White prayed about how they could minister to the existing community of believers that came mainly from the middle-upper class, as well as how to evangelize and use what ministry gifts God had given them. After reading an article in The *Alliance Life* about "Marriage Encounter" in Chile, a light came on for Doug, "That's it!" First Doug and Helen went to Chile, followed by the Wardens and other key couples of the Vila church to experience the "Marriage Encounter" weekend. They continued sending couples to Chile until there were enough Brazilians to sponsor the first "Marriage Encounter" weekend in São Paulo.

In May 1999 "Marriage Encounter" was launched in São Paulo with the couples that had gone to Chile, with the help of several Chilean couples plus Dave and Lou Ann Woerner, a C&MA missionary couple to Chile. Between 1999 and 2009 more than 600 couples went through the "Marriage Encounter" weekend. People from the Vila Madalena and the Airport churches collaborated together as did volunteers from Rudge Ramos, Paraíso and Alphaville. It became the key outreach tool of the Vila church. Many conversions took place. Today, key leaders in the Airport church, Vila Madalena and Alphaville are fruit of the "Marriage Encounter" ministry. With this step of faith in ministry, God's manifest presence seemed to be unleashed. Couples, who were not able to conceive, became pregnant and had children, a mother rose up from a coma, and a child was cured of chronic bed wetting. These needs and answers to prayer caused more people to come to Christ and to the Vila Madalena church.

"Marriage Encounter" became a ministry of grace that not only touched couples, but had a trickledown effect on families, and generations. Providentially, the Whites, on one occasion when they were in Chile, caught the tail end of a "Youth Encounter" ministry and caught a vision for ministry to youth in São Paulo. Carlos and Tomasa Borges, from the Vila Madalena church shared the vision and spearheaded the beginning of the ministry in 2002 with young people from the Vila church, including their daughter Ana, Vila Madalena pastor, Mike Davis, and by God's grace, Davis' future son-in-law, Otávio Garcia. These people and other key youth made a pilgrimage to Santiago, Chile. Later, Chilean youth came to São Paulo to help produce the first Alliance "Youth Encounter" in 2003. It was called JENTE, Jovens ao Encontro do Espírito (Youth Encounter of the Spirit). The abbreviation JENTE is a play on words in Portuguese because it sounds like "gente" that means "people." The Pan American Christian Academy, the school where most of the U.S. Alliance MKs studied, opened their facilities for the initial Youth Encounter weekend. Since then hundreds of young people have experienced the ministry. The workload has principally been shared with the Vila Madalena and Airport Alliance churches. Young people have come to Christ and relationships have been restored between youth and their parents. Both Marriage Encounter and Youth Encounter continue to this day. São Paulo Marriage Encounter spread to Belo Horizonte with the Lagoa Santa Alliance church, and Youth Encounter has spread to São José dos Campos and the Vista Verde Alliance church with the help of Encounter leaders from São Paulo.

In 1995 Dave and Sue Manske, and family, arrived in São Paulo and became part of the Airport Alliance church, having already worked in Brasilia, Porto Alegre and Curitiba. Dave had a passion for missions and helped the national church planting committee, the national missions department and the missions committee at the Airport Alliance Church. During their four years in São Paulo, Dave was an arm of encouragement to the Airport's sports ministries that sent out short term mission teams. During the same time, an effort was made to help a Brazilian church in Mount Vernon, NY, by sending out Celia Elvas from the Airport Church, also a graduate of the Alliance Bible Institute, along with Raquel Cândido from Porto Alegre. Dave helped in the strategy of the church planting effort in Fortaleza, in the northeast of Brazil, which was to be a predecessor and hopeful model for future missionary projects. The Manskes left São Paulo in 1999 to work in Fortaleza along with Pastor João Costa Junior and wife, Lenise. Pastor "Junior" was the son of ACEMBRAS first president, Pastor João Alves da Costa. Pastor João Junior had also served as president of ACEMBRAS. They went to Fortaleza with the goal of planting a church in the needy Northeast of Brazil.

Dave and Arlene Peters redeployed from the Airport church in 1996 to minister in Mexico City. At that time North American Alliance mission efforts were being reorganized. Brazil was administered by the U. S. C&MA with American personnel, and Mexico became a field administered by the Canadian Alliance with Canadian international workers. The Peters left a legacy, in particular, modeling how to grow a healthy team. This permeated the São Paulo missionary task force and has trickled down through the years to other teams and cities in Brazil. They emphasized:

- Team unity: a commitment to not speak negatively of one team member to another.
- Unity of vision: if there were strong differences of opinion, to talk and pray through them.
- Unity in decision making: not going ahead on major decisions without all being united.
- Unity and diversity of gifting. Dave also recognized that sometimes we have to work in areas where we are not gifted.

In the practical outworking of these principles, weekly breakfasts and prayer were held in each missionary home on a rotating basis. This bonded the São Paulo team together and the breakfasts continued after the Peters left.

1996 saw another departure from the Airport church. Romario e Jaqueline Santos, the young couple from the church, were sent to Lima, Peru with the Brazilian mission agency *Kairós* to do church planting in preparation for eventually going to India. They remained there for two years and planted a church. Another departure was from the church building of the Airport Church on Renascença Street. While trying to renegotiate the rent, the owner asked for triple the price, way beyond what the church was able or willing to pay.

Consequently, because of the need to vacate the building, the Airport Alliance Church found themselves looking for a new building at the beginning of 1997. The Sunday before the building had to be unoccupied, the leadership had no idea where they would meet the following Sunday. They had found nothing adequate. On Monday the pastor, Mike Davis, and two board members took to the streets, praying, walking and looking. They weren't able to find a building to rent to give the church permanent space. Instead they found *Kolpinghaus*, a German club, where they were able to rent a social hall for Sunday services only. Church furniture was stored in members' homes and weekday services took place in people's homes. On Sunday mornings chairs had to be arranged each week, as well as the set up and tear down of all musical equipment. The first Sunday that the church met in the *Kolpinghaus* space it was decorated with beautiful flowers left by a wedding that had just had their reception in the room. It gave joy for an inaugural service to a church body which felt homeless.

In the next month, February 1997, the Airport church sent their own soccer team to Cebu, Philippines to play in the "King's Cup," having been invited by CAMACOP, the C&MA national church of the Philippines. This invitation was the first of its kind in worldwide Alliance history, where one national church invited another national church to minister in their country without missionary involvement. They competed in a tournament, played exhibition games, and participated in an evangelism project with the Filipino churches.

On May 18, 1997, the opening service was held in a new building that the Airport Church found on Santa Catarina Avenue in Vila Santa Catarina. The building, like the one on Renascença Street, was a warehouse where the body of Christ could meet together and grow to maturity. During this time, offerings increased by 50% and there were ten members enrolled in the Bible seminary. In November of the same year, which coincided with the 10th anniversary of the Airport Alliance church, Pastor José Freitas became the lead pastor of the church. It marked a new era from being led by a missionary pastor to a national pastor who had a missionary heart.

Soccer ministries were part of Pastor José Freitas' DNA . They played a big role at the Airport Church from the beginning, and have continued until the time of this writing. Pastor José, with a degree in physical education and a theology degree from Word of Life seminary, was a man with an evangelistic and missionary passion. He helped propel this ministry. Not only were there sports ministries in the vicinity of the Airport Alliance church, but also internationally. Groups were sent to Spain and Morocco in 1989, a youth soccer school was started in 1995 at the neighborhood fire station. Adilson de Boa Morte restarted the neighborhood school in 2000. In 2003 Romario Santos, before going to India, worked with the soccer school and afterwards, it was headed up by Guilherme Lima. Between 2004 and 2009, there was the formation of Geração Vida Nova, (New Life Generation), a project initiated by the Airport church and today led by a non-profit organization which ministers to 200 children. Today this sports project is called IMBRAS, Instituto Muda Brasil, (Change Brazil Institute).

In 2003, 2004, and 2006 soccer missions teams were sent to Germany. In 2006 a group went to Spain. In 2010 Pastor José made a connection with the leader of "Ambassadors Soccer

International," Goran Tomic, when Goran was living in Brazil. The involvement allowed for a more structured sports ministry with a developed international organization. In 2012, Ambassadors were given space for an office in the newly built Airport Alliance church building. With Ambassadors, groups were sent to Russia in 2014, 2015, and 2016 accompanied by Pastor Leialdo Pulz, former Brazilian Alliance missionary to Russia. Generally these groups played local teams and shared their testimonies during halftime, as well as holding soccer clinics for children and youth, which opened doors for them to share the Gospel and perhaps make a link to a local church.

There were also short-term missionary trips that focused on evangelism and discipleship. Sandro Alves, Bible institute student and member of the Airport Alliance Church, completed an internship with a church in Santa Cruz, Bolivia in 1996. In 2000 two groups went out, one to Peru to work with Romário Santos, and another group went to Bolivia with Marcelo Dorigo and Charlotte Hisle. Starting in 2002, several trips and groups were sent to the Amazon in Roraima state to work alongside André and Tania Oliveira, Alliance Brazilian missionaries working among the Wai-Wai Indian tribe. These trips included people from the Airport and Vila Madalena churches. They ministered to children through Vacation Bible School and gave teacher training and Bible classes. They also helped build a small house for the Oliveiras and other missionaries visiting the tribe. One couple, Marcelo and Elaine Okassawara from the Vila Madalena church, became full-time missionaries there, and now serve with MEVA, Missão Evangélica da Amazônia (Amazon Evangelical Mission).

Survey trips were also made to the north of Portugal with the intent of gaining a vision to minister and open up Portugal as an Alliance field. These were spearheaded by the

Vision Team to Portugal—2002

national church's Alliance Department of Missions; some of the participants were leaders and members from the São Paulo Alliance churches. The first trip was made by a group coming out of São Paulo in 2002, and another in 2004, led by Dave and Judy Jones and Charlotte Hisle, but it was decided the time was not right to enter this needy country. A few years later in 2009, Danilo and Elaine Lima, Mike and Ruth Davis, and José Freitas returned with C&MA leaders from Europe and Latin America with the goal of opening a new field, a partnership between ACEMBRAS and the U.S. Alliance. In 2010 Mike Davis and missions director, Akira Fukuura of the Paraíso church, returned and registered the Christian & Missionary Alliance as a legal entity in Portugal. In September 2011, the Brazilian Alliance, represented by Danilo and Elaine Lima and the U.S. Alliance missionaries, Mike and Ruth Davis and Charlotte Hisle made Portugal their home with the purpose of planting a church or churches in the north.

Tatuapé Alliance Church is Birthed

Although missionaries continued as part of the pastoral team, in 1998 the Airport Alliance Church was officially organized as an ACEMBRAS (Brazil Alliance) church and became independent from the mission. Around the same time, Rev. Fred Smith, the C&MA Latin American Regional Director, strongly expressed his feeling that missionaries should be "apostolic," planting churches and not pastoring churches for more than two years. Soon several national pastors and missionaries sat down together to decide what area of the megalopolis of São Paulo would be targeted for the next church plant. Already there was a church presence in the southern zone, and the western zone. Two areas of interest were Butantã and Tatuapé. There was some fear that Butantã in the western region, near the São Paulo University, was very close to the Vila Madalena church. Tatuapé was in the eastern zone, and there were at least twenty Alliance people who lived in the area from three different Alliance churches. Consequently, it was decided to go to the eastern zone of São Paulo. In October 1999, a prayer meeting was started in a tea house in Tatuapé, a neighborhood which had recently sprung into prominence, featured on the front page of the news magazine *Veja*. A month later the group moved to a school auditorium. And Wednesday evening prayer meetings were begun; Sunday evening services began in March 2000. The initial team included Mike and Ruth Davis, Marshall and Teresa Erickson, Charlotte Hisle and SEMIBA student, Reyme Saraiva.

Home assignment schedules may have interrupted continuity in the ministry of the churches in São Paulo, but gave opportunity for new leadership to spring up and showed the flexibility of the missionary staff. Len and Diane Warden returned to Brazil and went to the Tatuapé church in 2000 while the Davises were in the United States. Mike and Ruth then returned from their home assignment in 2001 to go to the Vila Madalena church with the purpose of transitioning the church from missionary leadership to a national pastor. Kurt and Karen Baselides, a couple from the Porto Alegre Alliance church, were called to pastor the Vila Madalena church late in 2003 and became lead pastor in 2004, which coincided with the 10th anniversary of the Vila Church. Later in 2003 at the

Tatuapé Alliance Church, Len and Diane's son and wife, Jeremy and Berenice Warden, became a part of the pastoral staff. Len and Diane Warden left Tatuapé in 2004 for home assignment. Marshall and Teresa Erickson were also a part of Tatuapé, but had to return to the United States for family medical reasons. Jeremy Warden became the head pastor of Tatuapé and stayed until the church closed at the end of 2007.

While the Tatuapé congregation was forming, the mother church, the Airport Alliance church moved forward. In 2000, a second full-time pastor came on staff at the church, Edwin Del'Aquila. Edwin came from the Alliance in Peru, settled in São Paulo with his Brazilian wife, and graduated from the São Paulo Alliance Seminary. He served the Airport church until 2004.

In 2001, the Airport Church embarked upon a great adventure of faith. They bought two adjoining houses on 535 Baronesa de Bela Vista Street in Campo Belo, just one block from the Congonhas Airport, and close to the church's former rented facilities on Renascença Street. During the Carnaval weekend of that year, the church members banded together to make the move from the rented facility on Santa Catarina Street to what would become a more permanent home, a dream and a miracle. It is to the glory of God that these two houses were purchased and remodeled into a church. Today, it is one of the few Alliance churches in São Paulo with its own property and building. However, it has been an arduous task and a walk of faith for many years. In the same year of 2001, José Carlos dos Santos became a collaborating pastor of the Airport church, and Sandro Alves was contracted as a part time pastor. In 2005 Danilo and Elaine Lima, SEMIBA graduates, became part of the pastoral staff of the Airport Church. After their internship, they led a Baptist congregation in Parelheiros.

Northern São Paulo Zone Church Planting Attempt

Between 2004 and 2009 an attempt was made to plant another church in the northern zone of the city of São Paulo. The team which worked on this project, Len and Diane Warden, Alex and Julie Zell, Sanford and Wendie Hashimoto and part-time Brazilian pastoral couple, Wilson and Giselli Ferrante, started the work from scratch with zero contacts in the area. Len soon had a men's discipleship group started, which met in a restaurant. The chef, Miriam Dias, became interested in the Alliance ministry and became an integral part. Sunday services were held at a school in the northern zone of São Paulo. Later they met for a year in the Zell's home.

Another ministry that sprang to life at this time was "Integrity." This ministry had connections to Pastor Marty Berglund's Alliance church in New Jersey and led by Dr. Dennis Borg. The "Integrity" ministry began to intentionally reach out to businessmen, Christians and seekers. Groups of American Christian businessmen came to Brazil to link up with Brazilian businessmen, offering seminars related to business and visiting some of the men's workplaces. This ministry was not limited to the Alliance, or to the work in the northern zone, but there was a strong connection to Len Warden during the time he worked in the northern zone of São Paulo. There are still some Integrity groups functioning in the city of São Paulo today. The American arm of the ministry also sponsored trips for Brazilian men to travel to the US to visit businesses, Christian businessmen, where they were housed in their homes and participated in their churches.

Another idea for outreach ministries was the "English Encounter" initiated by Len and Diane Warden. Groups came from the United States to host an intensive weekend of English in a hotel. The English Encounter was probably inspired from the marriage and youth encounters that were happening at the time. The personnel from the U.S. roomed in a hotel with 1 to 3 Brazilians who were living the weekend as an English immersion experience. There were several Brazilians who came to Christ through the ministry. One that particularly is remembered is Marlene Ferrari, a lawyer, who went on to be baptized and become a member at the Vila Madalena and then onto the Paraíso church. She also became a student at the Alliance Bible Seminary.

Taboão Church is Birthed with a Remnant from Tatuapé

Thankfully there were celebrations of transformed lives that offset the woes of shutting the doors on a church plant. So was the case with the Tatuapé church. In March 2007; the Tatuapé Alliance church celebrated their seventh anniversary. One key couple that attended, Tadeu and Marilene Azevedo, were transformed as a result of Marriage Encounter ministries. They lived in Taboão, over 20 kilometers from Tatuapé, but felt a connection with the people in the eastern zone of the city at the Tatuapé Alliance church, people with whom they'd met at Marriage Encounter and they started attending. Not only did they attend faithfully but they brought 10-15 of their friends and family, using a van to pick them up. The church used two different buildings after their brief time in the school. Sadly, the congregation disintegrated following the loss of two key families who abandoned the church due to their displeasure over the discipline of a family member in another Alliance church in the city. The Tatuapé church held their last service in November of 2007. Those members who wanted to remain with the Christian & Missionary Alliance returned to the evening service of the Airport Alliance church, the mother church.

During the following two years, the Taboão group,

located 30 minutes southeast of the Congonhas Airport, continued meeting for prayer and Bible studies during the week in their area. Paul and Beverly Clark helped maintain these weekly encounters. In 2008, Doug and Helen White returned from a church planting effort in Rio de Janeiro and gave assistance to Marcelo and Gorete Dorigo with the Taboão contacts. At this time, the Dorigos were still living in Capão Redondo about an hour away from where they were pastoring in Taboão. By January 2009, Taboão began having Sunday services with Marcelo Dorigo as pastor. Doug and Helen White were assisting, as well as a seminary student, José Alves, and his wife, Luiza. The Clarks rejoined the pastoral team in Taboão in 2009 after their home assignment while the Whites transitioned from the Brazil field to US ministries.

Alphaville Alliance Begins

In 2002, Vila Madalena Alliance Church had several home prayer groups, plus the prayer meeting that was held on Wednesday nights at the church building. Two couples who were members of the Vila church and lived in Alphaville asked to host a prayer group in their homes. Alphaville is a region of gated communities located 25 kilometers northwest of the Vila Madalena church. Because of heavy responsibilities, and lack of other leaders, Mike Davis, then pastor, told the two couples, Osmar and Marisa Sampaio and Henry and Silvia Go, "If you want a prayer group in Alphaville, you may go and start it on your own. I give you my blessing." They did exactly that and the two couples began praying together. By 2003 the Davises began to join with the couples. Bible study was added to prayer as well as a lot of fellowship with food around the table. People were added to the group, including two or three couples from the "Marriage Encounter" ministry. It seemed that people were looking to know God and have genuine friendships. By January 2004 there were 16 regular attenders.

The Bible studies in Alphaville continued. José and Cremilda Rodrigues started attending with their daughter and son-in-law, Rogério and Soraya Torres. The Rodrigues maintained leadership of the Alphaville Bible study during the Davis' home assignment in 2005-2006. It should be noted that the Torres later moved to the United States where Rogério attended seminary and became an Alliance pastor in the Louisville, KY church. By 2007 the Bible study group that met in the home of the Sampaios in Residencial 11 gated community had grown sufficiently and a second Bible study was started in Residencial 2, the home of the Gos.

Sunday services began in Alphaville in September 2007 at the Hotel Bourbon on Almeida Cauaxi. These services were held once a month until the end of 2008 with an average attendance of about 40. In February 2009 they began holding services twice monthly, and then in June 2009 they started holding weekly services. The two weekly Bible studies continued, as did additional studies, such as Crown financial principles and the "Unique Woman."

In May 2007 Jo Kiel, Alliance missionary working in Caxias do Sul, and a trained fashion color analyst, was invited for a Mother's Day presentation at the Vila Madalena Church. Her contacts with women from Vila Madalena and Alphaville began three years of evangelism, 2007-2010, in the Alphaville region, as well as in other areas of São Paulo among contacts of members from the Alphaville Alliance Church, Nazarenes, and Presbyterians. Events were held in the Commercial Center of Alphaville, the Receita Federal (Internal Revenue Service) in Osasco and Alphaville, in gated communities in Alphaville near the Raposa Tavares Highway, hair salons, the "Kolpinghaus

German Club," and the "São Paulo Women's Business Club." More than 1000 women participated in the events over the three years and a large percentage said they prayed to receive Christ.

The color event was called "Inner and Outer Beauty." The outer beauty principles were derived from "Color Me Beautiful," a book and technique from the 80's. It said that women who dressed using colors that corresponded with their unique coloring, eyes, hair and skin, would look younger, rested and more radiant. Jo would go on to teach that true inner beauty comes from allowing Jesus Christ to transform one's life by removing sin, which is degrading, and allow His joy and peace to radiate from the inside out. The first evangelistic color event produced one solid contact, Mara. She had received an E-mail invitation intended for someone else of the same name who was an artist. However, "our" Mara also had interest in colors because she was an architect. More importantly she showed interest in Jesus and studying the Bible. She became a follower of Christ. Later she was diagnosed with cancer, but still wanted to be baptized. Due to the effects of chemotherapy, she was unable to be immersed but she donned the baptismal robes, and in humility removed her wig in front of the congregation in order to be baptized by sprinkling. She in turn hosted an "Inner and Outer Beauty" seminar in her home and was instrumental in opening doors for events at the "São Paulo Women's Business Club." Mara's given name was Maria, but Mara was her choice of names as a professional. After knowing Christ and battling cancer she said, "Don't call me Mara anymore. Mara means bitter. I'm not bitter. Call me Maria." She passed into the presence of the Lord in 2011, not bitter from cancer but better with her Lord.

In May 2008, the U.S. C&MA mission leadership

informed the Brazil Mission that the missionary staff would begin a five year phasing-out process and at the end of that period, the Brazil Alliance Mission would officially close. According to statistics from Patrick Johnstone's Operation World, 25% of Brazil's population was Evangelical. Consequently, U.S. leadership felt that the Brazilian church could multiply and develop on its own, and mission resources could be invested in needier places. Significant changes were coming for both the missionary staff and the Brazilian national Alliance churches. Upon hearing about this transition, plans were made to bring on a national pastor at Alphaville. The church prayed and Pastor Marcos and Fatima Tibúrcio were indicated as candidates. They had been on the staff of the Airport Church since 2007. Marcos is a gifted preacher and Fátima endeared herself to the women in Alphaville as a Bible study leader and counselor. Also, they had a major role in the "Marriage Encounter" ministry, a ministry which was foundational for the planting of the church in Alphaville. The Alphaville church was officially incorporated on May 15, 2011.

It now can be seen that the 1983 study team's recommendations have been realized. The São Paulo flagship church, the Airport Alliance, was successfully planted and now occupied its own newly-constructed building, and has birthed various daughter churches. Some of these churches in turn have birthed other churches, and the church planting cycle continues. National missionaries and pastors have been called and sent from these São Paulo churches and are supported by the Brazil Alliance Church (ACEMBRAS). The mission office was moved to São Paulo.

The Bible Institute, later renamed the Alliance Bible Seminary, SEMIBA, now known as the "A.W. Tozer Theological Seminary," transitioned out of Curitiba and reopened in São

Paulo in 1991. The seminary confers bachelor degrees, and master degrees, through the FATELA (Latin American Alliance Theological Faculty). The seminary purchased space from the Airport Alliance Church and today is housed on an upper floor of the church building, having its own classrooms, administrative space and a fully organized library. There is a sense of fulfillment in seeing come to pass what Jesus said "I will build my church" and to see believers of the church fulfill the Great Commission to go, teach, baptize and make disciples. The words of Simeon upon seeing Jesus, the promised Messiah, reflects some of the emotion within our hearts as we reflect on the years of ministry in this great city. "God, you can now release your servant; release me in peace as you promised, with my own eyes I've seen your salvation; it's now out in the open for everyone to see..." (Luke 2:28, MSG.)

CHAPTER TEN
TO THE REGIONS
BEYOND

ACEMBRAS

Beginning in 1975, and following more than two years of study and deliberation, the Pro-Tem Committee for the organization on the Brazilian Alliance Church drew up the legal documents consisting of Constitution and By-Laws. These were necessary for the official founding and registering of the autonomous Brazilian Alliance national church, the mission's goal since its beginning in the early 1960s. The work of the committee was to be presented to delegates from Brasília, São José dos Campos, Campinas, Curitiba and Porto Alegre at the "First Council of the Brazilian Christian and Missionary Alliance," held at the Alliance Church in Gama, Federal District of Brasília in 1978.

Previously, in 1976 and 1977, "Alliance Congresses" had been held in Brasília and Curitiba in order to give the delegates from around the country a sense of the larger Alliance church that was coming into being. These meetings were largely for fellowship and edification, while helping the delegates to understand not only the Four-fold Gospel message of the Alliance but also the global mission of the C&MA. The Alliance "roots and branches" all over the world existed to proclaim a Christ-centered gospel to unreached peoples worldwide.

Consequently, the first official C&MA Council was held January 6 - 8, 1978 at the Ebenezer Alliance Church in Gama, Federal District of Brasília. At that meeting, the constitution and by-laws of the Brazil Alliance, (A Aliança Cristã e Missionária Brasileira - ACEMBRAS), were read, discussed, debated, revised and approved. Rev. Tom Kyle, Board Representative, presided over the plenary sessions; he had taken over the mission leadership when the Joneses furloughed in mid-1977. The first Executive Committee of ACEMBRAS was chosen with Rev. João Alves da Costa of Gama elected president. Vice President was Pastor Sérgio Moraes Pinto of Porto Alegre. The secretary chosen was Mr. Noriyuki Kaji of Brasília, and Pastor Nelber Nuñez of Curitiba was chosen as treasurer. Member at large was Mr. Breno Bittencort of Curitiba.

Vila First ACEMBRAS Council Gama, FD

The July 26, 1978 Alliance Witness article quoted Missionary Richard LaFountain: "The business sessions were a delightful balance of delegates young and old who together wrestled with the heavy issues facing a newly formed national church." The youthfulness of the pastoral leadership pool for ACEMBRAS proved to be an ongoing issue in coming years.

The following year, January 1979, the Second Council of ACEMBRAS was held at the newly-dedicated Vista Verde Alliance Church in São José dos Campos. The council theme, "Go and Make Disciples" was reflected by the forty enthusiastic delegates that came from north and south. Missionary Ann Hemminger commented on the meeting: "It was a gratifying experience to see our national brethren expressing their ideas and initiating their own plans. There is no doubt in our minds as we reflect on the second annual council that for both missionaries and nationals a vision was caught. This vision saw not only the needs of Brazil but also in the regions beyond."

Following the official organization of the Brazilian C&MA, there was a significant growth spurt, with two churches in Manaus, far to the north in Amazonas, established by Colombian Alliance workers, Hernan and Edilma Osorio, requesting membership in ACEMBRAS. Far to the south, on the southern border of Rio Grande do Sul, in the town of Santana do Livramento, a new Alliance plant was begun by the Rivera Alliance Church. John and Loraine Todd in Campinas, São Paulo, were also at work on church planting, joined by C&MA Pastor Koon of China. In the far western region of Amazonas, in the river town of Benjamin Constant, another congregation was being planted by Rev. Daniel Tovar, a Colombian Alliance missionary who lived on the other side of the great Solimões River in the Colombian town of Leticia. This was a heady time when years of plowing, planting and persevering were finally bearing fruit. Vision for the vastness of Brazil and the larger "world out there" was coming into sharper focus. But this new-found wide-angle perspective also had its early roots.

Without Vision the People Perish

After the Sunday school class ended, one of the regular attenders, a long-time believer from a local Methodist Church, came to the missionary pastor with a perplexed frown on her face. "Pastor, I don't think I understood what you were saying today, about Brazilians being missionaries."

The first-term missionary thought to himself, "I guess I said something wrong or it came out sideways." "So, Dona Carmen, what is your question?"

The middle-aged lady with grey-streaked hair said, "Pastor, you said that someday Brazilian missionaries are going to be sent to other countries, sent by Brazilian churches. But how can that be?"

Again, the missionary said, "What don't you understand about that?"

"Pastor," she exclaimed, "Brazilians can't be missionaries!"

"Why not?" he asked.

With a rather exasperated expression on her face, she responded, "Aren't all missionaries either American or British?" With that, the young missionary pastor understood the problem.

Up to that time, 1970, the Brazil evangelical churches had sent out very few missionaries, mostly to neighboring South American countries like Paraguay, Uruguay and Bolivia. There was little or no missions vision in the Brazilian church. In fact, the largest Pentecostal denomination told its pastors that missions was not to be emphasized in their churches because of the great needs of Brazil, and the church could not afford the funds or human resources needed for missions. Dona Carmen had never seen a Brazilian missionary, and to her that term made no sense since she had never seen or heard of one in her church.

So the still-learning missionary sought to help make sense out of the idea of a Brazilian missionary. "Dona Carmen," he asked, "Where did Paul the Apostle, the great missionary, come from, what country? Was he British or American?"

Another perplexed frown creased the ladies weathered face. "I don't know where he came from."

The missionary explained: "Paul was a Jew from Asia Minor, modern day Turkey, and all of the other apostles, which means 'sent ones,' Peter, John, James, Andrew . . . all of them were Jews from the Holy Lands."

Seeing that the sincere Christian lady was trying to assimilate this idea, the missionary asked another question: "What language is your Bible written in?"

She looked at him strangely and replied, "Why, Portuguese, of course."

"Right, "he said, "It's in Portuguese and who reads Portuguese?"

By this time, this line of reasoning was beginning to irritate the lady. "We do, we Brazilians, and I guess the Portuguese do too."

"That's right; the Bible was translated into Portuguese, just like it was into English. That means that the people who can read Portuguese, like people in Brazil or Portugal, are supposed to know it and do what it says, right?"

Once again, Dona Carmen nodded her head in agreement. "So," the missionary went on, "What is written in Matthew 28:18-20?" The pastor knew that the dear lady really couldn't read; she had never gone to school as a girl raised on a farm in the interior of the country, but she carried her Bible to church faithfully and knew a lot of Scripture, including Matthew 28:18-20.

"That's the Great Commission isn't it? When Jesus tells His followers to make disciples of all of the nations, right?"

"Right as can be," was the missionary's reply. "Now why do you supposed that Jesus said that and why does that Great Commission appear in the Bible?"

Slowly the light was coming on in Dona Carmen's eyes. "You mean to say that anyone who can read the Bible, in whatever language, is supposed to obey it, including being missionaries?"

The missionary flashed a big smile and said, "100% right!" And with that, a seed was planted in the heart of a lady who had been a Christian for years. And Dona Carmen represented hundreds of thousands of other Brazilian Believers, as well as their pastors, who gradually were having their eyes opened to the fact that God's last command to His church is the church's first command today, to make committed followers from every tribe, tongue and nation till He returns. It was in this way that from early in the ministry of the Brazil Alliance Mission, "Missions and You" was taught and modeled.

An Outboard Motor

The students of the Alliance Bible Institute in Curitiba were on a steep learning curve, drinking deeply from God's Word. Theology, homiletics, hermeneutics, and Church history were served up to the aspiring future leaders and workers of the Alliance churches in Brazil. One of the classes prominently taught was Missions. However, principle and practice need to be closely related to be effective. And from a letter written in 1980 by a Colombian Alliance missionary, Pastor Daniel Tovar of Leticia, deep in the heart of the Amazon, such an opportunity came in a request for help. In his letter, Tovar described his cross-border ministry in three countries: Colombia, Peru and Brazil. Then as now, the "tri-country corner" was a haven for drug producers and pushers, a heaven for

Daniel Tovar
And the missionary canoe

consumers and a hell-hole of crime. Daniel's ministry was to the locals that lived among the drug lords and their constant battles.

Somehow by God's grace, Daniel befriended one of the local drug lords who took a liking to the courageous gospel preacher. He gave him a 30-foot dugout canoe to be used like a church bus to transport Daniel and the people he ministered to. However, the gift did not come with a motor; thus Daniel and his congregation spent hours rowing the heavy canoe back and forth across the Solimões River. Daniel's plea was for help to purchase an outboard motor.

The students at the Alliance Bible Institute in Curitiba decided to take on the fund-raising project and swung into action. Through sales, solicitations, and sacrifice, they were able to come up with the several hundred dollars needed to purchase the motor. Eventually they had the sum in hand and it was sent out to the enterprising missionary who bought a Yamaha outboard motor and used it to reach river dwellers in the three-frontier region.

Zaire/Cabinda

The 1980s saw years of war worldwide, and one of the

bloodiest and longest lasting occurred in Angola, where three warring "liberation fronts" ferociously tried to destroy each other, because the prize for victory included the forcible takeover of Cabinda, the oil-rich Portuguese protectorate that became one of the spoils of the long-lasting civil war. As a result of constant guerrilla activity in Cabinda's Mayombe rainforest, tens of thousands of refugees crossed over the Chiloango River into neighboring Zaire, now known as the Democratic Republic of Congo. This area of the lower Congo is where the C&MA Mission from North America had ministered for over one hundred years. The Alliance missionaries and nationals in Zaire spoke the French and Kikongo languages, and they had difficulty in communicating with the younger Cabinda refugees who primarily spoke Portuguese.

As a result, the C&MA mission in Zaire requested that the Brazil Mission and ACEMBRAS send over evangelists who could minister to those who had fled the fighting and were now living in rough refugee camps in the rainforest on the other side of the border. The request was received in Brazil and Pastors David Jones and Sérgio Pinto led a team to minister to the Portuguese-speaking population in the forests. From October 19 to November 14, 1986, the Brazil team ministered in four refugee camps: *Seke Zole, M'Fuique, Lundo Matende and Kimbianga*. For three weeks, the missionary evangelists from Brazil, accompanied by Zaire C&MA missionary, Jim Sawatsky, and the *Sango Malambo Trio*, preached nightly to hundreds of adults and children who left all they had behind in order to avoid the fighting. It was there in the camps, where the missionary team labored, that hundreds came to Christ—and many are still following the Lord today.

Despite both the members of the missionary team contracting malaria on the last day of their ministry and having to spend an extra week in Kinshasa recovering, the vision of those who lost all in the war but gained eternal life while in the camps helped fuel the flame of missions that was growing in ACEMBRAS. For the next several years, Bibles, Sunday school material and other Christian literature were sent to help those who had found faith in Christ in those dire circumstances, as well as a few Cabinda students at the Alliance Bible Institute in Kinkonzi and the Seminary in Boma.

"What Was That All About?"

There is a Portuguese proverb that says, "God writes straight with crooked lines." That certainly seems to be the case as relates to the refugee ministry trip to Zaire. The two men were sent from Brazil to minister to Cabinda refugees surviving in United Nations camps in the rainforests. Due to the constant fighting in Angola, the team was advised to not fly directly to Zaire via Luanda, capital of Angola. Although there were daily direct flights to and from Luanda to Kinshasa, Zaire's capital, which would have made the trip relatively direct and short, the travel agent in São Paulo advised the team to fly to the United States, from there to Lisbon, and then the final leg to Kinshasa, thus avoiding touching down in Luanda. U.S passports were not seen with friendly eyes by Angolan immigration agents in those days, since the United States was supporting one of the so-called liberation fronts in opposition to the ruling MPLA regime. Thus, the U. S. and Angola were not on good terms.

Accepting the agent's advice, the team flew to the New York's JFK Airport and then on to Lisbon, arriving in the middle of the night, October 18, 1986. Due to the eighteen hour flight layover, the team had almost a full day in Lisbon, with free hotel accommodations provided. After a few hours of sleep, Jones and Pinto decided to explore Lisbon, see the sights and visit evangelical churches while walking around town. After a full day of sightseeing and having a generally great time, the two missionaries returned to their hotel. They had seen Mormon missionaries, Jehovah's Witness teams, a Muslim mosque and dozens of Catholic churches, many of which were closed. However, they saw no evangelical churches of any size or kind. They didn't realize that most Portuguese evangelicals still remembered the traumatic Salazar years when evangelicals dare not put up any kind of sign announcing that a non-Catholic church was in existence. Consequently, only local evangelicals knew where the churches were located in back alleys and side streets.

As they compared notes in their hotel room while waiting their midnight flight to Kinshasa, they felt led to pray. "Let's open the window that looks out over the city and pray for Portugal." With the curtains rolled back and a clear view of the beautiful city painted with pastel shades by the setting sun, the team began to pray. And suddenly, both began to weep and cry over the lostness of this centuries-old city steeped in religion, but so utterly lost in spiritual darkness. As they prayed, they wept recalling the sight of the elderly Portuguese women climbing the steep steps on their way to Saturday confession and mass. Their faces, lined by years of toil and sorrow, and their black clothes pointed to perpetual mourning for lost loved ones, left a deep impression on the missionaries' hearts. When the women finally came out from the church after confession and forgiveness given by the padre, after partaking of the "holy wafer," they slowly walked back down the stone steps. One of the team commented at the time, "Look at them, they just confessed and received forgiveness, yet their sorrow and soul-weariness continues on their face."

That memory haunted the two men as they cried out to

God and asked Him for mercy on Portugal. And for a long period of prayer and intercession, the two missionaries wept over the land that had always been the butt of Brazilian jokes and sarcastic remarks. However, they saw no humor in a city where dead religion seemed to have no living witness to the saving grace of Jesus Christ. Then they finished their prayer, wiped their eyes, and closed the window. One of the team asked with confusion in his voice, "What was that all about?" It would take some years before understanding what God was going to do in and through them.

AMACOS

The 1980s were difficult times in Brazil and the rest of the South American continent. Political turmoil, a "lost decade" for the economy of Brazil and a generation that had lost hope. For the first time in Brazil's history, tens of thousands of Brazilians left for better economic prospects in Europe, North America and Japan. And it was in that very period of despair for the future that God began to stir up a missionary vision in the heart of churches all across South America, and in the heart of the C&MA Churches across the continent.

In Brazil, several national mission agencies were already established: *Missão Antioquia, AVANTE, ALÉM, Kairos,* and a few others. Brazilian youth joined their peers from other countries to prepare for missionary service in the newly founded missions training schools in São Paulo. Even Alliance youth from Peru came to Brazil as a result of the *Lima Al Encuentro con Dios* campaign of the 1970s and 80s to prepare. At last, it seemed that C&MA Missions DNA was bearing fruit.

In Chile and Argentina, the Alliance church presidents felt that the time had come to reach out to "the regions beyond"

**AMACOS Leadership Meeting
in Buenos Aires**

as had the missionaries who came to their countries almost a century before. A meeting was called in Buenos Aires in 1992 where the presidents of the Alliance Churches of Argentina (Pastor Rogélio Nonini), Brazil (Pastor Sergio Pinto) and Chile (Pastor Eládio Medina) met with Rev. Peter Nanfelt, the head of the U.S. Alliance Mission and Rev. David Volstad, C&MA Regional Director for Latin America. They gathered together for prayer and planning. The result of this historic meeting was the founding of AMACOS (Alliance Missionary AGENCY of the Southern Cone), the first nationally-led Alliance missions effort in the history of the Alliance in the Southern Continent. At this foundational encounter it was decided that the three churches would combine their vision and efforts in order to begin "doing missions" on the continent, and Bolivia was chosen as the first mission field of this new effort.

A Chilean missionary couple was chosen and commissioned, and the cooperating churches combined to fund their work. At that same meeting, Pastor Eládio Medina challenged those gathered to ask themselves, "Shouldn't we look farther, beyond South America, to a needy country with people not reached by the gospel of Christ." The Brazil representatives spoke up: "We know a place that is desperately needy with little true gospel light – Portugal."

During the years between their fleeting first visit to Portugal on the way to Zaire, the burden and vision, born in the hotel room when they threw open the windows and began to pray, had only grown over the years. They shared their experience from 1986 with the other AMOCOS leaders, who listened intently. After prayer and discussion, it was decided that the team should make a survey visit to Portugal and to report back at the next meeting of AMACOS leadership.

Pinto and Jones traveled to Portugal in August 1992, traveling throughout the country, visiting major cities, interviewing evangelical leaders, including the president of the Portuguese Evangelical Alliance, Pastor João Cardoso. Pastor Cardoso was very encouraging and invited the Alliance to enter Portugal. He promised full support and even offered to provide the all-important letter of invitation that would enable the mission to become legally organized and recognized by the government, a very positive sign.

One memorable interview was held in Lisbon with Pastor Fernando Resina de Almeida, director and editor of *Livraria Nûcleo*, then one of Portugal's major Christian publishing houses. In response to the question, "If you were coming to Portugal as a missionary to establish an evangelistic, church-planting mission, where would you start?" the veteran pastor replied, "The North of Portugal, because that is the neediest of all regions of our countries; it is the heartland of the Catholic church and the most resistant area."

A second question was posed, "Why are there so many more missionaries in Lisbon as compared with the rest of the country?" He smiled and replied, "The weather is very nice in Lisbon, and there is an MK school located in the city." Without saying another word, his honest reply brought a sense of chagrin to the missionary questioner as he reflected on that candid response. Consequently, the missionary survey team began to look northward.

Their visit to Porto and the region of Northern Portugal confirmed Resina's verdict; the rocks and mountains of the north proved to be as hard as the rocky soul soil found there. Braga, not far from Porto, considered to be the "Vatican" of Portugal due to the presence of Portugal's Cardinal, presided over millions of Roman Catholics. Fátima, to the south, was one of the major Roman Catholic pilgrimage sites. The number of evangelical churches and missionaries in the region were much lower than their counterparts in Lisbon and the south of Portugal. It was considered the "cemetery of missionaries" for those who came from Brazil.

At the next AMACOS meeting in 1993, a project, PROPOR, was presented in its original form. This project was analyzed by the members present and was adopted as a joint project between U.S. Alliance missionaries and missionaries sent out and supported by AMACOS-related churches. The prospect of working in Portugal was growing and gradually gaining momentum.

In 1994, a revised proposal, "PROPOR '97", was written by Jones and Pinto for the next AMACOS meeting. It was accepted with a view toward a partnership between the United States Alliance, AMACOS and an eventual participation with the Brazil Alliance. However, while the Project was well received, it was considered premature and put on hold. Later, a word came from the Word: "Then the LORD replied: "Write down the vision and make it plain on tablets so that a herald may run with it. For the revelation awaits an appointed time; it speaks of the end and will not prove false. Though it linger, wait for it; it will certainly come and will not delay (Habakkuk 2:2-3). So the vision was written down and the "watchmen" waited for God's timing.

After about a decade, the burden of Portugal still

weighed heavy on the heart of the watchmen, and another vision trip to Portugal was taken in 2002. The enthusiasm and renewed vision generated by this visit was encouraging. Following that, in October 2004, a team of missionaries from the Brazil Mission staff, David and Judy Jones with Charlotte Hisle, flew to Portugal where they met with Rev. John Corby, then Regional Director for the Alliance mission in Europe. After meeting with leaders of the Portuguese Evangelical Alliance and traveling to the North of Portugal investigating areas where there was little or no evangelical witness, it seemed that the hour had come for the Alliance to enter Portugal.

Already in the town of Paredes, located west of the city of Porto, two Chilean Alliance missionaries, Liliana Morales and Vilma Bustamonte, had arrived there a few years before and worked among the women and children. Eventually Vilma left and Lili continued on alone. The visit with John Corby was very positive and it appeared that the vision for reaching Portugal was about to be realized. However after further consultation, the U.S. Alliance mission decided that entry to Portugal would be in partnership with ACEMBRAS, and there were neither the needed funds nor trained personnel ready for this venture. So the vision was kept warm in hearts while waiting for God's timing.

Five years later, another ACEMBRAS and U.S. mission survey team visited Portugal with the prospect of establishing the missionary partnership. A follow up visit in 2010 established the Alliance legally in Portugal and 2011 saw the long-awaited Pro-Por dream fulfilled with the missionary team of Danilo and Elaine Lima, Mike and Ruth Davis and Charlotte Hisle. The words given years before, "Though it linger, wait for it; it will certainly come and will not delay," proved to be prophetic and accurate.

Alliance Missions Department - DMA

What is currently known as the *Departamento de Missões Aliança* - DMA (Alliance Missions Department) was originally known as the "Alliance Missions Commission," until the DMA's creation at the ACEMBRAS 1997 Council. It took several years for the various missions projects, basically initiatives of local Alliance churches, to become unified under the Department. Agreed-upon candidate standards were established, policies and procedures developed, and principles for partnerships with other mission agencies were defined. This process was emphasized in 2010 and resulted in a more efficient and clearer presentation of the global task of missions to the local churches. Early on, the missions page, "The Regions Beyond" was a standard feature of the church magazine, *Aliança em Revista* (Alliance in Review). Later, the missions periodical, *Tíquico*, communicated and promoted the work of the missionaries.

As the internet increasingly became the primary means of communications, the DMA and missionaries were able to communicate more frequently and efficiently with the churches regarding what God was doing on the various fields in order to receive prayer and financial support. This more organized approach accenting the missionary vision of the Brazilian Alliance, using the Faith Promise as the primary funding vehicle, saw the missions focus sharpen and become more effective. The following records the various missions outreaches worldwide that today are supported by the Brazil C&MA under the DMA.

Back to Japan

Since the earliest days of the Alliance in Brazil, missions had been taught in the church and Bible Institute. The seed that Christ's last commission was the church's first command had been planted, and eventually that principle began to bear fruit in the 1980s. This was about the same time that a compelling vision for the lost worldwide began to impact the Brazilian evangelical church in general. Influences from abroad, such as Operation Mobilization's ship, *Doulos* and its visit to the major ports of Brazil excited the imagination of young Brazilian followers of Jesus who sensed God's leading to be a part of this movement.

It was at this same time, the "lost decade," that many Brazilian youth began to lose heart in the country and its future. Thus, the *dekassegui* movement began in South America. Meaning literally, "to be working distant from home," the term designated anyone who would leave the country of birth to work temporally in another region or country. The word came to describe Brazilians of Japanese descent that moved to Japan to work. The term also was used to describe Japanese from other South American countries who also made the pilgrimage back to Japan to find work.

In one of those ironic twists of God's sovereign leading, the country that first sent an Alliance missionary to Brazil also became the first one to receive Brazilian missionaries returning to the land of the rising sun. The way that God orchestrated this move was not apparent at first, but His ways and thoughts eventually became understandable.

In 1985, one of the bright young men who had been saved under the ministry of Pastor Izumi of the Rudge Ramos Church won a scholarship from the Japanese government to do his Masters degree in engineering at the Yokohama National University. While studying, he attended the Idogaya Evangelical Holiness Church in the city while he roomed at the university's dormitory for foreign students. A group of Christian

303

students from the university met for Bible study and fellowship. During his time while working on his masters, Jurandir Yanagihara, was one of the leaders.

When Jurandir was able to pass the difficult entrance exam to work on a PhD, he returned to Brazil and married his fiancée, Mami, in March of 1988. Together, they returned to Japan and rented a house not far from the university. There they were able to have visitors and invited the students and "dekasseguis" who were in the area to receive them and hold services. It was through this unpretentious manner that the ministry which became the *Communidade Sal da Terra*, "Salt of the Earth Community" was born. In the words of Jurandir Yanagihara:

> "The Salt Community" was the first evangelical community of Brazilians in Japan. It was founded by Pr. Jurandir "Jura" Yanagihara, coinciding with the beginning of the exodus of the Nikkei community from Brazil towards Japan in search of better living conditions. It all began in 1988 with Bible study and prayer meetings held at our home in Yokohama, bringing together Brazilians married to Japanese and young workers from the metropolitan area of Tokyo. These meetings in the homes were multiplying, with several weekly meetings being held in different cities of the metropolitan region. The extent of the ministry and the number of people involved had been increasing and it became necessary to rent a larger location to bring everyone together. The first service of the Salt Community took place in 1989 in a church in

Tokyo, with more than 70 people participating. Considering that the region of Yamato at that time had a large industrial complex attracting many Brazilians, and a Japanese Presbyterian Church in the city opened its doors to providing a permanent home for meetings, the services were transferred there.

The great exodus of Brazilians in the late 1980s and early 1990s, coupled with the fact that they still encountered major barriers to their adaptation to the new culture, caused the evangelistic work of the Salt Community to flourish. Even with the return of Jurandir and Mami to Brazil in 1991, the work continued to grow to the point of gathering more than 150 people at a given moment. With the wide territorial extension of the ministry and the need for greater attention and care, three groups were formed in different cities, each of them being cared for by a missionary from a Brazilian church.

In 1991, after completing his PhD and seminary degree, Jurandir and Mami returned to Brazil where they were asked to pastor the Rudge Ramos Church when Pastor Eduardo Yassui and his wife, Hiroko, went to Japan for an internship ministry in Matsuyama, home church of Missionary Mutsuko Ninomiya. The Rudge Ramos Church was in the process of officially joining ACEMBRAS and did so later in that same year. Thus, the "Salt" group that remained in Yamato became the focal point for ACEMBRAS's first missionary project promoted by the newly-created Department of Missions, the Japan Project. Pr. Luis Ueda became the first missionary sent out by ACEMBRAS. In 1998 the Comunidade Sal da Terra officially became part of the ministry of the Christian and Missionary Alliance of Brazil.

Luis Hideki Ueda graduated from SEMIBA (The Alliance Bible Seminary) in 1996. Following graduation, he served in the Rudge Ramos Alliance Church, and eventually was sent out by ACEMBRAS to Japan to give leadership to the Salt Community

in February of 1997. While there, he met a young lady from Peru who attended the meetings. She returned to the United States to be with her mother. Two years later, Luis married Tani Yuri Yoshikawa, on September 14, 1999 in Denver, Colorado. They returned to Japan and

**The Ueda Family
Luis, Lucas and Tani**

served until March 2001, when they went back to Brazil to pastor the Rudge Ramos Alliance. At that point, Pastor Joel Konno and Andréia were sent out by ACEMBRAS to pastor the Salt Community congregation in Yamoto. Five years later in February 2006, Luis and Tani returned to Japan with their son, Lucas, to pastor The Salt Community, where they remain till the present time.

On March 11, 2011, a huge 9 point undersea earthquake heaved up the sea floor more than forty miles off the eastern coast of Honshu Island, moving the island more than eight feet eastward, and causing a tsunami wave more than 130 foot tall which struck the coastline with devastating force. Considered Japan's worst ever earthquake and tsunami, the Fukushima Nuclear Plant suffered massive damage, three nuclear meltdowns, chemical explosions and widespread nuclear pollution and damage. At a time like this, some might wonder, "Where is God in all of this? The answer to that question is, "He is there in and through His people."

In the words of Luis Ueda:

"Our first trip to Iwaki (locale where the nuclear plant was damaged by the tsunami), occurred on March 29, soon after the army opened the highway. First of all, we took food to the local population and cleaned streets and houses. In April, we began to go farther north (Ishinomaki and Kessennuma), where there weren't so many volunteers, and there we met Pastor Mineguishi of the Baptist Church, which was doing an excellent job of caring for people. At first, we went to clean streets and rebuild houses. We did this for several months.

In December of 2011, we went with one hundred volunteers, the majority members of the Brazilian churches. We took food, clothing, organized a party and celebrated Christmas. From that time on, we went once a month for the next four years, taking food and holding evangelistic teas. Many people heard the gospel during that period. We visited 3,502 temporary houses. With the help of various churches and ministries, we were informed that in those four years, four churches had been restored and four more founded.

Despite the initial resistance felt when those aided realized that these were Christians, little by little those receiving the love of Christ through His people came to understand that these volunteers cared for them. Often survivors would ask the volunteers to come into their homes and they shared the trauma caused by the disaster. Prayers were offered for comfort and strong bridge-relationships were formed that permitted the volunteers from the Salt Community and other evangelical churches to share Christ. Some gave their lives to Christ; hundreds more received the first gospel seed which will bear fruit in due season.

The Amazon

As the missions wave began to break on the shores of Brazil in the 1980s and 90s, young men and women all over the country were touched by its power. ACEMBRAS pastors began to preach and teach missions as an integral part of the local church's life. In the Vista Verde Alliance Church in São José dos Campos, Pastor Sérgio Pinto, following the powerful experience among the refugees in Zaire that impacted his life and ministry, renewed his Great Commission focus before the growing congregation. In the words of Pastor Pinto:

At the Vista Verde Alliance Church, we were intensely motivated, with seminars by the late Pastor Edson Queirós, on the theme of the local church's responsibility to do missions. Also the winds of AMACOS were still blowing on me. In addition, years-old challenges given by Rev. David Volstad led me to put the Lord in the first place and to pass these challenges to the church. We also had strong influences, from Pastor

Ariovaldo Ramos on the Global Mission of the Church. With these two focuses, we set out to form a local missions commission that would be responsible for executing projects and motivating the church to carry them through. At the time, a young woman from our church, Patrícia Rocha showed strong indication as a candidate for one of the projects. She was studying in the CETEVAP (Center for Theological Studies of the Valley of the Paraiba) where she excelled in her studies, achieving, according to the faculty, a level of excellence in her preparation.

Having participated in a short-term missions project in Argentina, with the support of the Vista Verde church, Patrícia returned from that experience very interested in linguistics. As a result, she was sent by the church to the Federal District for training. Once again she completed her studies with excellent results. Thus, a working agreement was drawn up between MEVA and the Vista Verde Alliance, to send and support Patrícia to work with the Yanomami people group in Roraima. The Vista Verde Mission Commission literally got their hands dirty sending a team from São José to build a house for her in the middle of the Amazon jungle. It was a great challenge for Vista Verde church, which had set out to put into practice what we had learned, "Missions is the responsibility of the local church." Today, that initial project, which has undergone modifications, continues and is under the responsibility of the DMA.

Following a short-term missions visit to Argentina, Patrícia felt the Lord's call on her life to take the Word of God to at least one of the more than one hundred and eighty tribes

IGREJA ALIANÇA
vivendo o chamado juntos

Família Rocha: D. Terezinha, Patricia, Nikole e Poliana

Servindo o Senhor entre os índios Ianomamis

then in Brazil without the Scriptures. Sent out initially by the Vista Verde Alliance church in 1999, and the Alliance church in Taubaté, Patrícia eventually came under the DMA's administration, working in partnership with MEVA (the Evangelical Mission of Amazonia). Patrícia has become an exceptionally-gifted linguist, and for more than seventeen years has been working among the Yanomami, a people group discovered only in the 1980s, untouched by the "civilized world," and more importantly, unreached by the saving message of Christ. She has been working on the translation of the New Testament into Yanomami, with almost ninety percent complete, with only the Gospel of John and 1 and 2 Corinthians to be completed. Her goal is to see the New Testament completely translated by 2018. With her two adopted daughters, Poliana and Nicole, and Patrícia's mother, Terezinha, the Rocha Family has served a total of eighteen years in Roraima, near the border with Venezuela.

As a trained language consultant, she also works with other translators of tribal languages in Brasil; and recently, the Lord opened Patrícia's eyes to faraway horizons to begin ministry in Mozambique, in southeastern Africa, to help the evangelical churches to teach the Word of God and reach the still-untouched people groups in that needy nation.

André e Tânia Oliveira, Laura and Letícia

Another Alliance missionary couple hails from Rio Grande do Sul. André and Tânia Oliveira, with their two daughters, Laura and Letícia, have been serving in Boa Vista, Roraima for almost twenty years. One might ask the question: "How did a couple from the far south of Brazil ever get a heart to reach the indigenous peoples of Brazil's far north?" The answer to that question harks back to a Santa Fé Alliance church retreat held in 1989 in the interior of the state, near an Indian reservation where a New Tribes missionary couple had a retreat center. They worked among the Caingangue Indians, and a joint service was held with the Caingangue believers. At the end of the service, one of the local leaders stood and spoke to the Santa Fé members, "We are so grateful for the missionaries who have come from so far away to tell us about Jesus. But I have a question. You live right here. Why didn't you come to tell us of Jesus?" Strong conviction fell on all those from the "Missionary Alliance" Church. They returned to Porto Alegre determined to become a missionary supporting and sending church. From that time on, the Santa Fé Alliance began holding annual missions conferences where the youth were challenged to respond to God's calling on their lives.

Brenda Kurtz was leading the youth ministry at that time. André came to the youth meetings and accepted the Lord in the early 90s. Then as a teenager, he had attended the Caingangue retreat where a seed was planted. Later, during one of the missions conferences, he responded, and from there went to the Theological Institute in Gramado. There he met Tania, who was from a Baptist church located in a small town close to the Argentina border. While in Gramado, they were introduced to MEVA, and there they felt that it was among the indigenous people groups in the Amazon that the Lord wanted them to minister.

Sent out in 1998 to work with the Waiwai tribe, the first indigenous people group in Brazil to have the complete Bible, and considered an evangelized tribe, the task before them was to prepare Waiwai "missionaries" to reach across cultural and tribal barriers to evangelize unreached peoples that are still found in the deepest reaches of the Amazon rain forest.

Since the Brazilian Indian Service, FUNAI, prohibited foreign and Brazilian missionaries from seeking to evangelize these primitive indigenous peoples, for fear that their "primitive cultural life style" would be "ruined" by the entrance of people from the outside, MEVA and other Brazilian mission agencies decided to train and send out evangelized Christian tribals who could not be prohibited from reaching out to other indigenous people groups. Thus the 2 Timothy 2:2 principle of "teaching one to teach another to reach another" took hold, with the message of Christ crossing language and cultural barriers that formerly were battle lines.

Following that experience, André studied anthropology at a local university and began to work in the training of other Brazilian missionaries, not only in the north of Brazil, but at other seminaries and missions training schools. More recently, he became vice president of MEVA and helped give leadership to this growing and effective Brazilian mission with which the DMA partners. The Oliveiras are another of the DMA's veteran group, those who have served for several terms, gained valuable ministry know-how and are reaching their peak years in terms of experience and effectiveness.

**André and Tánia Oliveira
and daughters**

Silvio and Simone Albuquerque, Sarah and Rebecca

Rio Grande do Sul has shown itself to be a very fertile "seed bed" for missionaries. Silvio and Simone Albuquerque were members of the Santa Fé Alliance Church planted by the missionary team led by Richard and Marilyn LaFountain and Steve and Diane Renicks. Simone's parents had accepted the Lord at Santa Fé, and she too gave her heart to the Lord there as a child. Silvio accepted the Lord as a teenager. Meeting at the church, they started dating and were married. Simone's parents decided to move back to the interior and her father turned over his half of a family business to Sílvio. Simone went on to become a dentist. As they sensed God's leading they studied at the Porto Alegre extension of SEMIBA. Charlotte Hisle was very instrumental in their discipleship. They worked with the missionaries on the Petropolis church plant and continued to work there even after the missionaries left Porto Alegre.

Simone also had attended the Caingangue retreat in 1989, and like André, she too was impacted by the challenge of the church leader. Like the Pulz Family who served in Russia, as well as André and Tânia Oliveira, ministering to indigenous peoples of Roraima, Silvio and Simone received their vision for missions from the Santa Fé pastors. In 2007, Silvio and Simone sensed God's timing and began to prepare to leave Porto Alegre for the far north.

Silvio worked as a systems analyst and Simone as a dentist. While serving on the leadership team at the Morada do Vale Alliance church just outside of Porto Alegre, God suddenly opened the door. In February 2013, they left for the field to serve with MEVA. They received language training and cross-cultural studies during their first years. Boa Vista, the capital of Roraima, served as their home base, from which they could visit villages, give primary dental care and gain a general idea of the work.

In 2014, they felt direction from God to look toward the Yanomami region, where Patrícia Rocha also was serving. After taking part in a MEVA project, MICAL (Ministry for the

Training of Indigenous Leaders), they sensed that they should follow that direction. Knowing that they would need to move into the region where the Yanomami live, they developed the *Halikato-U* Project. The purpose of this project is to live in the Halikato-U village of the Yanomami, learn the

The Albuquerque Family
Sílvio, Simone, Rebecca and Sarah

language and culture in order to preach the Word, evangelize, disciple and train leaders in the community. The intention was to live in the region for at least five years.

All of this meant they had to build a house in the village, dig a well and learn to live a much simpler, even primitive life style than they were used to living in Porto Alegre. They are now living and learning as they work with the local population with their two daughters, Sarah and Rebecca.

Nilson and Milena Rodrigues de Sousa, Nathan and Daniel

Nilson and Milena Rodrigues came to Christ at the age of seventeen. Nilson was from Bahia and Milena from Maranhão, in the far northeast. They were married in 1999 and sensed God's calling on their lives in 2002 while members of the

Gama Alliance church in the Federal District of Brasilia. Their pastor, Abisai Nunes de Lima, encouraged them as they prepared. Nilson studied at the Baptist Theological Seminary in Brasília and they both took part in the "Mark Project" preparatory course at the Word of Life Seminary in São Paulo.

They joined *Asas de Socorro*, the Brazilian sister mission of the Missionary Aviation Fellowship – MAF, in 2008. Asas de Socorro works in partnership with MEVA, New Tribes of Brasil, YWAM, and SIL/Wycliffe in Brasil. After three years of study, Nilson became a certified mechanic in airplane maintenance, with a specialization in the area of electronics and avionics. They live and work at the Asas airbase in Anápolis, Goiás, as well as having served at the Asas de Socorro base in Manaus, Amazonas. Milena works in administration at the Asas head office as secretary for the Partnership in Ministry team. They are supported by their Gama Alliance home church. Both of their sons were born in Brasília and attend elementary school.

Nilson and Milena Rodrigues de Soüsa and Sons

Marcelo and Elaine Okassawara

Marcelo and Elaine Okasawara, both from São Paulo state, are not missionaries sent out by the DMA. However, their salvation story and missionary calling have deep Alliance roots. Elaine was a member of the Vila Madalena Alliance church and began to date Marcelo, a young businessman from the interior.

Elaine was very concerned about the relationship since she liked Marcelo but felt conflicted since he was not a believer. Praise God, Marcelo found Christ at the "Quality of Life," church retreat, organized by missionaries Douglas and Helen White.

As a new convert, Marcelo devoured the Word, soon felt deeply that God was leading him into missions. Following their marriage, Marcelo was able to free himself from the family business, and the Okasawara Family moved back to the interior of São Paulo. Since there was no Alliance church in their city, Marcelo and Elaine began to fellowship at a local Baptist church. In God's timing, the Okassawara, with their two children, Clara and Felipe, were sent out to minister in the far northern state of Roraima among the people of the *Alto Arraia*, where there has been a powerful move of the Holy Spirit. In one year, more than ten percent of one village in the area had been converted. All of the tribe has received copies of the Scriptures, and they are seeing the seed bear much fruit.

India

The Airport Alliance Church became home to many young converts who had come to São Paulo to try to break into the upper tiers of professional "Futebol," the Brazilian national pastime. Many of these young men never made it to the top of the sport, but more importantly, they did find a home at the first church in Brooklin at the Princesa Isabel site. David Peters, missionary leader of the São Paulo Encontro com Deus ministry, with his wife, Arlene, discipled many of these athletes who later became part of the church as members and leaders.

It was to this church that a young man, Romário de Jesus Moraes, began to attend. He came from a difficult home, and had a rough childhood and teen years that led him far from

God, and deep into a tragic lifestyle. However, by God's grace, the lost sheep was found by the shepherd and became a fervent Christian. He soon sensed a desire to serve God and began to study at the Instituto Bíblico Aliança. About this time, he met a young lady, Jaqueline, who also was a Christ follower with a burden to share Jesus with others. They married and began to follow God's leading on their lives toward missions.

In November 1996, they were sent to Peru with the Kairos Mission to serve as missionary interns on the outskirts of Lima. During the two years there, they planted a church in the slum-town of *Canto Grande*, where they gained valuable experience in language acquisition, evangelism, church planting and cross-cultural communication. They then returned to São Paulo and continued to prepare for missionary service. About that time, God laid on the heart of this young couple a great burden for the countless millions of India, where so little witness for Christ was found in many regions of the country. Sensing that sport's universal appeal could be a means of reaching these areas of limited access to the gospel in India, they began to pray and prepare. Romário, who has the same name of one of the greatest of Brazil's soccer legends, began to

The Moraes Family in India

prepare to go down this avenue. He took the necessary training courses and gained certification as a bone-fide "futebol" coach, qualified to teach the sport and train players.

Thus, in 2003 Romário and Jaqueline Moraes, with their three daughters, Anabel, Mariana e Larissa, were sent out by the Department of Missions (DMA) of ACEMBRAS to begin a new and innovative missionary initiative, the "India Project," in the city of Kolkata (Calcutta) in West Bengal state. This project proposed using soccer as the principal outreach tool to open doors and hearts to the Good News.

Beginning with no knowledge of the local language, Bengali, and a modest command of English, the Moraes Family tried to relate to the youths, taking advantage of every opportunity to be with them. Their house and family became a reference for all of them. Even Portuguese-language movies were watched, although no one understood anything. Through the Holy Spirit, God used the language of love and sports to reach them. Almost two years later, eight youths understood the Word and gave their lives to Christ. It was the beginning of everything that exists today.

In 2007, after having seen the transformation of their son, free from alcohol, a Hindu family decided to lend part of the property to start the church, now known as the Sonarpur Christian Fellowship. There, a small hut of straw was built and services were begun. Seven months later, through the donation of a generous brother from Sao Paulo, a lot was bought and they started the construction of the church headquarters. Currently it has three floors, where 300 people attend almost daily activities, with the highlight being a Sunday School with 150 children attending each week.

During these years, Romário and Jaqueline worked to disciple and develop the spiritual formation of the young leaders. Four of the first eight who received Christ were sent to the William Carey Seminary and became pastors. They are now married with their own families and serving the Lord. Other leaders are being trained and are responsible for the progress of the work today, including the former alcoholic son of the family who "lent the land" for the first straw-hut church. He finished Bible School recently and is a faithful worker, and all his family became Christians.

In summary, the ministry today consists of three football academies, the main church, three congregations and four home Bible studies. The ministry has two full-time pastors and two part-time workers. The churches and workers are under the supervision of Pastor Ashok Andrews from Kolkata Christian Fellowship, their faithful partner since 2006. During their time in Kolkata, Romário and Jaqueline supervised the Academies and counseled the workers.

After twenty years of ministry, Romário and Jaqueline, now with two daughters in college, sensed God's leading to a new region of India, in the city of Pune, second largest city in the state of Maharashtra, on the Indian Ocean coast. Considered the "Oxford of the East" because of the several prestigious universities there, Pune is also highly industrialized.

Arriving there in mid 2016, the Moraes family began the process of adaptation to a new language and culture in their new place of service. The Pune Project will be developed in three phases: During their first year, they will work on building relationships, establishing an activity center and office and beginning two courses, one in soccer and the other in music. Their mid-range goal is to develop these activities, start new ones featuring basketball, table tennis, art and dance, enroll, as well as training new workers from inside and outside the country, opening new sport academies in other regions, and sharing the Word. Their long-range goals are to evangelize, plant a new fellowship, disciple the believers, and develop new leaders for the future of the work.

The vision that burdened the heart of Romário and Jaqueline Moraes for more than twenty years, continues to burn today, wider and with more knowledge and understanding of the great challenges that lie before them. Despite Romário's constant battles with health issues over the years, and the struggle to raise three young daughters in a very difficult culture, the faithful God who called them has already brought much to pass and will continue to do so as they reach out to the millions on the Indian subcontinent. The Moraes Family serves as an example for young Brazilian Alliance youth as they seek God for their part in the fulfillment of the Great Commission of Christ.

Russia

Their personal "history" as children of God was being written. They may have recognized that a Divine hand was writing on the pages of their lives even though they often only saw crossed-out, smudged and wandering narratives. They learned that only after giving one's life to Christ does their story begin to truly make sense. Today, they can now see that their story has a beginning, a middle and purposeful conclusion. Every story is its own story. Leialdo and Roni Pulz, "gauchos" from the far-southern state of Rio Grande do Sul, certainly must have wondered as God wrote His story on their lives.

Leialdo was born in Novo Hamburgo and raised in a spiritist home, but found no peace of mind or heart in a religion that taught works salvation, reincarnation, and communication with the dead. He was hungry for God, and he found the "bread of life," in Jesus Christ as his Savior and Lord while still young. By the time Leialdo was twelve, God had put a great burden on his heart for Russia, then called "The Soviet Union." Thus he began to study the language on his own, using tapes and books purchased from the Russian Language Institute in the nearby city of Porto Alegre.

The more Leialdo studied, the more burdened he felt for the people of that needy country. When The Soviet Union imploded as a political entity in 1991, he sensed that God was leading him to prepare to be a missionary. After high school, Leialdo entered the missions program at the Janz Team Bible Theological Seminary in Gramado, Rio Grande do Sul. While studying, the pastor of his church in São Leopoldo told him that his church would not send out, nor support Leialdo. Despite that discouraging word, Lei continued to follow the calling that God had put on his life.

While at Gramado, he met Roniângela, administrative assistant to the director. She was from the hill country north of Porto Alegre. She was raised in a nominal Catholic home broken by divorce. Like Leialdo, as a youth, she had searched for God and had become a Christ-follower. Some time later, she began attending the Santa Fé Alliance Church in Porto Alegre, where she was discipled, baptized and became an active member. While there, she heard God's call on her life and decided to prepare for ministry.

As the two got to know each other, they sensed that God was bringing them together. Following marriage, Roni helped her husband finish seminary in 1997. They then moved to the Federal District of Brasília, serving two years in the Gama Alliance Church and another three years in Taguatinga, where they completed their home service. While serving the church in Taguatinga, God began a slow but sure process of making the long-awaited Russia dream a reality.

In May 2002, the Department of Missions of ACEMBRAS sent Leialdo and Roni to Russia on a one-month, short-term mission. While there, they visited several cities in the State of Krasnodar where Leialdo preached and shared in the Alliance-related churches. They visited the Lampados Bible College in Krasnodar, with Leialdo translating for Roni as she shared her story. At Novorossiysk, they participated in a conference for national pastors. Leialdo's years of self-study of the Russian language made a great impression. The field director was amazed at his language ability and said that his language competence exceeded many of the U.S. missionary staff who had studied in formal language schools. The whole experience was a strong confirmation of God's call on their lives to Russia.

Following two years of home service in Porto Alegre, and another two years with the Paraíso Alliance Church in São Paulo, Lei and Roni were sent out to Russia with their two daughters Vanessa and Raíssa, in August 2005. After arriving in Krasnodar, field headquarters for the C&MA Mission and the national Evangelical Christian and Missionary Union, they began language study and worked with local Russian churches in the areas of preaching, teaching, discipling, as well as working with praise and worship teams. In 2007, they began a soccer project, the Christian Football League, with a local pastor. This

IGREJA ALIANÇA
Vivendo o chamado juntos

Família Pulz
Leialdo
Roni
Vanessa
Raíssa

Servindo o Senhor na Rússia

evangelistic ministry, built on a soccer platform, which was wildly popular in Russia and around the world, has opened closed doors all over The Russian Federation. Several teams from Brazil have gone there and shared the Gospel while holding soccer clinics in schools, for churches, in hospitals and other non-religious settings. This evangelistic tool is proving to be effective in unlocking doors formerly bolted and resistant to the message of Jesus Christ. It is now considered a model to be imitated by Alliance national churches worldwide to take the Gospel to those unreached by more conventional means.

In 2011, the Pulz family returned to Brazil to work in the Alliance Bible Seminary (now A. W. Tozer Theological Seminary) in teaching and administration. Presently Leialdo is director of the school and Roni is administrative assistant at the Tozer Seminary.

Portugal

In the 1990's Elaine was invited by her aunt to visit the Airport Alliance Church, which was then located on Renascença Street. A few years later, other relatives took her to the Vista Verde Alliance Church in São José dos Campos, where she made a public profession of faith under the ministry of Pastor Sergio Pinto. In 1999 she started attending the Airport church which had moved to Santa Caterina Avenue, and her walk with God became solid. That same year, during a missions' conference at the church, after hearing an *Avante* missionary speak, she sensed a call to overseas ministry. Because of this commitment she went on two short-term missions' trips; one to Bolivia in 2000 and then a second in 2001 to the *Wai-Wai* tribe in the Amazon.

Danilo had attended evangelical churches since his early childhood. As a young man he received an invitation from his

Danilo and Elaine Lima

aunt to visit the Brooklin Alliance Church (later named the Airport Alliance), where he started attending. In 1989, at a youth camp of the Alliance church, he confirmed his decision to follow Christ.

In 1998 Danilo went to Bahia to work with his father and brother in a simple fishing village. Once there, he suffered a near fatal accident while driving a pickup truck loaded with a ton of shrimp and ice. A donkey wandered onto the road, right into the path of the truck, and they collided. Immediately after the accident, when Danilo realized he was still alive, he felt God talking to him, "If you had died, what have you done for Jesus?" Soon he started sharing his faith and distributing Bibles that Pastor José Freitas sent him from São Paulo. Previously there had been no evangelical church in this community, although a pastor from another village came every two weeks to hold home meetings. In collaboration with this pastor's ministry, Danilo led people to Christ. Donations were given to construct a church building. Twenty years later this church continues its ministry with leaders that Danilo knew as adolescents.

Pastor José invited Danilo to return to São Paulo in 1999 and study at the Alliance Bible Institute, which he did. There at the Airport Church, while studying at the Alliance Bible Seminary, Danilo and Elaine met and realized that they had both been called to serve the Lord. While studying at SEMIBA, they were challenged to consider Portugal as their eventual place of missionary service, and a seed was planted in their minds, which took time to bear fruit. By 2005, they were married and began their ministry together. In 2008 they were invited to be a part of Project Portugal and arrived in Portugal in 2011, where they serve with their family as part of a bi-national Brazilian - U. S. Alliance missionary team.

Conclusion

The Word of God teaches that good seed will produce good fruit according to its kind. When good seed is planted it produces roots that penetrate deeply in the soil and serve as a foundation for the trunk, which grows up and puts out branches where the fruit can grow and flourish. Jesus said that His desire is that we, branches of His living vine, produce fruit, more fruit, much fruit and fruit that lasts. From around the world, God planted and grafted in roots and grew branches that today are reaching out to other continents and lands, preaching the same Christ-centered message and reaching the lost worldwide. To God be the glory!

CHAPTER ELEVEN
GOOD ROOTS
PRODUCE
GOOD FRUIT

Trees take time to take root and produce good fruit. No doubt those who plant and cultivate sometimes wonder if the tree will flourish, and viewing from close up makes it hard to have proper perspective of its growth and potential. Consequently, because of the relatively small number of churches and members in ACEMBRAS, spread over a country larger than all other South American countries, those who worked in the Brazilian "vineyard" should not be criticized for sometimes feeling embarrassed, when comparing the Brazil Alliance with other Alliance churches on the continent.

At the same time, by the early 2000s, the Alliance Church of Brazil was noticed by Alliance church leaders worldwide. For its relative size, ACEMBRAS had fielded one of the largest missionary teams of any church belonging to the Alliance World Fellowship. The ACEMBRAS Department of Missions was supporting missionaries in Japan, Russia and India, as well as several couples in the Amazon. A few years later in 2011, the first bi-national team of Brazilians and Americans began to work in Portugal. At the same time,

ACEMBRAS continued to evangelize and plant churches in Brazil as a priority, because lost people everywhere need to know Jesus and planting new churches is one of the best ways to lead people to Christ and develop new supporters for Great Commission outreach.

In 2007, the Brazil Mission staff had been commissioned to develop a field exit strategy and set a target date when the mission staff would depart Brazil and the national church, ACEMBRAS, would continue its ministry on its own. After much prayer and discussion, a date was set – 2020. Thus, both mission and national church could work together to strengthen, build up and broaden the church base, recruit and train new workers and leave ACEMBRAS ready to carry out its Great Commission responsibility.

However, God's ways and thoughts are not necessarily ours, and the carefully developed chronogram was unexpectedly changed a year later. From April 8 to 12, 2008, the Alliance World Fellowship held its quadrennial conference in Santiago, Chile. More than 350 delegates from 52 countries attended the conference, representing 91 different countries where Alliance ministry is present. A delegation from Brazil attended since it was held on the same continent. As a result, the Alliance mission was represented by Field Director, Tim Bubna and his wife JoLee, while ACEMBRAS had sent its president, Pastor José Freitas and his wife, Glaucia.

While at the conference, Bubna was informed that the exit strategy had been altered and the date for departure, instead of 2020, was moved up to 2013. This decision was made by the C&MA leadership, because Brazil was considered a "reached," evangelized country. Because of the C&MA's "unreached peoples" commitment to take the Gospel to nations where little or no knowledge of the message of salvation was present, the difficult decision was made to speed-up the exit strategy.

Bubna was given the difficult job of determining which of the missionary staff would begin the transition phase from the field to the States. By the end of that year, the first couple, Steve and Diane Renicks, had left for America. Over the next few years, Doug and Helen White, Sanford and Wendy Hashimoto, Alex and Julie Zell, Jeff and Jo Kiel, Paul and Beverly Clark and Charlotte Hisle, had exited Brazil. In 2013, Bubna sold the mission office and field director residence and "officially" closed the field. After more than sixty years of ministry since the first Alliance missionaries from Japan and Brazil had arrived, the Alliance Mission of Brazil ceased to officially exist.

Thus what had been an original strategic exit plan, became a much more urgent departure. How would ACEMBRAS react to this unexpected and unwelcome news? Would there be hurt, recriminations, a feeling of broken trust and abandonment? These were questions that would test the strength of the relationship between national leaders and the mission. Yet, happily, the Brazil Alliance responded with gracious acceptance. While not overjoyed with the accelerated exit, they understood the rationale presented by the North American mission leaders and made the necessary adjustments. For the members of the Brazil Mission, it was a great comfort to see that the results of their labor had produced good and lasting fruit. As a result of this unexpected change of the departure date, an aggressive goal to plant thirty new churches by 2020 was set by ACEMBRAS leaders.

In late 2014, International Ministries of the C&MA decided to extend the transition timeline in order to assist the national church in its ambitious church planting program of doubling the number of churches. Therefore, veteran missionaries, Len and Diane Warden completed their ministry with the church plant in Lagoa Santa, MG. Following home assignment, they returned to assist and advise ACEMBRAS for another term. International Ministries sensed that this would represent a better-written final chapter for the Mission's work in Brazil. (See APPENDIX for the rest of the story.)

Roots that had been planted decades before from Japan, North America, Argentina, Colombia, Chile and even far-off China, all with the same Christ-centered message and "then-the -end-shall-come" driving mission produced a national church with vision and purpose. From the earliest days of A. B. Simpson's vision for an "Alliance" of believers who would take that full-gospel message to all men and women everywhere, Brazil had been on his radar screen. In his earliest missions publication, *The Word, the Work and the World*, he wrote of longing to see this young nation, just climbing out of its "splendid cradle," become a land free of the domination of a corrupt priesthood and churches where sins were "forgiven" weekly while the people continued in them. And, by God's grace, after two early aborted attempts to plant such an "Alliance" in Brazil, a church rooted in His vision and purpose exists and grows and is producing lasting fruit. And, to God be the glory, it will continue to do so, until that "end comes."

APPENDIX

The need for an Appendix became apparent as the last chapters of this book were being written. More material from former mission colleagues came in; in addition, there was the need to cover other aspects of this history which had not been previously treated adequately. Personal contributions make up the largest part of this section, but other matters will also be included.

C&MA Missionaries to Brazil with arrival date, totaling 66 missionaries; 30 couples and 7 single women.

1. Rev. Mutsuko Ninomiya from the Japan Alliance Church – 3/25/59
2. Rev. Paul and Mrs. Claudia Bryers – 1/16/62
3. Rev. Samuel (10/11/62 · deceased 9/12/1975) & Mrs. Vera Barnes – 01/63 – deceased 3/31/94

4. Rev. David and Mrs. Marilyn Sundeen – 9/7/63
5. Rev. John and Mrs. Beverly Nicholson – 9/7/63
6. Rev. Alwyn and Mrs. Edythe Rees – 7/27/64
7. Rev. Emmit (deceased 5/6/1991) and Mrs. Sandra Young – 8/7/64
8. Rev. Thomas (deceased January 2009) and Mrs. Mary Kyle – 8/27/65
9. Rev. David and Mrs. Judith Jones – 8/12/67
10. Rev. James and Mrs. Ann Hemminger – 9/12/69
11. Rev. Darrell and Mrs. Jan Smith – 09/26/70
12. Rev. Robert and Mrs. Shirley Kallem – 1/18/74
13. Rev. James and Mrs. Billie Jo Medin – 1/18/74
14. Rev. Lawrence and Mrs. Ida Jenks – 7/26/75 (deceased 5/10/96)
15. Rev. John and Mrs. Loraine Todd – 06/30/76
16. Rev. Richard and Mrs. Marilyn LaFountain – 1/11/77
17. Rev. Stephen and Mrs. Diane Renicks – 8/09/79
18. Rev. Sanford and Mrs. Wendie Hashimoto – 3/19/80
19. Miss Regene Bartel (Martin) – 3/18/83
20. Miss Rebecca Otero (Anderson) – 07/17/83
21. Miss Brenda Kurtz – 10/04/84 (deceased 11/13/12)
22. Rev. Leonard and Mrs. Diane Warden – 08/08/86
23. Rev. Michael and Mrs. Ruth Davis – 10/09/86
24. Rev. Timothy and Mrs. Jo Lee Bubna – 12/03/1986
25. Rev. Jeff and Mrs. Jo Kiel – 01/07/87
26. Rev. David and Mrs. Arlene Peters – 07/01/87
27. Rev. Paul and Mrs. Beverly Clark (deceased 1/7/13) – 12/14/87
28. Rev. Douglas and Mrs. Helen White – 01/13/88
29. Rev. David and Mrs. Sue Manske – 4/9/89
30. Miss Charlotte Hisle – 01/04/89
31. Miss Barbara Bradshaw – 01/90

32. Rev. Dwayne and Mrs. Rhonda Buhler – 09/06/90
33. Rev. Alex and Mrs. Julie Zell – 10/04/95
34. Rev. Bryan and Mrs. Vickie Joyce – 10/17/97
35. Rev. Marshall and Mrs. Theresa Erickson – 08/98
36. Rev. James and Mrs. Nikki Chung – 08/08/2000
37. Miss. Ruth Strubbe – 01/2003

WORKERS APPROVED BY GOD

From the earliest years of the Alliance Mission in Brazil, the preparation of national workers had high priority for the mission. As soon as the first church-planting campaigns resulted in new believers, it was expected that God would call and raise up men and women for training in ministry. The following is an abbreviated sketch of a much more complete and compelling story to be told in full by others. However, this small contribution will provide a timeline and basic outline of the growth of this ministry.

As a result, the earliest effort to train workers began in 1971, shortly after the second successful church plant in Curitiba. With the Boa Vista and Capão de Imbuia churches underway, there were those ready and willing to be trained. Thus, the Alliance Mission entered a working relationship with the Maringá Bible Institute of the United Missionary Church. Two extension courses for academic credit were approved by Maringá and were begun in Curitiba. One class, "The Life of

Christ," was taught by Emmit Young at the Boa Vista church with nine students, and David Jones taught a course on Evangelism at the Capão with five students.

Sensing a growing need, Board Representative, Thomas Kyle, charged David Jones in mid-1973 with the responsibility of organizing and beginning the "Alliance Training Center," called *CETRA* (*Centro de Treinamento da Aliança*). From the earliest years, the Scriptural admonition that Paul gave in 2 Timothy 2:15: "Be diligent to present yourself to God as one approved, a worker who doesn't need to be ashamed, correctly teaching the word of truth," became the goal. Thus, the school that eventually became the A. W. Tozer Theological Seminary located in São Paulo had a rather humble origin. Yet, the founders did not despise the day of small beginnings.

CETRA was housed in a rented hall in downtown Curitiba, with courses taught three nights a week. In the second semester of that year, the Joneses were sent to Porto Alegre and Darrell Smith became director and the school was moved to another rental site on Praça Osório. In 1975, James Medin became director of *CETRA*, and the following year the name was changed to *Instituto Bíblico Aliança* (Alliance Bible Institute). The first two students graduated in 1976, Alberto Casapietra and Maria Ângela de Lapa.

In 1977, there were seven students registered with five in the pastoral course and another two in the music program. Classes met three times a week, with four subjects being taught over a fifteen-week semester. IBA followed a three-year program, two-semesters year, with four teachers on the faculty: James Medin, Thomas Kyle, Larry Jenks and Ann Hemminger.

In 1978, enrollment increased to twenty-three students, with thirteen in the pastoral course. The faculty grew to seven teachers and the program was growing. Due to financial restraints, the downtown location was closed and IBA was moved to the Capão da Imbuia church. The move resulted in a drop-in enrollment to sixteen students, with only three in the pastoral course by year's end. Upon return from furlough, David Jones was named IBA director in mid 1978.

Despite the challenges facing the school, the first IBA extension center was opened in Porto Alegre in 1979, and that same year two other extension centers were opened in São José dos Campos and Brasília. In the second semester of 1979, a second-floor property was purchased in downtown Curitiba, in the Galeria Andrade. The new facility was remodeled, and by 1980 enrollment had jumped back up to thirty-two students. Due to the arrival of out-of-town students, a "dormitory" was set up on the Capão church's property for students coming from Brasília and São José dos Campos to study. It is important to note that this "jump" came as the result of the first "official" time of fasting and prayer ever convened by the Mission. It was called specifically so that God would send more students to IBA, and He answered in a big way.

In 1981, James Medin returned to direct the school. He was followed by Lawrence Jenks in mid-1982, who continued as director till 1985 when the Jenks family furloughed. In 1983, two students arrived from Manaus bringing the total student enrollment up to thirty-six, with twenty-four studying full-time. By this time, the students were coming from various Alliance churches as well as the Holiness, Nazarenes, Independent Presbyterians, Lutheran, Baptists, Four-Square, Anglican, Presbyterian, Lutheran, Mennonite Brethren and Evangelical Alliance churches. In addition, another fifty students were studying in the three extension programs.

Over the next several years, the student body plateaued in number. In 1986 through 1990, Lawrence and Ida Jenks were assigned to work at the Theological Institute of Gramado, of the Canadian-based Janz Team Mission. Several Alliance students graduated from Gramado, including Minister Gardenia Alves, now planting a church in Cocalzinho GO, Pastor Paulo Koon of Campinas, as well as Pastor Leialdo and Roni Pulz and Missionaries André and Tânia Oliveira. In 1990, the Jenks returned to the United States. Soon after, Larry became a professor at Toccoa Falls College in Georgia.

Mrs. Ann Hemminger became director of IBA following Lawrence Jenks and continued in that capacity from 1985 till 1989. Over that period, there was an average of twenty-six students at the IBA facility in Curitiba. Besides serving the Alliance, IBA continued to train students from the many other evangelical churches. Many of those graduates serve in Curitiba, Santa Catarina and Rio Grande do Sul as pastors, seminary professors and church planters.

After the last class of eight graduated in November of 1988, the decision to close IBA was made because the Hemmingers were returning to the U.S. for furlough mid-1989, and because of the lack of new students. In 1989, the Division of Overseas Ministries/C&MA, decided to transfer the mission staff from Curitiba to São Paulo. This resulted in the sale of the IBA property in Curitiba and closing of the school. There were students from denominations other than the Alliance at that time who were not able to graduate. Despite the difficult decisions made regarding the closing of IBA, the Hemmingers were gratified because they could invest in so many lives.

At the same time, the new mission initiative to enter São Paulo with an "Encounter-type" of program with aggressive evangelism and discipleship and a strong missionary team was showing good fruit. By early 1990, there was a growing interest on the part of several youth from the church-plant to prepare for ministry. Led by David and Arlene Peters, who had transitioned from Colombia where they had been part of a successful Encounter effort, the Alliance Church in the Brooklin neighborhood on Princesa Isabel had several young people sensing God's call on their lives. Peters contacted Dave and Judy Jones, who had just closed the Alliance Bible Center in Brasília in September because of the 800% increase in rent in just six months. After more than seven years in the "Pilot Plan" of Brasília, the Joneses were waiting for God's direction on their lives. Peters asked Jones to come to São Paulo and join the Encounter team, with the intent of beginning a ministry training program.

This request to relocate to São Paulo to reopen the Alliance Bible Institute in São Paulo resulted in the Joneses traveling south to be part of a youth retreat in November of 1990. While there, it became apparent that there was a group of quality youth with great ministry potential. The Joneses sensed that God was directing them to move to São Paulo to develop a new program and curriculum. An innovative proposal for training in Bible and theology was presented to the São Paulo team and at ACEMBRAS's 14th General Council. The Book of Acts was chosen as the 'spinal column' of an integrated program of biblical theological study designed for those called to ministry who had already demonstrated gifting for ministry at the Princesa Isabel church, or elsewhere. The program was designed as a four-year course of study, three nights a week with two and a half hours of class time and thirteen week semesters. The proposal was accepted and the Joneses moved to São Paulo in early January 1991.

The first class began on March 8, 1991 in the basement of the building on Princesa Isabel with twelve students registered. Soon after opening, IBA was accepted by *AETTE*, a

Brazilian evangelical accrediting agency for Bible institutes and seminaries. The library of 1,000 books which had been inherited after IBA had been closed in Curitiba was upgraded to 3,000+ in short order. By the next semester, the classrooms and library were moved across the street at Princesa Isabel into the same building where the Alliance Mission office relocated after the move from Curitiba. Faculty members included Arlene Peters, Paul Clark, Ann Hemminger and David Jones. By the end of 1993, the goal of 3,000 books for the library had been attained. The student body varied from twelve to fifteen.

In mid 1994, the Joneses furloughed and Paul Clark became the director for IBA. The Joneses moved to the Alliance National Office in Colorado Springs, Colorado, and Paul gave leadership to the Instituto for the next several years. Over that time, IBA moved as the school grew and vacated the building where the mission office was located. Over the years, the faculty grew, with Mike and Ruth Davis teaching as well as Tim and Jo Lee Bubna, David Manske, Beverly Clark and Alex Zell. Pastor Jurandir Yanagihara came on the board as vice president in 1997. Charlotte Hisle, who had been one of the principal teachers for many courses, served as interim director when the Clarks furloughed in 1998. The next year, Rev. Yanagihara became the first Brazilian director of SEMIBA and continued until he was elected president of ACEMBRAS. Paul Clark returned to the school as Academic Dean in 1999 and continued in his new role until Jurandir was elected president.

In 2002, the school moved into expanded facilities in Conceição, not far from the Metrô Station, where it remained for several years. In 2003, a Bachelor of Theology was added to the course offerings. An extension program restarted at the Vista Verde Alliance in São José dos Campos. Video conference classes in Taubaté e Bauru were begun in 2005. In 2009 as the

Airport Alliance church was building a new multi-story facility on Baronesa de Bela Vista, discussions began between the church leadership and SEMIBA with the idea of joint financing of the construction. Funds held by the Mission after the sale of the old IBA facilities in Curitiba in 1990 were added to other funding and construction began in 2010. That same year, Pastor Joel Jun Konno, former IBA graduate in the 1990s, became vice-director of the school. By February 2011, the new SEMIBA facilities, located on the second and third floors of the Airport Alliance church were inaugurated. That same year, Missionaries Leialdo and Roni Pulz returned after two terms in Russia as ACEMBRAS missionaries and began to work at SEMIBA in teaching and administration. The following year, 2012, the Clarks left Brazil due to Beverly's medical emergency.

In 2001, after serving in the C&MA National Office, the Joneses returned to Brazil. Part of their assignment was to introduce the *Faculdade Teológica Latino-American (FATELA)*, the Alliance's masters-level graduate school begun by Dr. Fred Smith, regional director for South America. At that time, *FATELA* served the Alliance churches in several South American countries. As a distance-learning program that met several times a year, the students did classroom preparation at home, going to São Paulo for a week of intensive classes, after which they would return home to work on their class project. Six modules were held a year. Jones translated the *FATELA* administrative material, developed a Portuguese-speaking faculty drawn from national evangelical leaders such as Dr. Russell Shedd, Pastor Ariovaldo Ramos and Pastor Ricardo Barbosa, among many others, as well as Alliance leaders from all over South America, i.e., Dr. Miguel Palomino – FATELA director for South America and Dr. Frank Hankins of the Alliance Seminary in Guayaquil, Ecuador. Begun in 2002 with nine students, this graduate program continues to serve the evangelical church in Brazil and works in close collaboration with the A. W. Tozer Theological Seminary.

As was the case with the planting and growth of the Brazilian Alliance Church, the discipleship and preparation of national workers for the work of the Kingdom had shown the "roots and branches" that lead to its development. Despite the changing conditions and spiritual climate over the years, workers approved by God have been trained and sent out by the Alliance ministerial training program, in its various iterations. May God continue to bless and expand this vital ministry.

THE SECRETARIES

As the mission grew in the 1980s, the administrative burden became increasingly heavy, and the Mission leadership realized the need to help the Field Chairman with administrative assistance. Thus, the first of the mission "secretaries" (now administrative assistants) was sent down to handle office and accounting responsibilities. In large part, besides fulfilling their office tasks, these called and sent women also became fully involved in ministries according to their gifting.

Regene Bartl

Regene Bartl, a Toccoa Falls graduate, came to Brazil in March 1983 and was assigned to work in the Mission Office as the mission staff was growing. Following her year in Campinas language school, where she proved to be a good language learner, she soon was involved not just with mission office work, but also became an active worker in the local Alliance churches. In time, she trained with Evangelism Explosion and became an effective soul winner as well as a trainer of others.

Following the close of the Curitiba office, Regene moved to Porto Alegre, where the mission office was relocated under the leadership of Steve Renicks for a few years. When the

mission office was eventually moved to São Paulo in 1991, Regene moved with the office and soon was part of the growing Airport Alliance congregation. There, she put her experience with EE into good use. She served for two terms before returning to the United States and her marriage ceremony was performed by her field colleague, Jeff Kiel, in Alabama. She was a vital part of the mission and sorely missed after she left the field in 1996.

Barbara Bradshaw

Barbara arrived on the field in January 1997 and worked in the mission office in São Paulo following language study. As an active part of the Airport Alliance, she worked in the "Favela" project of the church that came to the aid of dozens of families burned out of their shanty-town homes by a terrible fire that hurt so many families. Barb also worked in some of the English Encounter weekends led by Len and Diane Warden. Barb served the Alliance in Brazil for two terms, returning to the United States in May 2003. after "a wonderful 8+ years with a wonderful mission family!"

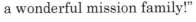

Ruth Strubbe

"Ruthie,"as she was known, had served previously at Alliance Academy in Quito before coming to Brasil in January 2003. Due to her limited time for language study, Ruth was largely involved in Mission Office work, even though her smiling face and buoyant demeanor were present in the Airport Alliance church where she worshipped. Ruth served for three years before returning to America.

MISSIONARY STORIES

Jeff and Jo Kiel

Jeff and Jo Kiel served from 1987 to 2010 with the Brazil Alliance Mission. They ministered in the State of Rio Grande do Sul, in the cities of Porto Alegre and Caxias do Sul. Like most other Alliance missionaries, they were "generalists" and served in many capacities: Evangelism, church planting, discipleship, leadership development, construction of buildings, administrative work in the mission, pastoring, leading seminars and much more. The following are accounts of their ministry.

In her third term, Jo developed a unique women's evangelistic ministry, "Color Me Beautiful" and "Inner and Outer Beauty." Using cosmetics and colors that complimented a woman's natural complexion, Jo introduced hundreds of women to Jesus, the Master Painter, who made them beautiful on the inside. She presented the seminars in shopping malls, tennis clubs,

Jeff & Jo Kiel

B R A Z I L

colleges and universities, and church evangelistic teas. Others have been trained to lead the seminars and women all over South America have been reached with the gospel through this evangelistic tool.

Jo's Story: I want to tell the story of Rosana, my first adult convert during my first term of service in Porto Alegre. Rosana was the right-hand assistant to the leading Spiritist medium in POA. She would go to the cemeteries; and while taking the knife to kill the animal for blood sacrifices, she would say," God help me!" The medium would tell her, "Don't say that, you're ruining everything." Right before she was to receive blood baptism to become a Spiritist medium, she said, "God if you exist don't let me do this." And He didn't. She walked away and she started working for us.

She was done with religion; she told me that her first day on the job. I said, "Religion is not where it's at, Rosana; it is a personal relationship with Jesus Christ." She asked many questions and came back; for 14 months, this went on and she began attending the Alliance Church in Porto Alegre. On July 15, 1990, Steve Renicks preached, gave an altar call, and Rosana was touched. I almost ran up the aisle to be with her, and she said: "Jo you know why I am here." I shared with her John 1:12 and she said, "Oh yes, Jo, I want to become a child of God." Then I shared I John 1:9 and she said, "Oh yes, I am a sinner." We bowed our heads, and she prayed and said "Amen." I did not have to ask her as she said, "Jo, if I go to the furthest end of the Amazon and I never see another person again, I will never forget Him as He is right here in my heart." A few months later we were packing up our apartment to leave for furlough. I usually prayed before we ate, but she said: "Jo I want to pray." She said this: "Thank you God for taking me from darkness to light; thank you for putting me on Your path; thank You for sending Jeff and Jo to Brazil because I am going to be in Heaven someday because they came." There is no greater joy for anyone than to hear something like that.

Jeff remembers: "After I finished the message that Sunday morning, one of our Brazilian pastors gave a very impassioned plea for the kids to come forward and seek the fullness of God's Spirit in their lives. Many of the youth came forward; I would estimate about sixty or more. Many of them came to the altar while others knelt or even lay prostrate on the bare concrete floor. Almost all were weeping and intensely seeking the fullness of the Holy Spirit. The impassioned praying went on for over an hour before Pastor Beto ended the service, since it was already past noon and lunch was ready to be served. I praised God for the presence and manifestation of His Spirit among us. I have seen many manifestations of God's Spirit in my twenty-four years in Brazil, but none as powerful as this. We all went home rejoicing in the refreshing renewal we received from God's work in our lives."

Alex and Julie Zell

Alex and Julie Zell arrived in Brazil on October 3, 1995. They moved into the 8th floor of an apartment in Campinas where they studied Portuguese. They asked the field director what to do in case of a fire. Tim Bubna said, "Everything is concrete and block and mortar. They never have fires here." That night after he left them, the ice cream factory across the street burned to the ground. "What did we get ourselves into?" they wondered. God protected them again and again.

One time, Alex was detained from going to São Paulo while living in Itatiba and could only leave at 7:30 p.m. The next day, the newspaper reported that there were two fatal accidents on the Bandeirantes Highway that he would have traveled, one at 6:39 and one at 8:30! Praise God for His protection. Another near miss happened when our girls were playing in the winter garden in the middle of our house. Strong winds knocked out our power and the girls screamed and ran to the kitchen. Thirty second later, the wind ripped loose the glass roof tiles above where they had been playing, and they came crashing down, splintering into hundreds of pieces. The glass shards embedded in the hard, tile floor like a shotgun blast. God spared our three girl's lives one more time.

Julie and Alex worked in Vila Madalena during our first term. Daughters Jody and Linsey were both born while there.

So, Julie learned the language and took care of babies during that term. I taught Pastoral Compendium (*Seja um Obreiro*) at the church and Greek 1 at SEMIBA. During our second term, 2000 to 2004, we were assigned to Itabia, about 50 miles (83 kilometers) from the city of São Paulo, to work with the local pastor. After one year, he became jealous of God's blessing on our lives and limited our preaching and teaching. Julie and I had a home Bible study and worked with the youth. God blessed with converts and disciples. When we arrived, there were about twenty people, mostly women and children. When we left, twenty men gave us roses and thanked our whole family for staying through the hard times. We love those brothers and sisters. The church had two more pastors and then became unsustainable and eventually closed.

Our third term began in 2007, after my leave of absence to begin working on a PhD. in Deerfield, Illinois. I served as National Coordinator for FATELA Brasil, the Alliance's masters program. We worked in the North Zone of São Paulo with a home Bible study and then with the Japanese-Brazilian Paradise Alliance Church. We helped them as we were able, but Alex was heavily occupied with his PhD. research project, as well as coordinating the FATELA program and teaching duties at SEMIBA. Julie was always counseling women and exercising her gift of hospitality. Together, we made an excellent team. Melisa, our oldest daughter, participated in the church drama team. Jodi sang in some cantatas and Linsey adopted aunts, uncles and grandparents that were there. We left Brazil two days after the first FATELA graduation on February 28, 2011.

James and Nicki Chung

One of the unique feature of the Alliance ministry in Brazil is the fact that the many "roots" that produced such a variety of branches came from many different lands. As seen in the first chapter, Missionary Mutsuko Ninomiya came from Japan. The early North American missionaries came from Canada and the United States. Over the years, staff came from other lands, such as Rebecca Otero (Anderson) of Puerto Rico. Sanford Hashimoto was born in Hawaii of immigrant parents, raised in a native Hawaiian neighborhood and learned English as his third language while still a child.

James and Nicki Chung arrived in Brazil in August 2000 with their two children Jonathan and Timothy. Their third child, Joanna, was born the next year in São Paulo. Like their colleagues, they studied Portuguese in Campinas, struggling to learn the language and finally felt triumph when they could

speak not only in the past tense but also in the present tense, after four months. James was glad that they could now talk with their neighbors about what was happening and not just what had happened!

They were sent to minister to mainland Chinese immigrants who worked in downtown São Paulo in the "23rd of May" commercial area dominated by street vendors. The Chungs were involved in a church planting project among these hard-working people who came to Brazil to earn their fortune. Most of the immigrants spoke just enough Portuguese to do business, but their children grew up in a challenging bi-cultural, bi-lingual milieu. Most parents did not want to send their children to Brazilian schools, preferring to put them on the streets with their cheap products where they were subject to thieves, corrupt city officials looking for bribes and police who loved to swoop in and sweep their goods off their stands into the streets. One of their best memories of ministry involved a young man named Tiago. In James' words:

> A young man came to São Paulo when he was 15. His name was Tiago. He could only speak Chinese. The number one goal of these families was to make money in São Paulo. His parents put him into business as a street vendor. He had no experience and didn't like it at all . . . He argued with his parents every day. His merchandise was stolen. His business was bad, and he could not make any money during his first few weeks in São Paulo. However, he really liked to go with me on visitation and ministry. Therefore, I persuaded his parents to give him two years for school. However, they didn't believe he would do well in school. After two conversations, they finally let him try for two years. I helped him register at a local high school and started to teach him basic Portuguese (that's all I learned, basic Portuguese). A few months later, he was still struggling with the language and felt discouraged. I enrolled him in a local

tutoring center run by a Chinese Christian organization. He worked very hard and got back on track with his other Brazilian classmates very soon. He also began to serve in our praise and worship team. A few years later, he was accepted by a local college and graduated with B.S. in physical therapy. He is now studying in a local seminary and serving as a Chinese pastor of a new Chinese congregation with a Brazilian Korean church in São Paulo. He is now married to a Japanese Brazilian and they have two girls. We are thankful to God who saves and grows His people."

During their six years of ministry in Brazil, before being reassigned to work in Hong Kong, James and Nicki sensed at various times the manifest presence of God on their lives and ministry. When they look back at their short but fruitful time in Brazil, they "tagged along the journey with God and witnessed His goodness and faithfulness. We were so blessed to be on that journey with God." Chungs have recently relocated to the United States and James is president of the Chinese Church Association (C&MA) and lives in New York city.

David and Sue Manske—Fortaleza

The *Projeto Nordeste* (Northeast Project) was birthed by ACEMBRAS's church planting committee (Joao Costa Junior, Toshiaki Yassui, Luis Ueda, José Freitas, David Manske and Steve Renicks) and was given the task of developing a church planting strategy. First envisioned in 1997, over the course of a couple years, the study group looked at going to the new state of Tocantins; at "filling the gap" between the states of Rio Grande do Sul and Paraná/São Paulo; at "stitching up the border" along Argentina, Paraguay and Uruguay (pioneer work already was in Uruguaiana). Other areas were considered, including Fortaleza, Ceará in northeast Brazil. After serious discussion considering the pros and cons of these options, the team set aside a couple of days for prayer. Everyone came back with the confirmation of going to Fortaleza. A very comprehensive project was written up, submitted to the Mission and ACEMBRAS and endorsed officially by both.

The effort was intentionally "missionary:"

1. ACEMBRAS churches were to join in a cohesive effort. This initiative was to draw the churches and their leaders together in support of a new work (prayer, funding and personnel) for a specific period of time, distant from their local context, but still in Brazil.
2. The funding would mostly come from ACEMBRAS, with some Mission funds. The Brazil Alliance churches would raise money for this project, and because of this experience,

eventually transitioning to Great Commission Fund giving to support ACEMBRAS missionaries being sent out by the Department of Missions.

3. Team structure: The national pastor was to be the lead pastor of the work to avoid transition problems later, and the missionary was to be an advisor/overseer of the whole project which would work to develop new leaders and church planting projects. Fortaleza would be a hub, sending workers out into the interior of the Northeast where there was a need for evangelical churches and could provide a type of location for confirming the missions call of future workers.

4. The project would be overseen by both the ACEMBRAS president and the Mission field director.

David Manske and Luis Ueda visited Fortaleza before the Costas arrived on site. They interviewed pastors in local churches, gathered demographic information, prayer walked and talked with city officials regarding the local church situation. The Northeast Project team was chosen, with Rev. João Costa Junior and wife Lenise as the lead national pastor and Missionaries David and Sue Manske chosen as the Mission team members. The team arrived in Fortaleza in 2000, as part of ACEMBRAS's Project 2000.

Once on location, the team began in-home Bible studies, English classes, literature distribution, monthly gatherings to socialize, share about our purpose and share a "lite" presentation of the Christian life. They started public Sunday night services in a local restaurant, with a monthly gathering for a larger group. Pastor João Costa held Bible studies in his home, while Manskes led English classes using Christian material by Max Lucado and Chuck Swindoll among others. Both couples did one-on-one discipleship and developed non-

354

Christian contacts. Manskes and the Costas interacted with other local church leaders. Manske became a member of Rotary Club, while Pastor Costa taught some classes at the local Presbyterian seminary. A short-term team flew up from Rudge Ramos during the winter when Manskes were on home assignment to give assistance and encourage the Costas.

The vision of the project was to reach unchurched people with the Gospel and build a fresh expression of what the church really is. The effort failed despite the investment of time and effort. Reasons for this failure include the following conclusions:

1. A possible underestimation of Catholic resistance to a new evangelical church.
2. The team being seen as "outsiders" since there were no members from Fortaleza or Ceará among them.
3. The project apparently did not resonate with the Alliance churches
4. The team would have been stronger if more experienced evangelists and church planters had also been on it.

The Manskes returned to the United States in 2003 to take up a new ministry; no other mission personnel were available. The Costas continued on for a time, becoming bi-vocational as funding diminished. After another year or so, the project was discontinued at their request. (Compiled from material by Timothy Bubna and David Manske)

Doug and Helen White—Rio De Janeiro

In March 2005, Alexander Fajardo, son of a Colombian Alliance pastor, and his wife Susan, working in Rio de Janeiro, contacted Pastor José Freitas about starting a work in the city. Doug White and José followed up the request by going to Rio, to meet with Alex and get to know the city better. While there, Doug visited a church service where he felt God calling him to minister. He went forward for the altar call. In July 2005 Doug and Helen White moved to Rio to the area of Barra da Tijuca, an area that had a lot of people from Portugal.

Doug and Helen developed friendships in their building, also by walking the beach, and Helen became a part of a hydro-gymnastics class. On Sunday mornings they attended Union Church, an English-speaking congregation, led by a Brazilian pastor. On Sunday evenings, the same pastor and Doug started a Portuguese speaking congregation that met in the Union Church building. On Wednesday evenings Doug and Helen hosted a prayer meeting in their apartment attended by Alexander and his family, a couple teachers from the international school and a young Japanese girl.

One of the blessings that came out of the work was the future ministry of Marcos and Andrea Alírio who work in Brasilia today in the Santos Dumont con-dominium as pastors. During the time that the Whites were in Rio, Marcos and Andrea became a part of the prayer meeting that met in Whites' apartment. At that time Marcos and Andrea felt called into ministry. Upon closing the work in Rio in 2007 permission was granted to use the money that had been collected in offerings to help Marcos attend seminary, which he did at Bethel seminary in Rio de Janeiro.

The White Family: Rachel, Doug, Aaron, Caleb and Helen

Aimée's Story
by Richard LaFountain

Aimée's Asthma

It seems that Aimée was destined for trouble in this world. As a little girl, she had trouble with bouts of asthma which made us fear for her life. She would get so bad that she could hardly breathe. We'd watch anxiously as her little chest tried to draw in oxygen. Many times we'd have to rush her to the emergency room to get help.

One night I was on my knees praying with her at bedtime. She prayed her normal prayer but left out asking God to heal her asthma. So, I reminded her not to forget to pray for her asthma. I waited but she said nothing. I said it louder thinking that maybe she didn't hear me. Nothing. So, this time I looked right at her and repeated that she should pray for her asthma. As I looked at her, tears streamed down her face, and with broken sob she said: "Daddy I don't think God hears my prayers. I don't think he's going to heal my asthma." At that point, I'm sure I said something spiritual or something positive; I don't remember. But my heart was aching for my little girl's lost faith.

I went back to my room and

angrily wept and prayed with my wife as I related what had just happened. How can God ignore childlike faith? Why wasn't God answering her cry? Why does God remain ominously silent when we have such desperate needs?

This shook my faith. It troubled me as I prayed and mulled over this problem for weeks. Then one sunny morning I get a frantic call from a backslidden couple who had left the church years before I even came to that church. It was a petty argument over something not important. She was calling me to tell me her husband had just had an apparent stroke and was paralyzed from his neck down. I urged her to call an ambulance immediately, but she refused saying her husband insisted on calling me first to pray over him for healing.

As I drove to their house I was angry. It was a man who deliberately alienated himself from fellowship with the church over some petty argument that took place many years ago. I'm supposed to pray a prayer of faith over him, while my innocent little daughter continues in anguish with asthma? I had no faith that God would hear my prayer for this man much less answer his prayers. On the way there, God clearly directed me to Hebrews 10:25 concerning "neglecting the assembling of ourselves together" and about "roots of bitterness that may defile many" from Hebrews chapter 12.

I arrived at their little house to find the man still on his back on the floor and unable to move. As a young Pastor, I wondered how I was supposed to rebuke his sin instead praying for him. To my surprise he said "Pastor I called you first because God said he has a word for me from you. What is the word that God gave you for me?"

Wow! Talk about an open door. I immediately knew those passages were from God, not from my angry heart. So, I open the word and preached about grieving the Holy Spirit through disobedience. Immediately the man broke into sobbing tears of repentance asking God for forgiveness. At the end of his prayer he said, "OK Pastor, now you can pray for me"

I was in a dilemma. There I was still angry and very much without faith that God would heal this man, but like Peter after the night of fruitless toil fishing, I thought, "nevertheless at your word we will let down our nets." I then obeyed and anointed him with vegetable oil (I had no vial of anointing oil) and prayed for his healing. To my utter shock and amazement, the man began to move his arms and legs. Soon he rose to his knees and stood up stretched his arms above his head while shouting "hallelujah!" Then to prove his healing was true he did jumping jacks and then got down and did push-ups. With a grateful heart, he and his wife promised to be in church the next Sunday. God had done a miracle. God healed a paralyzed man.

I walked away from that situation confused. Why had God seen fit to heal this disobedient man but not my daughter? It didn't make any sense to me; to this couple's credit they did attend church that Sunday. But to their discredit that was the only time they ever attended because in that service they saw the family that they were angry with and never returned.

Aimée's Broken Arm

We don't have to admit that at times Aimée was uncoordinated, like the time she got roller-skates and decided to learn on our sidewalks. Our home in Brazil was enclosed by high walls, as most homes are, to deter thieves. That meant that we had plenty of cement patio and sidewalks all around the house. Once Aimée was comfortable with that flat surface, she decided to skate in front of the house where there was a slope leading down to the sidewalk. She was OK going down but coming back up she slipped and fell hard on her right arm.

We heard her scream and saw the tears, but what shocked us most was seeing her arm broken and crooked. It wasn't a compound fracture where the bone broke through the skin, but it was broken like a snapped twig. My knee-jerk reaction was to do what I had seen in first aid books and videos. I grabbed her arm and pulled hard to reset the bone. Bad move! It didn't work. It only made things worse and gave her more pain.

We rushed her to the hospital, had x-rays taken and the bone was reset and put in a cast. The doctor knew we were scheduled to return to the United States on furlough in just a few weeks but I could see that he wanted to see Amy again to be sure the bone was mending properly.

Weeks later we returned to the doctor just before furlough. He removed the cast. What we saw broke our hearts for Amy. The arm was still broken and misaligned, almost like it had never been set properly. The doctor put a removable brace on it and told us to see an orthopedic surgeon in the States as soon as possible. He suggested that the surgeon might break the bone and reset it or do surgery and have pins placed in it. I felt so bad for Amy. I felt like it was my fault for attempting to reset her arm.

So, we prayed fervently that Amy wouldn't have to go through another trauma of surgery or breaking a bone. It took a couple weeks before we could make an appointment with an orthopedic surgeon in the U.S. We told him what happened and how the doctor removed the cast, and it was still broken and misaligned. The doctor said, "Well let's have a look." When he took off the splint and removed the wrappings, he found her arm was perfectly healed and straight. We were amazed. X-ray showed the bone was set properly and mended perfectly. God had answered prayer.

Aimée's Love for Her Friends

We spent a good year at home on furlough in 1991 to 1992. We preached at lots of churches and shared our vision and burden for Brazil. Aimée shared that burden for Brazil for her neighborhood friends and was determined to share Christ with them.

We needed to buy a car but didn't have enough money to do so; however, a friend told us that if we went to Argentina, a neighboring country, we will get a better exchange rate and make up the difference. My neighbor was an Uruguayan immigrant and naturalized citizen of Brazil. He thought it was a good idea to exchange our car savings in Argentina. It so happened that he was going to visit his parents in Uruguay and would be happy to accompany me that far and lodge me at his home. We all had been praying for Leopoldo and his wife and family and were looking for opportunities to share Christ with them. So, after praying about it, we decided I should go with him.

Before going however, Aimée had saved her money and wanted to buy Bibles for her three neighborhood friends. We decided to spend the day together since I had to go downtown to exchange money and pay bills. I would take care of my business and then we would go to the Christian bookstore and find appropriate Bibles. We spent a good deal of time considering different Bible translations before finally deciding on a Portuguese version of Good News for Modern Man. That night as I prayed with her before bed, I asked her if she had been able to give the Bibles to the girls. She said in emphatically, "No daddy, it's not time yet. When the time is right, I'll give them the Bibles. "

The Accident

The next day I was scheduled to leave with my neighbor for Uruguay and Argentina. I wasn't looking forward to leaving the family so soon after returning to Brazil, and I dreaded the long bus trip to Uruguay, and then a boat ride to Argentina. As Marilyn and I stood in the doorway saying goodbye, she said, "I don't want you to go. I've had a bad feeling about this trip like something will happen or you're going to die." I agreed, I too had a foreboding in my spirit about this trip, but we prayed about it and decided it was more about spending time with Leopoldo than exchanging money. We agreed, and I left for an eight-hour bus ride and then a ride across the bay to Argentina.

The trip was long and I don't remember if I was able to share Christ with Leopoldo and his family. The next day I headed on to Argentina on an *alescafo,* a hydrofoil boat, that crossed the bay to Buenos Aires. I was scheduled to meet friends there at the Alliance's Buenos Aires Bible Institute.

When I arrived, the missionaries had an urgent message to call home. There had been an accident and my daughter Amy had been hit by a car and was in serious condition. I immediately called Marilyn and found out from her that Amy was crossing a busy street with her friends to buy bread and was hit by a speeding car. She had been rushed to the hospital with serious injuries and was in intensive care. I'll never forget the terror in Marilyn's voice and she said to me: "Dick you need to get home now. She's dying!"

There were no flights to Brazil until the next morning. I spent a sleepless night in tears and prayer pleading with God to spare her life, or allow me at least to arrive home before she would die. That night as I read the Scriptures God gave me an insightful promise from Psalm 45:7-15:

7 You have loved righteousness and hated
   wickedness
   Therefore God, your God, has set you above
   your companions
   by anointing you with oil of joy.

8 All your robes are fragrant with myrrh and aloes
   and cassia;
   from palaces adorned with ivory
   the music of the strings makes you glad.

9 Daughters of kings are among your honored
   women;
   at your right hand is the royal bride in gold of
   Ophir.

10 Listen, daughter, and pay careful attention:
   Forget your people and your father's house.

11 Let the king be enthralled by your beauty;
   honor him, for he is your lord.

12 The city of Tyre will come with a gift,
   people of wealth will seek your favor.

13 All glorious is the princess within her chamber;
   her gown is interwoven with gold.

14 In embroidered garments she is led to the king;
   her virgin companions follow her-
   those brought to be with her.

15 Led in with joy and gladness,
   they enter the palace of the king.

I got the first flight in the morning and told the stewardess of my urgent need to get off the plane immediately when it landed. They were gracious. They put me in the first seat and I was the first to exit. My friend and missionary colleague, Steve Renicks, was there to greet and rush me to the hospital.

Oh the horror of seeing my daughter in ICU horribly bruised and swollen, her hair shaved and head wrapped in bandages, and being kept alive by a respirator and tubes. The doctor informed us that Aimée had suffered dramatic brain trauma in the accident and there was no longer any cerebral activity. The machines were keeping her body alive but she was gone. They informed us that we needed to give them the order to disconnect the life-support system. We could not make that decision. The doctor told us that she had a strong young heart and that her heart could continue beating for several months while being maintained by the life support system.

We went home to pray and grieve together. I remember that none of us wanted to go to sleep. Andrew and Angelica slept in our bedroom with us that night. As we were going to sleep, we prayed and asked God that if Aimée was indeed already in heaven, would He command her heart to stop so that we didn't have to make that decision. At 1:10 AM in the morning the hospital called to tell us that Amy's heart had stopped beating on its own. She had gone to be with Jesus.

Strange Events in Her Death

There were some strange events, miraculous coincidences to this story. First, the driver of the car that hit Amy was a Baptist pastor who was rushing to get a senior pastor's wife to a church meeting. His name I can never forget, Pastor José Couto.

José had stopped immediately, called an ambulance and gave first aid until they arrived. He also refused to leave Aimée's side as she was taken to the hospital for emergency surgery. In fact, despite urgings from the medical professionals, he stayed until I arrived. The doctors and staff warned him that he shouldn't be there, that the father would attempt to kill him once he discovered that he was the driver. José assured them that this was not the case, that we were both believers and that we would embrace as brothers.

As I entered the intensive care unit I thought it was odd that all the medical professionals were eyeing me carefully as I walked in. Steve Renicks had told me who the driver was, that he had been with Amy nonstop since the accident. Upon entering the ICU and being introduced to José, I embraced him with tears and we wept together. I assured him that there was no animosity or hostility in my heart towards him. Who among us has not been careless in our driving when rushing to an appointment? I was glad that Aimée had a fellow Pastor by her side during this trauma.

Second, Aimée's girlfriends, whom she wanted to win to Christ, were with her when she was hit by the car. They related to us that when they arrived at the crosswalk, a city bus had stopped to board passengers and was blocking their view of traffic. The girls said they didn't see a car coming but must've heard or sensed it. One of the girls had put her arm out to block Aimée from stepping out into traffic, but Aimée was just beyond the reach and she had already stepped out to look around the bus.

It was for these girls that Amy had purchased the Bibles the day before. Little did we know that Aimée had already signed the Bibles and written her testimony in the inside covers. We gave those Bibles to those girls at Aimée's funeral.

Third, Marilyn and I both had been warned by the Holy Spirit that on our return to Brazil great trials awaited us. I was so impacted by this impression from the Lord that I wrote it in my devotional journal while I was still in the States. I remember it because the feeling was so strong that I called Marilyn into my study where I had been praying. I remember sitting her on my lap and showed her the Scriptures the Lord had given to me and I asked her "Are we still willing to return to Brazil?" We both considered it and said a unified, "Yes!"

Fourth, the corner on which Aimée was struck by the car was the same place that I had previously identified as the location of our future Alliance Church in Parque Santa Fe.

Fifth, Marilyn's parents were able to arrive in time to be with us for the funeral. Aimée was hit by the car on August 4, 1982 and died on August 6. In Brazil, it is required by law that since embalming is rare and expensive, the deceased must be buried within 24 hours of their death. Marilyn's parents had to get visas approved and airline tickets within 36 hours of hearing of the accident. Miraculously the Brazilian Consulate broke all regulations in approving their visas and expedited their trip to Brazil. They arrived a half hour before the funeral.

Steve Renick's Addendum to Aimée's story:

Dick,

Thank you for writing Aimée's story. There was a lot that I did not know about the beginning years and recounting her time in Brazil brought back many feelings surrounding her accident and death. There is one more thing that I wanted to add about Marilyn's parents getting their visas to Brazil.

There were no airline seats available out of JFK in New York and they had missed their flight to Miami. The person at the consulate had gone to the airport with them, went into the Varig office and got them on the plane that was supposedly full. When we were back in the States for our furlough after Aimée's death, we spoke at Diane's home church in Riverdale, NJ. We showed our slides and shared about the work in Brazil. Our last slide was of you and Marilyn. We told what had happened, and asked the church to pray for you. At the end of the service, a Brazilian woman who was attending the church service that night approached us and said, "I always wondered if they made it in time for the funeral." She worked in the Brazilian Consulate in New York and was the person who had stamped the visas and had gotten them on the Varig flight. She broke down in tears as she realized how God had used her in that situation. I always stand amazed at God's love, mercy and providence.

Steve

HISTORICAL PHOTO ALBUM

Mutsuko
Ninomiya

Paul and Claudia
Bryers

Samuel and Vera Barnes pioneered Alliance work in Brazil.

Called to Pioneer

Sam and Vera
Barnes

Dave, Lesley and Marilyn
Sundeen

John and Beverly
Nicholson

A Reminder To Pray For

THE THOMAS KYLES
Laurie, Mary, Lynnette, Tom

BRAZIL

Tom and Mary
Kyle

Dave Sundeen and
Paul Bryers
Baptism in Gama
1964

Alliance Church
in Goiânia
1964

Missionary
Mutsuko Ninomiya
1964

Brasília Team 1964:
Nicholsons, Youngs
and Sundeens

Tom and Mary
Kyle
1966

Evangelistic Tent
Avenida Paraná
Curitiba
1967

Junior, Elza, Elzita
and Pastor João
Alves da Costa
1969

Vacation Bible School
Boa Vista
Curitiba
1969

Construction of
Capão da Imbuia
Church
1971

Presidents of the Brazil
Christian and Missionary Alliance

Rev. João Alves da Costa

Rev. Hernán Osorio Gomes

Rev. Juan Nelber Nuñez

Pastor Marcos de Lima

Rev. Sérgio Moraes Pinto

Rev. João Alves da Costa
Junior

Rev. Eduardo Toshiaki
Yassui

Rev. José Freitas

Rev. Jurandir Yanagihara

Rev. Abisaí Nunes de Lima

Second Council of
ACEMBRAS
1979

Third Council of
ACEMBRAS
1980

PRAYER CARDS

Darrel and Jan
Smith

Bob and Shirley Kallem
Bretta and Brad

Jim and Billi Jo
Medin
Jennifer and
Jackie Jo

THE LaFOUNTAIN'S

B R A Z I L

B R A Z I L

Dick & Marilyn, Aimée & Andrew

Richard and Marilyn
LaFountain
Aimée and Andrew

". . . that at all times they ought to pray and not to lose heart."

Regene Bartl

Serving with:
The Christian & Missionary Alliance
P.O. Box 35000
Colorado Springs, CO 80935-3500

BRAZIL

Field Address:
Caixa Postal 18085
04.699 São Paulo, SP
Brasil

Regene Bartl

P R A Y

O R A D

Ivette Rebecca Otero

Ivette Rebecca Otero

Field address
en Brasil

The C. & M.A.
Caixa Postal 1299
80.000, Curitiba
Paraná, Brazil

At home
en Puerto Rico

Arecibo Gardens
St. I, B19
Arecibo, P.R. 00612

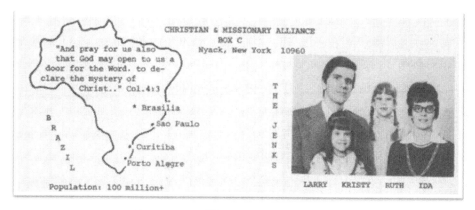

Lawrence, Kristy, Ruth and Ida Jenks

Sanford and Wendy,
Ginger and Tracy
Hashimoto

Steve, Diane, Paul
and Timmy Renicks

WARDENS

Len, Diane, Jeremy,
Angelynn and Evan
Warden

THE DAVIS FAMILY

Michael   Ruth Ann
        Blaine

Mike, Blaine and
Ruth Davis

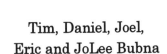

Tim, Daniel, Joel,
Eric and JoLee Bubna

Jeff and Jo
Kiel

Jeff & Jo Kiel

B R A Z I L

Serving Jesus Christ in
BRAZIL
With the Christian & Missionary Alliance

Paul & Beverly Clark
Laura, Rebecca & Karen

"I urge you brothers, by our Lord Jesus Christ, and
by the love of the Spirit, to join us in our struggle by
praying for us."   (Romans 15:30)

Home Address: Field Address:
The C&MA   Caixa Postal 1299
350 N. Highland Ave.   80.000 Curitiba
Nyack, NY 10960   Parana, Brazil

Paul, Beverly,
Laura, Rebecca
And Karen Clark

Doug, Helen
And Aaron
White

Sue, Katie, Ian and
Dave Manske

Charlotte Hisle

Dwayne and Rhonda
Brett and Kayla
Buhler

Bryan, Vicki, Caleb,
Jonathan and
Andrew Joyce

Marshall and Teresa,
Kiersten, Cassie,
Caleb and Katie
Erikson

IN MEMORIAM

Samuel G. Barnes
deceased September 12, 1975
Vera Barnes
deceased March 31, 1994

Alwyn Rees
deceased November 8, 1995
Edythe Rees
deceased December 8, 2010

Aimée F. LaFountain
deceased August 6, 1982

Emmit Young
deceased May 6, 1991

Ida F. Jenks
deceased October 5, 1996

Thomas B. Kyle
deceased January 30, 2009

Brenda J. Kurtz
Deceased October 13, 2012

Beverly R. Clark
deceased January 7, 2013

BIBLIOGRAPHY

Araújo, Cristina Gonçalves. 2004. *História do Protestantismo em Goiás (1890-1940)*. Tese de Mestrado – Universidade Federal de Goiás. Goiânia.

Barnes, Vera. 1965. *Miles Beyond in Brazil*. Harrisburg, PA. Christian Publications Inc.

Clark, David B. rev. 2011. *Origin and Growth of the Missionary Church Association in Jamaica*. Fort Wayne, Indiana. Private printing.

Clark, David B. s.d. *Diary of Raymond B. Clark*. Fort Wayne, Indiana. Unpublished manuscript.

Clark, R. B. 1923. *Bananal or Among Pagan Indians in Brasil*. São Paulo. Imprensa Methodista

Cook, William Azel. 1909. *Through the Wilderness of Brazil by Horse, Canoe and Float*. New York. American Tract Society.

Cooke, Lloyd A. 2017. *A Godly Heritage: Jamaican Planter Families Planting the Church at Home and Abroad*. Maitland, FL. Xulon Press.

Glass, Frederick C. s.d. *Adventures with the Bible in Brazil*. London. Pickering & Inglis.

Howe, Barbara L. 2010 . *Forgotten Voices: Women in Ministry in The Christian and Missionary Alliance in Canada*. The C&MA of Canada.

Millard, Candice. 2005. *The River of Doubt – Theodore Roosevelt's Darkest Journey.* New York. Anchor Books.

Matos, Alderi S. 2004. Os Pioneiros – Presbiterianos do Brasil (1859-1900). São Paulo. Editora Cultura Cristã.

Konno, Joel Jun. *Memória em Movimento – Quando a História e a Bíblia se Encontram iluminando a Vida Hoje.* São Bernardo do Campo, São Paulo. Graftipo.

Vandevenne, Jean. 2001. *Only One Life.* Fort Washington, PA. CLC Publications.

Warren Harris Gaylord. 1906. *In the Rebirth of the Paraguayan Republic: The First Colorado Era, 1878-1904.* (reprint 1985) Pittsburgh, PA. The University of Pittsburgh Press.

Wilding, Rettie. 1979. *Semeando em Lágrimas.* Goiânia, Goiás. Casa Editora APLIC.

And the seeds continue to germinate...